Raniero Cantalamessa, O.F.M. Cap.

The Holy Spirit in the Life of Jesus

The Mystery of Christ's Baptism

Alan Neame, Translator

A Liturgical Press Book

 THE LITURGICAL PRESS
Collegeville, Minnesota

232.95 ?
catt

Cover design by Ann Blattner
Cover icon: Baptism of Christ, Greek Icon, 14th century

Published originally in Italian under the title *Lo Spirito Santo nella vita di Gesù* by Editrice Àncora Milano.

2   3   4   5   6   7   8   9

Library of Congress Cataloging-in-Publication Data

Cantalamessa, Raniero.
    [Lo Spirito Santo nella vita di Gesù.   English]
    The Holy Spirit in the life of Jesus: The mystery of Christ's baptism / Raniero Cantalamessa ; Alan Neame, translator.
        p.   cm.
    ISBN 0-8146-2128-7
    1. Jesus Christ—Baptism.   2. Baptism.   3. Baptism—Biblical teaching.   I. Title.
BT35.C3613   1994
232.9′5—dc20
                                                                93-14101
                                                                CIP

Contents

3

Chapter One

"God Anointed Jesus of Nazareth with the Holy Spirit and Power"

The baptism of Jesus and the mystery of the anointing

At the beginning of St. John's Gospel, the evangelist solemnly affirms that "from the fullness" of the Word incarnate we have all received grace upon grace (cf. John 1:16); St. Paul affirms the same thing where he writes that in Christ "dwells the whole fullness of the Deity" and that, in him, we share in his fullness (cf. Col 2:9f.). The Fathers of the Church understood these expressions in a very precise way: from *the fullness of Holy Spirit* of Jesus, we have received and receive grace upon grace! In him, bodily, dwells all *the fullness of the Holy Spirit* and in him we share in this fullness! For instance, St. Irenaeus writes: "The Spirit of God descended on Jesus and anointed him, as he had promised in the prophets, so that we might draw on the fullness of his anointing and so be saved";[1] and another writer, a little later, says the same thing with the imagery of the spring and its streams: "The Holy Spirit is he who came upon the Lord as a dove after He had been baptized and abode in Him. In Christ alone he dwells fully and entirely, not wanting in any measure or part; but in all his overflowing abundance dispensed and sent forth, so that other people might receive from Christ a first outpouring, as it were, of his graces. For the fountainhead of the entire Holy Spirit abides in Christ, so that from him might be drawn streams of grace and wondrous deeds, because the Holy Spirit dwells affluently in Christ."[2] "From his fullness," St. Athanasius says unambiguously, "we have received the grace of the Spirit."[3]

The mystery of the anointing, which we shall try to study more deeply in the course of these meditations, speaks to us about this great event of grace; it speaks to us of Jesus, who at the incarnation and still more specifically at his baptism was filled with the Holy Spirit by the Father so that Jesus in turn could fill us with

5

the Holy Spirit, since we share in the mystery of Christ's anointing. This alone is enough to show how important this mystery is for the life of the Christian. In this first meditation I shall try to give a general outline of the whole mystery and the way it is understood by the Church, leaving to subsequent meditations the task of going more deeply into certain specific and concrete aspects of the Holy Spirit's activity in the life of Jesus and the Church.

1. *"Christ, because anointed by the Father"*

What, we may wonder, in the life of Jesus is the concrete fact that makes the anointing a 'mystery,' that is to say an historic event charged with significance for our salvation and, as such, celebrated by the Church in her liturgy? For the earliest Christian thinkers there were no two ways about it: it was Jesus' baptism in the Jordan, when he, "coming up out of the water, saw the heavens being torn apart and the Spirit, like a dove, descending upon him" (Mark 1:10). The apostle Peter in his sermon in the house of Cornelius the centurion says, "After the baptism that John preached . . . God anointed [*echrisen*] Jesus of Nazareth with the Holy Spirit and power. He went about doing good and healing all those oppressed by the devil" (Acts 10:37f.). Before his baptism, there had certainly been other anointings in the existence of the Son of God: there had been the anointing (or, at least, the coming) of the Holy Spirit at the actual moment of the incarnation, thanks to which Jesus was holy from the moment of his birth onwards; according to some of the Fathers, earlier still there had been the cosmic anointing, that is to say the anointing the Word had received from the Father with a view to the creation of the world, so that, as St. Irenaeus says, he in his turn could "anoint and adorn all things," thus conferring his own splendor on the universe.[4]

These theologians of the earliest times were not therefore unaware of the Holy Spirit's presence in Jesus from the moment of his human birth; they did however attribute a different and decisive significance to the solemn anointing received by Jesus in the Jordan to mark the beginning of his messianic mission. According to some of them, just as at the incarnation the Word had become "Jesus," so at his baptismal anointing he had become "Christ," that is to say God's Anointed One, the Messiah: "He is called Christ because anointed with the Holy Spirit by the Father.''[5] As they saw it, the mystery of the anointing was so important that the very name of 'Christians' was derived from it: "This is why we are called Christians (*christianoi*)," writes one of them, "because we are anointed (*chriometha*) with the oil of God."[6] Christians, according to this explanation, did not so much mean "followers of Christ," as the pagans at Antioch who had been the first to call them this intended (cf. Acts 11:26), but rather "sharers in Christ's anointing."[7]

The anointing Jesus received in the Jordan was Trinitarian in nature, since all three divine Persons concurred in it: "In the name of Christ is implied He that anoints, He that is anointed, and the unction itself with which He is anointed. And it is the Father who anoints, but the Son who is anointed by the Spirit, who is the unction."[8] St. Basil too insists on this fact: "To name Christ," he writes "is to confess the whole Trinity, because it indicates the God who anointed, and the Son who was anointed, and that wherewith He was anointed, namely the Spirit, as we have learnt from Peter in the Acts: 'Jesus of Nazareth, whom God anointed with the Holy Spirit' (Acts 10:38). And in Isaiah we read, 'The Spirit of the Lord is upon me, because He has anointed me' (Isa 61:1); and the Psalmist, 'Wherefore God, even your God, has anointed you with the oil of gladness' (Ps 45:8)."[9] His quoting of the text from Acts clearly shows that St. Basil still situates the mystery of the anointing at Jesus' baptism in the Jordan.

Yet a dangerous heresy, the Gnosticism, soon comes to disturb these tranquil certitudes of the faith. In the Gnostic view, Jesus was one person and the Christ another: Jesus denoted the man born of Mary, whereas Christ denoted the deity that descended on Jesus at the moment of baptism. Thus the baptism came to negate the reality of the incarnation and this could not but give rise to a strong reaction on the part of the Church. Other heresies came later to reinforce the reasons for "discrediting" the baptism of Jesus: Arianism used Jesus' baptism as a pretext for asserting that if any change occurred in Jesus at the moment of baptism, this meant that he was subject to change and therefore not a changeless God like the Father; the adoptionism of Paul of Samosata made Christ's actual divinity depend on the coming of the Holy Spirit, as though Jesus were one of the prophets, though certainly the holiest one, in whom the power of God had worked. Against these, St. Gregory Nazianzen declared excommunicate "anyone who says that Jesus Christ was judged worthy of filial adoption in consequence of his baptism."[10]

Added to the nuisance of all these heresies there is also an external factor: the strong tendency towards ontologization, characteristic of the Greek culture to which the people of those days, including the theologians, belonged. In this view, what matters, in everything, is "what it was at the beginning," the *arché* of things, that is to say their metaphysical constitution, not their becoming and their history; what matters is the essence, not the existence. In this context, the question naturally arises: how can the Word incarnate become at baptism something new, which he was not already at the moment of incarnation? Can one attach weight to the history of Jesus and the concrete facts of his life without calling into question the fact that he was perfect human being and perfect Savior from the moment of his birth?

Under the pressure of these questions, we see attention being transferred, little by little, from the events and concrete mysteries of Jesus' life (he was born, was baptized, died, rose again) to the moment of the incarnation. The problem of the *foundation* of salvation (that is, how the Savior *is made*) becomes more important than the problem of the *unfolding* of salvation (that is, what the Savior *does*). In this new climate, the mystery of Jesus' baptism retains and even increases in importance and solemnity, in the Greek world especially, but in a very different sense from before. The baptism is now a Christological mystery only in the active sense (Christ operates in it) and not in the passive sense as well (it operates in Christ). Jesus' baptism in other words is important and efficacious for us, but not for him. "The descent of the Holy Spirit on Jesus in the Jordan," says St. Athanasius, "was for our benefit because he bore our body; and it did not happen to make the Word perfect but to make us holy."[11]

Jesus' baptism in the Jordan comes to be seen and celebrated as the feast of the institution of Christ's baptism. In the homilies delivered on this feast we find the essential theological elements of this mystery becoming fixed, which later figure in the Byzantine liturgy and the art of the icons up to our own day: Jesus was baptized so as to bury all the old Adam in the waters and to sanctify the Jordan, so that, just as he was flesh and Spirit, so he would bring us to salvation by water and the Spirit; coming up out of the water, he carries the world up with him; he sees paradise opening, which Adam had closed, while the Spirit attests his divinity.[12] The Holy Spirit intervenes at Jesus' baptism, we now see, more to attest Christ's dignity than to anoint and consecrate his humanity.

The concept of Jesus' anointing as the work of the Holy Spirit does not disappear from theology, but is transferred from the baptism in the Jordan to the moment of the incarnation, eventually becoming identified, purely and simply, with the incarnation itself. The anointing loses its true Trinitarian character, which we showed above; he who anoints is still and ever the Father, and he who is anointed is still and ever Christ's human nature, but the chrism with which he is anointed is no longer, properly speaking, the Holy Spirit but the Word himself. In Christ, the human nature is anointed, that is to say sanctified, by the divine nature, by the very fact of the hypostatic union. At the incarnation, says St. Gregory Nazianzen, Jesus "was anointed with the divine nature, and the unction of his human nature was not other than the divine nature itself."[13] The function of the Holy Spirit with regard to the person of Jesus is only that of causing his human nature, by miraculously effecting, in Mary, the incarnation of the Word.

The most obvious result of all this is a certain weakening of the pneumatic dimension of Christology, that is, the attention accorded to the Holy Spirit's activity in the life of Jesus. There are exceptions, one of them represented by St. Basil, who speaks of a "continuous presence" of the Holy Spirit in Jesus' life,[14] but usually the decisive point of insertion of the Holy Spirit into salvation history is no longer at Jesus' anointing, but at Pentecost. Pneumatology tends to part company with Christology and locate itself after the latter, rather than within it. (The recurrent danger of contrasting the work and age of the Holy Spirit with that of Jesus — as in the case of Joachim of Fiore — exists only in this new perspective, not when the Holy Spirit is correctly considered as "the Spirit of Jesus.")

Among the Latins, with the advent of Scholasticism the mystery and the very concept of Christ's anointing by action of the Holy Spirit on the day of his baptism disappears completely from theology, never figuring as a separate topic in any of the various *Summae,* starting with that of St. Thomas. With the Second Vatican Council, this mystery has resurfaced in the Church's consciousness: "The Lord Jesus, 'whom the Father has made holy and sent into the world' (John 10:36), has made his whole Mystical Body share in the anointing by the Spirit with which he himself has been anointed."[15] We are only dealing with preliminaries here, however. The Holy Spirit's presence and activity in Jesus' life have not as yet, even in conciliar texts, received the attention they once claimed in the Church's theology; nor, for that matter, was it possible for this to happen instantly. We have not yet stressed an explicit relationship between the mystery of the anointing and Jesus' baptism, nor have we restored to this moment in Christ's life the importance it enjoys in the New Testament texts.

2. What is the significance of Jesus' baptism?

The mystery of the anointing is like a sunken treasure, only now beginning to re-emerge on the surface. The Second Vatican Council drew up guidelines, indicated where to excavate. We must go back and excavate in the ground of the Bible and of the most ancient tradition of the Church but with the tools furnished by the latest exegesis and theology. If we can indeed hope to throw a little new light on the mystery of the anointing, this will not be because we are relying on our private intuitions, but because, owing to the progress made in biblical and patristic studies, we can interrogate Scripture from a more favorable vantage point, and because we are no longer inhibited by those heresies which in the past induced people rather to disregard Jesus' baptism. Let us make our humble pilgrimage back to the Jordan then and try to understand what it was that, one unique day in world history, took place on its banks.

Exegetes today never weary of pointing out the great existential significance that the experience connected with his baptism in the Jordan had for Jesus. This importance, in their view, does not depend only on what Jesus *accomplished* on that occasion (sanctifying the waters of baptism), but also and principally on what *was accomplished* in him. What was done that day in Jesus? "At baptism something happened that modified the course of Jesus' life. . . . We are entitled to suppose that this was the moment when Jesus accepted his vocation" (C. H. Dodd). Not because before then he had not accepted it but because only at this point in his "growth in wisdom and grace" as a human being had it manifested itself to him in clear and concrete terms. "It was at the moment of baptism that Jesus must have acquired the certainty that he had to assume the role of the Servant of Yahweh"

(O. Culmann). Indeed, the heavenly voice proclaims regarding Jesus those words that, in Isaiah 42:1, are applied to the Servant of Yahweh: "Here is my servant whom I uphold, my chosen one with whom I am pleased, upon whom I have put my Spirit. . . ." It is at this moment, therefore, insofar as it is given for us to know, that the fusion occurs in Jesus' consciousness — in his *human* consciousness — of the two figures of the Messiah and the Servant of God, which fusion will henceforth determine the messianic identity and originality of Jesus and give an unmistakable stamp to his every word and action.

This revelation from the Father did not however find Jesus unprepared; his decision to go and be baptized by John, lining up, so to speak, with sinners and becoming, as it were, one of them, was already one step towards taking upon himself the sins of the human race: a fundamental feature of the Servant of Yahweh's mission (cf. Isa 53:6). The scene of Jesus baptized in the midst of sinners is a prelude to the scene of Jesus crucified between two thieves. All his life spent hitherto in Nazareth in obedience to the Father and to human beings had been one long, consistent apprenticeship for this moment. The Father's revelation at the moment of baptism falls on soil already prepared, creating a new situation for which a new "fiat" is required on Jesus' part; and this he immediately utters by resisting the devil's temptations, which are designed to push him in a direction exactly opposite to that of his mission. The Father's call and Jesus' response anticipate and succeed one another in an interpenetration of obedience and love between the human will and the divine will. The Holy Spirit comes to anoint (which in biblical language means to consecrate and invest) Jesus with the powers necessary for his mission, which is not simply the mission of saving the human race but of saving it in a particular way precisely laid down by the Father: the way of self-abasement, willing obedience, and expiatory sacrifice. To skip this moment in Jesus' life would mean putting off his redemptive "fiat" until the night in Gethsemane, locating it only at the end and not also at the beginning of his messianic activity. At the moment of the incarnation, the unique, free consent of a creature to salvation is Mary's "fiat"; but beginning with the baptism and temptations in the wilderness, there is something new in salvation history: the free and human consent of a God! Human but of God; a yes of fully human quality, but of divine power.

11

To this new and fundamental stage in Jesus' life there corresponds a new and fundamental anointing with the Holy Spirit, and this is precisely what we refer to when we speak of the mystery of the anointing. It creates something new in Christ's spiritual itinerary, so much so indeed that, as we have seen, the very name "Christ" was derived from this moment. We are talking about a functional newness, that is, in the mission; not a metaphysical one, in the depths of the person. It manifests itself by grandiose and immediate effects: miracles, preaching with authority, the ushering in of the kingdom of God, victory over demons. From this we can see why the Gospels assign such importance to the episode of Jesus' baptism, notwithstanding the fact that it constituted a problem from an apologetic point of view, since it seemed perhaps to admit a certain imperfection in Christ and inferiority to the Baptist. The importance they attached to the baptism also derived from the fact that in the most ancient phase of gospel tradition, it constituted the starting-point, the "beginning" (*arché*) of the gospel and the story of Jesus (cf. Mark 1:1, 9; Acts 10:37), a beginning that in Matthew and Luke was to be shifted to his virginal birth from Mary, and in John to his eternal birth from the Father. To have the Gospels without this initial episode of Jesus' baptism would be like having the Acts of the Apostles without the initial account of Pentecost: the interpretative key for an understanding of the rest of the book would be missing.

3. *From the anointing to the outpouring of the Spirit*

Only now, having taken account of the importance baptism had for Jesus personally, can we also consider the importance it assumed for the Church and fully evaluate what the Fathers had to say on the subject. "The descent of the Holy Spirit on Jesus in the Jordan," St. Athanasius writes, "was for our benefit . . . to make us holy, so that we might share in his anointing and of us it might be said: 'Do you not know that you are the temple of God and that the Spirit of God dwells in you' (1 Cor 3:16). For when the Lord, as a human being, was washed in the Jordan, we were the ones to be washed, in him and by him, and when he received the Spirit, we were the ones who, thanks to the Lord, were made recipients of the Spirit."[16] The anointing of Christ was an anointing "for our benefit" in the sense that it was *intended* for us. St. Peter, wishing to explain the miracle of Pentecost to the gathering crowds, said, "This Jesus . . . received the promise of the Holy Spirit from the Father and poured it forth, as you see and hear" (Acts 2:32f.). At Pentecost and, before that, in the paschal mystery, Jesus poured out on the Church that Spirit which he had received from the Father at his baptism. Hence it is called the "Spirit of Christ." At Pentecost, says the Vatican II document I have already quoted, the Lord Jesus "has made his whole Mystical Body share in the anointing by the Spirit with which he himself has been anointed."[17] One same Spirit therefore flows in Jesus and in us, as the same sap flows in the vine and in the shoots.

Of course, there is only one Holy Spirit; but here we are talking about the Holy Spirit in terms of history of salvation (*oikonomia*), not in trinitarian terms (*theologia*), in the sense that the Holy Spirit comes to us through the history of Jesus and not, so to speak, directly from eternity; he comes through the Church. This does not mean that we forget the ultimate source of the Holy Spirit, which (as Orthodox Christians love to emphasize) is the Father. For the Holy Spirit comes to us exactly as he came upon Jesus, that is to say as the Spirit sent by the Father, as "the Spirit of the Father"; his eternal source is not forgotten merely because we look at his immediate source in time.

In the Holy Spirit, through Jesus, we directly (without barriers extraneous to the divine nature) reach the Father himself. God, says the Apostle, has sent into our hearts "the Spirit of his Son," the Spirit of Jesus who cries *"Abbà, Father!"* (cf. Rom 8:15). The fact that the Holy Spirit within us cries "Abbà, Father!" is the best proof that he is the Spirit that was in Jesus of Nazareth; indeed, on his own account, as the Third Person of the Trinity, the Holy Spirit could not cry to God and call him Father, since he, unlike Jesus, is not the Son; for he proceeds from the Father (and from the Son) by inspiration, not filiation.

When we invoke the Spirit, we should not, so to say, look up to heaven or anywhere else; the Spirit comes not from there but from the cross of Christ. This is the "spiritual rock" from which living water pours over the Church to quench the thirst of believers. As the rain, in its season, falls abundantly from the sky, collecting in the rocky recesses of the mountains until it finds an outlet and becomes a spring gushing continuously night and day, summer and winter, so the Spirit that came down and collected entirely in Jesus during his earthly life, on the cross found an outlet, a wound, and became a fountain gushing to eternal life in the Church. The moment when Jesus on the cross "handed over the Spirit" (John 19:30) is, for the evangelist, also the moment when "he poured out the Spirit"; the same Greek expression should be understood, according to John's idiosyncratic usage, in either sense: literally as "breathing" and mystically as "giving the Spirit." The episode of the water and blood, which follows immediately afterwards, accentuates this mystical meaning. And not long after this, the mystery is as it were represented in plastic form when, in the upper room, the Risen Jesus "breathed" on the disciples and said "Receive the Holy Spirit!" (John 20:22). Paraphrasing some words of Jesus ("I have given them the glory you gave me"), St. Gregory of Nyssa has Jesus say, "I have given them the Holy Spirit you gave me."[18]

But an unbidden question springs to mind: why the long interval between the moments when Jesus received his anointing in the Jordan and when, on the cross and at Pentecost, the outpouring of the Spirit occurred? And why does St. John the Evangelist say that the Holy Spirit could not be given while Jesus "had not yet been glorified"? St. Irenaeus gives this answer: the Holy Spirit had first to become accustomed to dwelling among human beings; he had, so to speak, to be humanized and historicized in Jesus, so as to be able, one day, to sanctify all human beings from within their human condition while respecting the times and modes of human behavior and suffering. "The Holy Spirit," he writes, "descended upon the Son of God, made the Son of man, becoming accustomed (*adsuescens*) in him to dwell and rest among the human race, so as to be able to work the Father's will in them and renew them from their old habits into the newness of Christ."[19] Through Jesus, the Spirit is able to make grace "take root" in human nature; in Jesus who has not sinned, the Spirit can "come down and remain" (John 1:33), and get used to staying among us, unlike in the Old Testament where his presence in the world was only occasional. In a sense, the Holy Spirit becomes incarnate in Jesus of Nazareth, even if in this case "becomes incarnate" means something different, i.e., "comes to dwell in a physical body." "Between us and the Spirit of God," writes Cabasilas, "there was a double wall of separation: that of nature and that of the will corrupted by evil; the former was taken

14

away by the Savior with his incarnation [and, we may add, with his anointing], and the latter with his crucifixion, since the cross destroyed sin. Both obstacles being removed, nothing further can now impede the outpouring of the Holy Spirit on all flesh."[20]

The same author explains how the wall of separation constituted by *nature,* that is, by the fact that God is "spirit" and we are "flesh," came to be removed. The Savior's human nature, he says, was like an alabaster vessel which in one way contained the fullness of the Spirit, but in another way prevented his perfume from spreading abroad. Only if, by some miracle, the alabaster vessel were itself transformed into perfume would the perfume inside no longer be separated from the outside air and no longer stay shut up in the only vessel to contain it. Now, this was exactly what took place during Jesus' life on earth: the alabaster vessel, which was the pure human nature of the Savior, was itself changed into perfume; in other words, by virtue of his full and total assent to the Father's will, the flesh of Christ gradually became spiritualized, until at the resurrection it became "a spiritual body" (1 Cor 15:44), the "Christ according to the Spirit" (cf. Rom 1:4). The cross was the moment when the last barrier fell; the alabaster vessel was then shattered, as at the anointing at Bethany, and the Spirit poured out, filling "the whole house," that is to say the entire Church, with perfume. The Holy Spirit is the trail of perfume Jesus left behind when he walked the earth! The martyr St. Ignatius of Antioch admirably combines the two moments we have been considering — that of the anointing and that of the outpouring of the Spirit — where he writes: "The Lord received a perfumed (*myron*) ointment on his head, so that he could breathe incorruptibility on the Church."[21]

4. *The mystery of the anointing in the Church and in ourselves*

It remains to examine how the mystery of the anointing acts now, concretely, in the Church and in ourselves. St. John explains how we can know that we remain in Jesus and he in us even after his ascension into heaven: "He has given us of his Spirit" (1 John 4:13). The Holy Spirit is the mystery of Jesus' permanence among us; he makes himself present by making Jesus present, so that St. Paul can say in an elliptical yet true phrase, "The Lord is the Spirit" (2 Cor 3:17); that is, the risen Lord Jesus lives and manifests himself in the Spirit. "As the Father," writes St. Basil, "makes himself visible in the Son, so the Son makes himself present in the Spirit."[22] This belief was such a familiar one for the earliest generations of Christians that they celebrated Pentecost not so much as the event of the Holy Spirit's descent upon the apostles on the fiftieth day after Easter, but rather as the new presence of Jesus "according to the Spirit," inaugurated by his resurrection, the "spiritual" presence of Christ in his Church, of which the fifty days after Easter were a manifestation. Pentecost was not the feast of the fiftieth day, but of the fifty days; it began on Easter Day itself and gave the name to the fifty days following: "To the feast of Easter," writes St. Athanasius, "we shall add the feast of Pentecost, through which we pass, as though through a succession of feastdays, while we celebrate the Spirit who is now always near us in Christ Jesus."[23]

The Church is therefore led by the Spirit of Christ. Furthermore, in a certain sense, the Church is brought about by sharing in Christ's anointing; in other words, we are "Christ's body," that is, the Church, because we are animated by the Spirit of Christ: "Not only has our Head been anointed," says St. Augustine, "but we ourselves too, who are his body. . . . We are all the body of Christ because we all share in the anointing and, in him, we are all Christ's and Christ, since in a certain way the whole Christ consists in both Head and body."[24] We are a "messianic people," as Vatican II says, because we are an anointed people, a people consecrated with the Spirit.

This rediscovery of the mystery of the anointing is already starting to yield fruit in theology. H. Muehlen defines the Church as "the continuation in history of the anointing of Christ with the Holy Spirit." The Church, he says, is not, except in the broad sense, a prolongation of Christ's human body, that is to say of the incarnation, but it is, in the strict sense, a prolongation of the Spirit of Christ, of his anointing and of his grace. It is from the anointing that Christ receives "capital" grace (*gratia capitis*), the grace he has and conveys as Head of the Church, and not so much from the hypostatic union, from which he only receives his "personal" grace, that is, the unique and incommunicable holiness he has as only begotten Son of God made flesh. In this sense, the Fathers of the Church whom I mentioned earlier insisted that from the "fullness of the Holy Spirit" of Jesus we have received grace upon grace. Of course, Christ's baptism cannot be divorced from his incarnation; without the latter, the baptism would have no real significance for us; nevertheless, it adds something of extreme importance for us which impels us to a deeper love and contemplation of this mystery of Christ's life.

The Church has various means at her disposal for putting us in contact with the baptism of Jesus and the mystery of his anointing. One is the liturgical feast of Jesus' baptism, bringing the historical event to life again, as is the very nature of the feast. But even more important is the sacramental means of baptism and, more particularly, of anointing: whether the anointing that survives today as a complementary rite to baptism, or the anointing that has gradually come to be an independent sacrament, i.e., confirmation, with chrismation or unction.

Referring to this particular aspect of baptism, St. Paul says, "The one who gives us security with you in Christ and who anointed us is God; he has also put his seal upon us and given the Spirit in our hearts as a first installment" (2 Cor 1:21f.). In the golden age of the Fathers of the Church in the fourth century, this moment of sacramental anointing was the most favored opportunity for illustrating to the faithful the ineffable mystery of their sharing in the anointing of Christ: "As partakers of Christ," the bishop of Jerusalem told his people, "you are rightly called Christs, i.e., anointed ones. It was of you that God said, 'Touch not my anointed' (Ps 105:15). Now, you became Christs by receiving the seal of the Holy Spirit . . . Jesus bathed in the river Jordan and after imparting the fragrance of his Godhead to the waters, came up from them. Him the Holy Spirit visited in essential presence, like resting upon like. Similarly for you, after you had ascended from the sacred streams, there was an anointing with chrism, which is a figure of that with which Christ was anointed, that is, of the Holy Spirit."[25]

The Church, I said, disposes of various means for putting us in contact with the mystery of the anointing of Jesus, but all these means remain inoperant unless to them we add our personal effort. To the *historical* plane (the baptism of Jesus in the Jordan) and to the *sacramental* plane (our own baptism and confirmation) must be added the existential or *moral* plane. Thus, all that the Word of God has revealed to us up to this point about the mystery of the anointing tends towards this operative plane, towards bearing its fruit in us. And the fruit is that we ourselves become the "sweet smell of Christ" in the world. When consecrating the oil which is to serve for anointing at baptism and confirmation at the Mass of the Chrism on Maundy Thursday, the bishop says: "May this unction permeate them and make them holy so that, freed from the corruption of their first birth and consecrated as the temple of your glory, they may breathe forth the perfume of a holy life." Origen informs us that the pagans of his day used to challenge Christians by saying: how can one man, who for good measure lived in an obscure township in Judea, fill the world with the perfume of the knowledge of God, as you Christians say (cf. 2 Cor 2:14)? Origen's answer was that Jesus can do this because he has consecrated a large number of disciples with the Holy Spirit and sent them through the world, and these devote themselves to saving the human race by living in purity and righteousness and by teaching the same doctrine as Jesus. Thanks to them, "the precious oil sprinkled on the head" of the true Aaron, who is Christ, runs down "onto the collar of his robe" (cf. Ps 133:2), that is, it spreads throughout the body of the Church and, through it, to the whole world.[26]

We are those disciples sent throughout the world to spread the "sweet smell" of Christ! To succeed, we too must "shatter" the alabaster vessel of our human nature: we must mortify the works of the flesh, the old Adam which acts as an inner barrier to the rays of the Spirit. The perfume of Christ is given off by "the fruits of the Spirit" (according to St. Paul, "love, joy, peace, patience, kindness, generosity, faithfulness, gentleness, self-control" [Gal 5:22]); if these are in us, then, without our realizing (and of course while we by contrast only smell ourselves giving off the stink of our sins), someone around us may get a whiff of the fragrance of the Spirit of Christ. The world has a great need to smell the perfume of Christ! It needs this to be preserved from corruption or, at least, for its corruption to become manifest and be judged: "For we," says the Apostle, "are the aroma of Christ for God among those who are being saved and among those who are perishing; to the latter an odor of death that leads to death, to the former an odor of life that leads to life" (2 Cor 2:15f.).

I end this meditation with the beautiful prayer assigned in the liturgy to the bishop, for the Mass of the Chrism on Maundy Thursday: "Father you have consecrated your only-begotten Son with the unction of the Holy Spirit and have made him Messiah and Lord; grant that we who share in his consecration may bear witness in the world to his work of salvation."

NOTES

1. St. Irenaeus, *Adversus Haereses* 3.9.3.
2. Novatian, *De Trinitate* 29.168 (CCL 4, p. 70).
3. St. Athanasius, *Contra Arianos* 1.50 (PG 26, 118).
4. Cf. St. Irenaeus, *Epideixis* 53 (SCh 62, p. 114).
5. Tertullian, *De baptismo* 7.1 (CCL 1, p. 282).
6. Theophilus of Antioch, *Ad Autolycum* 1.12 (PG 6, 1041).
7. Cf. St. Cyril of Jerusalem, *Catechesis mystagogica* 3.1 (PG 33, 1089).
8. St. Irenaeus, *Adversus Haereses* 3.18.3.
9. St. Basil, *De Spiritu Sancto* 12 (PG 32, 116).
10. St. Gregory Naziazen, *Epistola 1 ad Cledonium* 23 (PG 37, 180).
11. St. Athanasius, *Oratio 1 contra Arianos* 46; cf. also St. Cyril of Alexandria, *In Iohannis Evangelium* 5.2 (PG 73, 754).
12. Cf. St. Gregory Nazianzen, *In sancta lumina* 15-16 (PG 36, 351); St. Gregory of Nyssa, *In diem luminum* (PG 46, 580).
13. St. Gregory Nazianzen, *Oratio* 30.2 (PG 36, 105B).
14. Cf. St. Basil, *De Spiritu Sancto* 16 (PG 32, 140).
15. *Presbyterorum ordinis* 1.2.
16. St. Athanasius, *Oratio 1 contra Arianos* 47 (PG 26, 108f.).
17. *Presbyterorum ordinis* 1.2.
18. St. Gregory of Nyssa, *In Cantica canticorum* 17.22 (PG 44, 1116).
19. St. Irenaeus, *Adversus Haereses* 3.17.1.
20. Nicholas Cabasilas, *Vita in Christo* 3.1 (PG 150, 572).
21. St. Ignatius of Antioch, *Epistola ad Ephesios* 17.
22. St. Basil, *De Spiritu Sancto* 26.64 (PG 32, 185).
23. St. Athanasius, *Epistolae festales* 14.6 (PG 26, 1422).
24. St. Augustine, *Enarrationes in Psalmos* 26.2 (CCL 38, p. 155).
25. St. Cyril of Jerusalem, *Catechesis mystagogica* 3.1 (PG 33, 1089).
26. Origen, *Contra Celsum* 6, 79 (SCh 147, p. 376).

Chapter Two

Kingly Anointing

The Spirit urges Jesus and the Church on —
to struggle against Satan

St. John in his First Epistle reminds Christians of "the anointing
that comes from the Holy One": he says that it "remains" in us
and that it "teaches everything" (cf. 1 John 2:20, 27). The anointing received from the Holy One indicates that we share in Christ's
anointing; in the ultimate analysis it is identical with the Holy
Spirit received in baptism in that he acts in us as light that warms
and illuminates and as inner master of truth. The anointing, it
is said, teaches "everything"; but what exactly it teaches, Jesus
himself explains when promising the coming of the Comforter:
"The Advocate, the Holy Spirit that the Father will send in my
name — he will teach you everything and remind you of all that
I told you" (John 14:26). So the anointing teaches us Jesus; reminds us about Jesus; brings Jesus to life for us. It is vitally important therefore to find out from the Gospels just what the Holy
Spirit prompted Jesus to do during his life on earth, what steps
he made him take, what choices: for he is prompting the Church
to do exactly the same things now. Pentecost turns our attention
back to the Gospels. And this indeed is what we see happening
in the Church immediately after Pentecost: the believers at once
set to work, very carefully collecting information about Jesus,
gathering from witnesses his words and everything he had done
"in the country of the Jews and in Jerusalem" (cf. Acts 10:39).
The Gospels tell the things to be done; Pentecost, that is the Holy
Spirit, grace, gives the strength to do them.

The following meditations have this very purpose: to find out
from the Gospels what the Spirit prompted Jesus to do. We shall
do our best to establish the safest criterion by which to recognize
the true motions or promptings of the Holy Spirit in our own lives
and in the life of the Church.

Everything Jesus says and does in the gospel, he performs "in the Holy Spirit." He chose the apostles "through the Holy Spirit" (cf. Acts 1:2). St. Basil says that the Holy Spirit "was a continual presence in the life of our Lord, being his anointing and his inseparable companion" and that "all Christ's activity unfolded in the presence of the Spirit."[1] "Christ is born," writes St. Gregory Nazianzen, "and the Spirit precedes him; he is baptized, and the Spirit bears witness to him; he is put to the proof, and the Spirit leads him back to Galilee; he works miracles, and the Spirit accompanies him; he ascends into heaven, and the Spirit succeeds him."[2] St. John Chrysostom says that Christ during his life "was assisted by the most sweet and with-him-consubstantial Spirit."[3]

These are very lovely expressions which conjure up images of intimacy and friendship, but they cannot even remotely give us an idea of what really went on at the deepest level between Jesus and the Holy Spirit during the days of the Savior's life on earth. We might think of two brothers who, having lived for ages in intimate friendship in their father's house, meet again after a long interval, in a foreign country, among people who speak a different language, both of them committed to one same dangerous enterprise desired by the father they love. Who can know the secret understanding established between the two of them, the support each receives from the other, the sweetness of their intimate exchanges, the longing to get the work done quickly with which their father has entrusted them. No one, says St. Paul, knows the secrets of the human heart, except the human spirit within (cf. 1 Cor 2:11), and this is equally true of Jesus and his Spirit. We have to leave this "secret" inviolate, and be content with contemplating it in prayerful silence, to have some scent of it, if the Spirit be pleased to give it to us.

I said that Jesus' whole life unfolded under the action of the Holy Spirit; within this continual presence however, certain particular moments stand out, since the Gospels themselves explicitly relate them to a special prompting of Jesus by the Holy Spirit. We shall concentrate on these, so as to be sure of touching the real *cruces* of the Spirit's activity in Jesus' life and avoiding the risk of making an arbitrary choice.

There are three such moments in particular: the Spirit drives Jesus out into the wilderness to be tempted (Mark 1:22); the Spirit consecrates Jesus by anointing him to bring the glad tidings to the poor (Luke 4:18); the Spirit makes Jesus "exult" and say,

"I bless you, Father . . ." (Luke 10:21). In other words, the Spirit urges Jesus on, to struggle against the devil, to preach the gospel, and to pray to the Father and offer himself in sacrifice to him. In these three things we can see the effects of Jesus' threefold — kingly, prophetic, and priestly — anointing. At the consecration of the oil for the anointing at baptism and confirmation in the Maundy Thursday Mass, the liturgy stresses this threefold unction with the words: "So, Father, we ask you to bless this oil you have created. Fill it with the power of your Holy Spirit through Christ your Son. It is from him that chrism takes its name, and with chrism you have anointed for yourself priests and kings, prophets and martyrs." In the struggle with the devil, Jesus fulfills his *kingly mission,* in that he overthrows the kingdom of Satan and establishes the kingdom of God; he himself said, "If it is by the Spirit of God that I drive out demons, then the kingdom of God has come upon you" (Matt 12:28); his *prophetic mission* unfolds in evangelizing the poor; and his *priestly mission* is seen in his praying to the Father with inexpressible groans. Thus, in all these three things he performs his fundamental mission as Servant of Yahweh, which he received at his baptism and in which all other activities are included.

1. *"The Spirit drove him out into the wilderness"*

Let us now consider the first of these "motions" of the Holy Spirit on Jesus, in which his kingly anointing takes effect.

All three Synoptics say that, after his baptism, Jesus retired into the wilds; all three attribute this decision to the Holy Spirit: "At once the Spirit drove him out into the desert" (Mark 1:12). Luke, who is the most sensitive of all to the Holy Spirit's activity in Jesus' life, duplicated the mention of the Holy Spirit here, and says that "filled with the Holy Spirit, Jesus returned from the Jordan and was led by the Spirit into the desert" (Luke 4:1).

We know each of the three evangelists gives his own coloring to the episode, corresponding to the aim and character of his narrative. Matthew and Luke, for instance, point out a connection between Jesus' temptations and those of Israel in the wilderness, implying that Jesus is the new Israel, succeeding where Israel had failed; Mark however alludes to the difference in outcome between the temptations of Jesus and Adam, implying that Jesus is the new Adam who, having overcome the Tempter, readmits the human race to its lost paradise ("He was among wild beasts, and the angels ministered to him").

But we are not so much concerned now with the differences as with the common nucleus or basic significance which can be extracted by taking account not only of the episode of the temptations but also of the rest of the gospel. Jesus himself explains the meaning of his struggle with Satan in the wilds, saying, "No one can enter a strong man's house to plunder his property, unless he first ties up the strong man. Then he can plunder his house" (Mark 3:27). While in the wilderness, Jesus has "tied up" the Adversary: he has, we might say, settled accounts with him before setting to work, and can now carry his campaign forward into enemy territory, free of any kind of indecision or uncertainty about his aims or the means to be employed (C. H. Dodd).

Jesus frees himself from Satan, to free everyone from Satan; this is the meaning of the episode of the temptations, seen in the light of the whole gospel. And indeed, as we read on after this episode, we really do get the impression of an irresistible advance, as it were, of the front of light, as it throws back the demonic front of darkness. At Jesus' approach, the demons take fright, they tremble, they beg not to be driven out and try to make terms: "What have you to do with us, Jesus of Nazareth? Have you come to destroy us? I know who you are — the Holy One of God!" (Mark 1:24); "If you drive us out, send us into the herd of swine" (Matt 8:31). But the presence of Jesus permits no escape: "Quiet! Come out of him!" (Mark 1:25). The people are seized with awe and say, "What is this? A new teaching with authority! He commands even the unclean spirits and they obey him!" (Mark 1:27).

Most striking is the authority and power bursting forth from Jesus. Immediately people begin to ask: Where does this authority come from? The answer from the hostile is: From the prince of the demons! Jesus's answer is: From the Holy Spirit. "By the finger of God I drive out demons" (Luke 11:20); "by the Spirit of God" (Matt 12:28). So too Peter in the Acts of the Apostles makes a strict connection between Jesus' activity against the demons and the anointing with the Holy Spirit: "God anointed Jesus of Nazareth with the Holy Spirit and power. He went about . . . healing all those oppressed by the devil" (Acts 10:38).

But let us try to understand this statement rather better. What had happened in the wilderness for the person of Jesus, on his

23

return, to have such authority as could make Satan melt away before him? It was that Satan had been beaten on his own ground! Satan's next favorite ground, after sin, was human free will. He had made this his fortress: an impregnable fortress since the only thing that could drive him out of it was the human will, but owing to sin the human will had become enslaved to him (cf. Rom 6:16f.; John 8:34) and, being his slave, could not rebel against its boss and overcome him. Jesus pierced the defenses of this fortress and destroyed it. His potent, threefold no to the temptations blunted Satan's sting, rebellion against God. Then Satan did indeed fall "like lightning" (cf. Luke 10:18). That threefold no was in fact an unconditional, loving, threefold yes to the Father's will.

Satan's defeat thus begins where his victory first began: in an individual's free will. Jesus appears to us, at this moment, as the new Adam at last uttering that free yes for which God had created heaven and earth. A created will has so far expanded as to welcome the entire will of God within itself. Jesus' power springs from here; he acts from now on with the very authority and power of God; the demons sense that Jesus is "the Holy One of God," that is, that the very holiness of God is present within him, and a presence like this is something they cannot withstand. "Driving out demons in the Spirit of God" means "The devil was stripped of his power in the presence of the Holy Spirit."[4]

Death still remained under Satan's sway, but even this he lost by rashly dragging Jesus into it. The passion is the second episode in the great battle between Jesus and the prince of darkness; it is that "appointed time" when the devil, as St. Luke says, returns to the charge against Jesus (cf. Luke 4:13). "The ruler of the world is coming," Jesus said on the eve of his death. "He has no power over me, but the world must know that I love the Father and that I do just as the Father has commanded me" (John 14:30f.). Satan had lost all power over him in the wilderness, but now Jesus reduces to total impotence "through death, the one who has the power of death, that is the devil" (Heb 2:14). Satan was conquered in his last refuge; the great judgment of the world takes place and the prince of the world is "driven out" (cf. John 12:31). On the cross, Jesus, obedient to the Father's will even unto death, breaks the power of Satan, as an iron bolt is broken; from this moment, the Book of Revelation says, "the kingdom of the world belongs to our Lord and to his Anointed" (Rev 11:15).

2. *The Dragon and the Woman*

When, from this assertion of Jesus' victory, we pass on to examine the Church's situation immediately after that first Easter, we are very bewildered at first and acutely disappointed: everything goes on as before! The New Testament writers are the very people to tell us so, with disconcerting candor. St. Paul says, "Our struggle is not with flesh and blood but with the principalities, with the powers, with the world rulers of this present darkness, with the evil spirits in the heavens" (Eph 6:12). Peter writes in his turn: "Your opponent the devil is prowling around like a roaring lion looking for someone to devour" (1 Pet 5:8). The Book of Revelation gives a kind of scenic representation of this new situation: the devil (the Dragon), not having managed to devour the Son (Jesus), full of rage, hurls itself at the Woman who gave birth to the Son, forcing her to flee into the wilderness (cf. Rev 12:13-14). The Church (the Woman) too is led by the Spirit into the wilderness to be tempted by the devil! It could not be said more clearly: after Jesus, the struggle against Satan goes on, inside the Church, against the Church. Also, this struggle has become more relentless, for now Satan is "in great fury," since "he knows he has but a short time" (cf. Rev 12:12). And indeed, with the coming of Christ, his time has been cut short; the fullness of time having come, he has nothing left to look forward to except eternity, when every prospect of activity in the world will be finished as far as he is concerned and he will be forever confined in the eternal immobility which is his doom.

If the New Testament writers can tell us all this without betraying any surprise, this is because they have discovered what it all means. Being tempted is one aspect of Christ's sufferings. St. Paul's words: "In my flesh I am filling up what is lacking in the afflictions of Christ on behalf of his body, which is the Church" (Col 1:24) are therefore true also when said about being tempted: In my flesh I am filling up what is lacking in the temptations of Christ on behalf of his body, which is the Church! The members ought to share in the struggle of the Head, just as one day they will share in his complete victory and glory. This is a universal law: it holds good for every type of suffering, even for that special suffering, temptation and the struggle against the devil.

But here we discover that it is not entirely true to say the situation is unchanged and things are on the same footing after Jesus as before him. In the wilderness, Jesus bound Satan once and for all; then on the cross, "despoiling the principalities and the powers, he made a public spectacle of them, leading them away in triumph" (Col 2:15). Satan's power is no longer free, as it used to be, to act for his own ends; henceforth it is "enslaved." He thinks he acts for one purpose but instead achieves the very opposite; without wishing to, he serves the cause of Jesus and his saints. Satan henceforth is indeed "that power that always wills evil and does good" (Goethe). This is because Jesus has, as it were, upset and altered the target of his activity: henceforth it rebounds on himself; it has become a sort of boomerang. He tormented Jesus by having him convicted, scourged, and finally crucified; but Jesus, by accepting all of this in obedience to the Father and for love of the human race, transformed it into God's supreme victory and Satan's supreme defeat. Jesus is *victor quia victima*[5]; Satan by contrast is *victima quia victor:* Christ is victor because victim; Satan is victim because victor — the victim of his own victory.

This has always been so for the true followers of Jesus, for the saints, starting with the martyrs mentioned in the Book of Revelation (cf. Rev 11:7f.). God's victory is built in the midst of apparent defeat. The hardest thing to accept in all this is that, every time, defeat looks absolutely real and final, and God seems to give in to the Adversary on all fronts and, as it were, withdraw from the fray, leaving the Enemy in a position to wheel out his most terrible of weapons: doubt about God's goodness. "Where is your God? What father would not intervene if worth the name of father, and put an end to such sufferings as his son's?" The mortal defeat of Satan occurs when, in this situation, we disciples of Jesus, summoning up all our strength and as though crying out inwardly, say, "You are holy, Lord! Just and true are your ways. I surrender myself to you, Father, even though I do not understand you any more! Father, into your hands I commend my spirit!" The victory consists, in a word, in making the sentiments which were Jesus' our own.

There is another purpose for which God makes use of Satan's activity: to correct and humble his elect. Lest Paul should have become proud because of the great revelations he had received, he was given a thorn in the flesh, an emissary of Satan to beat him (cf. 2 Cor 12:7). St. Francis, having received the stigmata lest even he should grow proud, received so many tribulations and temptations from the devils that he used to say, "If the brethren knew how many great trials and afflictions the devils bring upon me, there is not one of them who would not be moved to compassion and pity for me."[6] St. Francis, however, used to call the demons "bailiffs," that is to say the material executors of the Lord's commands: "Just as the Podestà sends his policemen to punish a guilty man, so too does the Lord correct and chastise those he loves through his policemen, that is, the devils."[7]

Naturally this is only a vision *in positive* of the story of the Church's temptations; there is also a vision *in negative,* of yieldings, of partial or even total victories for the Enemy. Such things have come about whenever a Christian takes off from Christ's flock, to fight like a wolf rather than like a lamb; whenever the Church has attempted to establish God's kingdom by other means than those employed by Jesus in the wilderness. But people have had so much to say about this negative history in the past (suffice it to recall the tremendous indictment Dostoevsky puts into the mouth of the Grand Inquisitor!) that, for once, we may leave it to one side.

3. *The silence about Satan*

All this for better or worse, has conferred a dramatic quality of struggle on Christian life throughout the ages, and of struggle "not only against flesh or blood." Today, this tension has in great part and in many sectors of Christendom collapsed; silence has fallen about Satan; the struggle is now only against "flesh and blood," that is, against evils within human reach, such as social injustice, violence, one's own character, one's own sins. For evils within human reach of course a salvation suffices which is equally within human reach, achievable with progress and human effort; in other words, Christian salvation, coming from outside history, is not necessary. The inventor of demythologization wrote: "You cannot use electric light and radio, you cannot have recourse, when sick, to doctors and clinics and at the same time believe in the world of spirits" (R. Bultmann). Demythologization has exorcised the devil from the world, but in a different way than we read in the New Testament: not by driving him out but by denying his existence. No one, I imagine, has ever been so delighted at being demythologized as the devil, if it is true — as has been said — that Satan's greatest cunning is to make people believe he does not exist (Charles Baudelaire).

So, the present generation, after treatment in the two acid baths of demythologization and secularization, shows a strange and suspect allergy to hearing this subject discussed. More or less consciously, it has ended up accepting a soothing explanation: the devil is the sum total of human moral wickedness; he is the collective unconscious or, for sociologists, the collective alienation. When Pope Paul VI dared to remind Christians a few years ago of the "Catholic truth" that the devil exists, secular culture (or at least some part of it) reacted by rending its garments and exclaiming in shock: "How can he still go on about the devil at this point in time? How positively medieval!" Many of the faithful too and among them several theologians allowed themselves to be intimidated: "Well, yes, the idea that he's symbolic . . . the mythological explanation or the psychological one: any of these would do. . . ." For Christians, the question of the devil has become a typical example of ill faith; we pretend a certain thing doesn't exist because we haven't the guts to acknowledge that it does and take the consequences.

The Christian life, as I have said, has thus been de-dramatized, but by the same token banalized. And not only Christian life but Christ's life too becomes de-dramatized, for his victory becomes an empty one if we do not know who his true adversary was: Satan, against whom he strove with all his soul, who led him to the cross and on the cross was overcome by him. In making us the gift of Christian life at baptism, the Church presents it as a choice: "Do you renounce . . . do you believe in . . .?" as much as to say, "There are two dominions, two kingdoms in the world: you have to choose: which one do you want to belong to?" To have abolished one of the poles of choice, the negative one, possibly betrays in our secularized generation a fear of having to choose. We have chosen to eliminate anxiety at the root by eliminating choice, but we have not grasped that in so doing we offer our arm to an anxiety much worse.

For we have to choose — or wager — and we know it! As the unconscious, when repressed, generates neuroses, giving rise to every kind of psychological disturbance, so the devil, driven back among the myths and repudiated by the intellect, takes advantage of this to cause all sorts of spiritual neuroses in the modern psyche: agitation, fear, remorse, anxiety. A very curious thing is going on: Satan, driven out through the door, has climbed back through the window; driven out of religion and theology, he has come back in superstition. The modern, technological, industrialized world, especially where it is at its most industrialized and advanced, is crawling with gurus, witches, spiritualists, readers of horoscopes, sellers of spells and amulets, not to mention actual satanist sects. Something has happened similar to what the Apostle Paul reproached his pagan contemporaries with: "While claiming to be wise, they became fools and exchanged the glory of the immortal God for the likeness of an image of mortal man or of birds or of four-legged animals or of snakes. . . . And since they did not see fit to acknowledge God, God handed them over to their undiscerning mind . . ." (Rom 1:22, 28).

4. *The devil exists, all the same . . .*

So now we have a situation where, as St. Catherine of Siena once said, we need someone to utter "a roar" over the body of Holy Church, lusty enough to wake up the children lying asleep within her. Friends, now is the time to awake from sleep! The devil does exist and is more "full of rage" against the saints than ever. It looks as though he has got wind of something big about to happen in the Church and has thrown all his forces into the struggle to prevent or distort it; as though, unexpectedly, he finds he hasn't got much time left. He reacts violently when he hears the proclamation: "The wedding day of the Lamb has come, his bride has made herself ready" (Rev 19:7). He becomes mad with jealousy over anything to do with Jesus.

Jesus, it has been said, is in agony in the garden until the end of the world. This is true for the doctrine of the mystical body. It is also true that Jesus is in the wilderness being tempted until the end of the world! Were it possible to describe what Satan contrives against this Jesus who is still in the wilderness being tempted, a cry of horror would burst from our lips. The arguments he shrieks to detach believers from their God are a terrible school of theology; they show us how many of today's theological disputes, filling books, reviews, and newspapers and wasting the Church's time and energy are mere academic skirmishes, whereas the real battle is far more deeply seated and barely touched by them. Woe to the Church, were it not for those advanced ramparts which, suffering themselves to be scourged by Satan's angel, hold in check and break the force of his billows and prevent them from flooding the whole Church. St. Paul wrote some words to the Thessalonians which, I am convinced, have special meaning for us today, even though it may not be entirely clear what: "Now you know what is restraining [God's adversary], that he may be revealed in his time. For the mystery of lawlessness is already at work. But the one who restrains is to do so only for the present, until he is removed from the scene. And then the lawless one will be revealed, whom the Lord Jesus will kill with the breath of his mouth and render powerless by the manifestation of his coming, the one whose coming springs from the power of Satan in every mighty deed and in signs and wonders that lie" (2 Thess 2:6-9).

Why then do so few people seem to be aware of this tremendous subterranean battle taking place in the Church, while those few are often left very much to themselves and given to think they are battling with chimeras and the products of auto-suggestion? Why do so few people show any sign of hearing the "lion's" sinister roars as it prowls around, looking for someone to devour? It is simple! Because our scholars and theologians (and not only they!) look for the devil in books, whereas the devil is not interested in books but in souls; he is not to be found hanging about in university institutes, libraries, or the offices of the ecclesiastical top-brass, but on the look-out for souls. It is with souls, especially those who take the gospel seriously or, better still, those whom God has chosen for his mysterious plans, that he is forced to come out into the open. The strongest proof of Satan's existence is not to be found in the sinful or in the possessed, but in the saints. In them his activity stands out clearly in contrast, like black on white. So too in the gospel, the most convincing proof of the existence of demons is not to be found in the freeing of the possessed (which may sometimes in fact depend on contemporary notions about the origin of illness), but in the tempting of Jesus, when Satan is forced to take position, so to speak, "against the light."

One cannot expect an atheist or secularized culture to believe in the existence of the devil. It would be absolutely tragic if it believed in the devil while not believing in God. What can one know about Satan when all one has to go on is, not the reality of Satan, but the concept or the cultural, religious, and ethnological traditions about him? People in this position commonly treat the subject in a very assured, very superior manner, dismissing it all as "medieval obscurantism." But this assurance is only skin-deep, like that of people who pride themselves on not being frightened of lions because they have seen so many paintings and photographs of them and never felt frightened then.

No sooner do we leave the academic world and enter the world of souls and the heart of the kingdom of God than we alter our views on Satan. For we then discover where the poison comes from that is infecting the world, where a certain atheistic philosophy originates, exalting absolute human autonomy, where the lie erected into a system, the destruction of human life, blasphemy, rage against the name of Christ, all have their origin.

5. *The spirit in the air*

It is not however only in souls or in people as individuals that Satan's activities take place, even if only there do these activities come into the open. They also lurk and act through human institutions, situations, and realities of which they take possession. The New Testament has something extremely relevant to teach us in this connection: it speaks of a spirit that roves in the air, like an atmosphere that we inhale, and finds its favorite vehicle in public opinion and the mass media.

> In Ephesians 2:2, the prince of this world is curiously called "the ruler of the power of the air." And the apostle himself clarifies the meaning of the word "air." For him, it is "the spirit that is now at work in the disobedient," that is to say those people who have rejected the gospel. The consequence of this is that Satan acts in the world by fixing on the spirit that rules unbelievers. He acts through this spirit, having taken possession of it, and dwells in it. The spirit is simultaneously an atmosphere. He lives and acts in this spiritual atmosphere and wields his influence through it. From it and by means of it, as his dwelling-place and immediate field of activity, he acquires power over human beings and gets inside them. This is not of course his only way but it is clearly the one he prefers as the most effective way of extending his power. He becomes a spirit of great historic intensity, from which an individual finds it hard to escape. That one should conform to the spirit of the times, people regard as obvious. To act, or think, or say anything con-

trary to it is regarded as folly, or even as wrong or as a crime. So people no longer dare to confront things, situations, most particularly life itself, in a different way than the spirit of the age presents. The hidden ruler of this world — hidden precisely in the spiritual air, in the atmosphere of various periods — makes the world and existence appear in *his own* perspective, by making use of this atmosphere, which he controls."[8]

One might say that, just as Christ's unction exists, which "teaches everything," shows everything by the light of Christ (cf. 1 John 2:20, 27), so also there exists the Antichrist's unction, which teaches everything, gives everything its own, diabolic interpretation and, so to speak, the Satanic side of things. This deadly unction permeates everything, sticks to everything, and becomes the spirit of the particular age. When the Apostle exhorts us not to conform ourselves to the spirit of the age (cf. Rom 12:2), this is the spirit to which he is referring. One may safely say that the unbelief of today's world — where it is not imposed by violence from above — is caused by Satan, largely by that supine adaptation to the spirit of the times, by making people inhale the scent of his unction, which has the power to anesthetize our consciences.

6. *The discerning of spirits*

Of course there is always the problem of the discerning of spirits. This is a delicate matter in which we need prudence so as not to delude and confuse ourselves: to delude ourselves by indiscriminately ascribing all our own mistakes to the devil, without taking serious note of the evil we all have rooted inside us and hence without mortifying it; to confuse ourselves by attributing every kind of phenomenon to the devil in person and seeing him at work everywhere. Here the Word of God gives us sure criteria. Speaking about the devil, St. Peter advises us to "be sober and vigilant" (1 Pet 5:8). To be "sober" means to have a healthy and realistic view of ourselves and of the world in its complexity and ambiguity, so as not to see Satan at work where only illnesses are involved, even if they are very mysterious, or the consequences of sin; to be "vigilant" means not to let ourselves be lulled into a sense of false security by overlooking the fact that the devil still exists and that he never sleeps. St. John too exhorts us not to put faith — for good or ill — in every inspiration, but to put inspirations to the test so that we may know whether they truly come from God when they seem good, and truly from the devil when they seem bad (cf. 1 John 4:1f.). Sane discernment ought also to prevent us from making false and crude representations of Satan which a modern mind would automatically be inclined to refute on the grounds, this time, of a healthy demythologization. Satan is not a person, as a human being is, or as the Word is, once made flesh; so he cannot be represented or treated as though he were a concrete person. "In the New Testament, the demonic powers are called by the same term as designates the divine power of the Holy Spirit: *pneuma*, spirit. The Holy Spirit however does not speak directly and immediately within us but rather expresses himself *in* and *through* our intelligence, will, feelings. By analogy, it would be an error to suppose that Satan would speak directly and immediately within us and answer questions" (H. Muehlen). Not therefore a person, but only a personal power, that is to say a power endowed with intelligence and will, pursuing the very precise aim of destroying human beings' relationships with God and with one another.

Outside his own world, when he is at work in the human world, Satan has a merely parasitic life: he cannot subsist on his own as an autonomous person but always needs to attach himself to something or someone and deploy his activity through them. The New Testament suggests that he can attach himself to the spiritual faculties of human beings and through these act on the physical; he can also act directly on the physical, without being able to effect the faculties of the soul (at least the deepest part of the soul) as certain diabolical ordeals prove which we find in the lives of some of the saints. He can attach himself to objects in the world regarded as sacred or divine, as the stars and idols once were (cf. Gal 4:8f.; Col 2:18). He can also take possession — as St. John shows in Revelation — of the world of politics, as far as infusing the holders, the means, and the spheres of political power with his own will-to-power, and manipulating these to deadly effect by instilling his own spirit into them (H. Schlier). The following words, inspired by what happened during the Second World War, confirm St. John's insights in Revelation:

> In those days we came all too often into contact with demonic powers; we experienced and saw, more than was needful, individuals and whole groups of people seduced and led by mys-

terious, hellish powers; all too often we observed a spirit extraneous to people transform them to the very depths of their being as it egged them on to acts of cruelty, drunk with power and bursts of madness of which they had never known themselves capable before; an invisible hand proffered an invisible goblet of frenzy, passing it from people to people until the nations ran mad. I say we saw too much of this, we were too frightened by it, for us not to feel ashamed to go on doubting whether or not the devil existed. (H. Thielicke)

If we too could look at some of the political realities of our own day with the piercing, prophetic eye the author of Revelation focused on the empire then tyrannizing over the nations and persecuting the Christians, perhaps our evaluation would be no different, and many things to which we have become accustomed would appear to us under their true face: a satanic face, that is.

Our discerning of spirits must also take another point into account: the position the devil occupies in our religion. In Christianity, Satan does not have an importance equal to that of Christ; therefore it is not at all correct to say we believe "in" the devil. We believe in God and we believe in Christ (cf. John 14:1) but we do not believe in the devil, if believing means trusting someone and relying on them. We believe the devil exists, but we do not believe *in* him; he is an *object,* and for good measure a negative one, of our faith, like sin and hell, not the cause or *end* of it. We establish no personal relationship with him, as we do with Christ when we say, "I believe in Jesus Christ!"

God and the devil are not two parallel, eternal principles, independent each of other, such as may be found in some dualistic religions (Zoroastrianism, for instance). As far as the Bible is concerned, the devil is merely a creature of God's that has gone to the bad; everything that he is in a positive sense comes from God; his power, now as before, comes from God, but the devil corrupts it and misdirects it by using it against him. Only his malice therefore comes from his free will; all that he has of his own is his will to be independent of God and all that he seeks in the world is to drag us into this, his "will to be independent of God."

7. *Freeing ourselves from Satan to free others from Satan*

The problem of the discerning of spirits and of prudence does not exhaust the responsibilities of the Christian, still less of pastors and priests in this matter. It would be a fatal mistake for all our sobriety and vigilance to be used up in discouraging excessive credulity and facile exorcisms. These are distractions and false alarms of the Enemy, which we must be able to recognize, but woe be to us if once this is done the Church should believe she has done all she can to preserve her children from the roaring lion or, worse, should ignore the existence of this roaring lion that goes about looking for people to devour. Something more is needed. It is required of us who, owing to our priesthood, share in a special manner in the kingly anointing of Jesus that we boldly proclaim that the Christian life is a choice between two kingdoms, that our warfare is not only against flesh and blood. It is required of us that we proclaim in Spirit and in power that Jesus has overcome all powers, and that henceforth he is the one, true Lord and that there is nothing to be afraid of, "for the one who is in you is greater than the one who is in the world" (1 John 4:4). It is very important, while the struggle is still going on and the dragon seems to have the upper hand, that the Church should raise the triumph-shout of victory: "Now have salvation and power come, and the kingdom of our God and the authority of his Anointed One. For the accuser of our brothers is cast out, who accuses them before our God day and night. But they have conquered him by the blood of the Lamb" (Rev 12:10-11). By the purity of faith that it implies, this shout raised in the darkness makes Satan's throne tremble to its foundations.

Of us is required above all that we imitate Christ's struggle and victory on behalf of his body, the Church. In the wilderness he freed himself from Satan so that he could then free all of us from Satan. He bound him and cast him completely out of his life and thus could set about fulfilling his mission of bringing glad tidings to the poor, "healing all those who were oppressed by the devil." Jesus points out that one of the essential tasks of a good shepherd is to take the wolf on personally, to defend the flock from the wolf, thus distinguishing himself from the hireling who "sees the wolf coming and abandons the sheep" (cf. John 10:12f.). The Apostle tells us how to arm ourselves for this battle "with the world rulers of this present darkness":

> Put on the armor of God, that you may be able to resist on the evil day and, having done everything, to hold your ground. So stand fast with your loins girded in truth, clothed with right-

eousness as a breastplate, and your feet shod in readiness for the gospel of peace. In all circumstances, hold faith as a shield, to quench all the flaming arrows of the evil one. And take the helmet of salvation and the sword of the Spirit, which is the word of God. With all prayer and supplication, pray at every opportunity in the Spirit. To that end, be watchful with all perseverance and supplication for all the holy ones (Eph 6:13-18).

Apostolic zeal, strength of faith, word of God and incessant prayer in the Spirit: these are the arms recommended to us. Jesus freed himself from Satan by an act of total obedience to the Father's will, once and for all handing over his free will to him, so that he could truly say, "My food is to do the will of the one who sent me" (John 4:34). And so today, when we as God's servants abandon ourselves completely to the Father's will for the sake of our fellow beings and go on putting our trust in him even in the most complete darkness, the prince of this world loses any power over us and we too share in Christ's liberating power. His word and his life, in small matters as in great, according to the position in which the Lord has placed us, are a true exorcism, not however an exorcism by words but by deeds. Wherever we go, the Enemy is dislodged and put to flight, not by us (need I say!) but by the kingly unction that we bear within us and that makes us sharers in Christ's own holiness.

A somewhat new picture of Jesus is disclosed to the eye of faith after this meditation, an image radiating spiritual energy and courage: the Jesus anointed with the Holy Spirit and power, who courageously takes on the powers of darkness; the Jesus of the early moments of his mission; the Jesus who acts to usher in the kingdom of God and says, "Anyone who wants to be my disciple, follow me!" If we stay firmly united to this Jesus, we have nothing to fear from events and from the unrestrained powers of evil; Jesus stands in front of us, an insurmountable wall against which every power of darkness founders. To this Jesus, the Church entire, drunk with the scent of his unction, exclaims in the words of the bride in the Song of Songs: "Draw me! We will follow you eagerly!" (Cant 1:4).

1. St. Basil, *De Spiritu Sancto* 16 (PG 32, 140).
2. St. Gregory Nazianzen, *Oratio* 31.29 (PG 36, 166).
3. St. John Chrysostom, *Catechesis baptismalis* 3.26 (SCh 50, p. 166).
4. St. Basil, *De Spiritu Sancto* 19 (PG 32, 157).
5. St. Augustine, *Confessions* 10.43.69.
6. St. Francis of Assisi, *Mirror of Perfection* 99 (*St. Francis of Assisi, Writings and Early Biographies,* Chicago 1983, p. 1235).
7. St. Francis of Assisi, *Legend of Perugia* 92 (*Writings,* p. 1068).
8. H. Schlier, *Besinnung auf das Neue Testament,* Freiburg in Br. 1967, chap. 10.

Chapter Three
Prophetic Anointing

The Spirit urges Jesus and the Church on — to evangelize

Immediately after being tempted and overcoming the temptations in the wilderness, Jesus, St. Luke tells us, "returned to Galilee in the power of the Spirit and . . . taught in their synagogues" (Luke 4:14f). Jesus' evangelistic activity all begins at this moment, being thus put under the action of the Holy Spirit. But we have Jesus' own testimony about this. Let us listen to the gospel narrative:

> He came to Nazareth, where he had grown up, and went according to his custom into the synagogue on the sabbath day. He stood up to read and was handed a scroll of the prophet Isaiah. He unrolled the scroll and found the passage where it was written:
>
> > The Spirit of the Lord is upon me,
> > because he has anointed me
> > to bring glad tidings to the poor.
> > He has sent me to proclaim liberty to captives
> > and recovery of sight to the blind,
> > to let the oppressed go free
> > and to proclaim a year acceptable to the Lord.
>
> Rolling up the scroll, he handed it back to the attendant and sat down, and the eyes of all in the synagogue looked intently at him. He said to them, "Today this scripture passage is fulfilled in your hearing" (Luke 4:16-21).

The presence of the Holy Spirit in Jesus' life receives new light from this passage. We have two sources for knowing what the Holy Spirit worked in Jesus during his life on earth: the first consists in what the Gospels themselves say on the subject (for instance that Jesus "was led by the Spirit into the wilderness," that "he exulted in the Holy Spirit," and so forth); the second consists in what had been foretold by the prophets about the relationship between the Spirit of God and the Messiah and was applied by the evangelists to Jesus or, as in this instance, was applied by Jesus to himself.

Of the great texts that speak of the outpouring of the Spirit in the last days, only one, Joel 3, refers to the age of the Church; all the others — Isaiah 11:1f.; 42:1f.; 61:1f. — are applied in the Gospels to the earthly Jesus. Once again we discover that Pentecost starts in the gospel.

In these last mentioned texts it is said that the Spirit will be conferred on the Messiah in all his work, but especially in the work of evangelization. The Spirit of the Lord "is put" on the Servant so that he can proclaim the law with firmness, so that he can be "a light to the nations" (cf. Isa 42:1f.) and so that he can "bring glad tidings to the lowly" (cf. Isa 61:1). These are the ways in which the Messiah's prophetic anointing finds expression in action. But, in applying the prophetic mission to himself, Jesus widens it out of all proportion; "Today," he says, "this scripture passage is fulfilled." In Isaiah's case, it was in effect a figure; with Jesus now it is a reality. Thus, Jesus is not one of the prophets but the "fulfillment" of all the prophets. In the Old Testament prophets, the Spirit's presence was temporary and partial, linked to particular moments of inspiration; in Jesus it is full and permanent: "to him the Spirit is given without measure" (John 3:34, according to some codices). The difference is qualitative, not merely quantitative. We are speaking of a fullness that is at once eschatological (that is, definitive) and ontological (total and absolute) because, as Word, Jesus is, together with the Father, the very origin of the Spirit and, as man-God, offers a limitless capacity for welcoming the Spirit.

1. *The Spirit, force of the Word*

The Spirit, as I have said, was given to Jesus for the quite special purpose of evangelizing. The Spirit does not give Jesus the word to preach, for Jesus is himself the Word of God, but gives force to his word, and so is the very force of the word of God. What, in concrete terms, does the Spirit do to the word of Jesus? He confers authority on it ("He speaks with authority!") and efficacity. When Jesus speaks, things always happen: the paralyzed man stands up, the sea grows calm, the fig-tree withers, "the blind regain their sight, the lame walk, lepers are cleansed, the deaf hear, the dead are raised, the poor have the good news proclaimed to them" (Luke 7:22). The Spirit also confers a divine freedom on Jesus in his preaching, which places him above conflictual situations and party interests (Pharisees, Saducees, Zealots, Herodians), so causing even his opponents to admit: "You do not regard a person's status but teach the way of God in accordance with the truth" (Mark 12:14). A powerful breath once more pervades the country, after the long silence of the prophets. This breath, besides giving force to Jesus' words, also gives them unction, that is, sweetness, consolation, suavity: "Never before has anyone spoken like this one," say the guards who have been sent to arrest him (John 7:46). Above all, however, the Spirit gives Jesus the strength not to become downcast (cf. Isa 42:4). One could say the Spirit is given to Jesus more with a view to failure than to success (that same day in Nazareth, he had to flee for his life!); the mission of servant, accepted by Jesus at his baptism, passes by way of rejection, failure, and defeat.

It is certainly a marvelous thing to see Jesus going right ahead, without regrets or second thoughts, consenting to pass — he, the Son of God — from disappointment to disappointment, from rejection to rejection, from obstruction to obstruction. When, in one such situation, some of the disciples suggested he should call down fire from heaven, Jesus "turned and rebuked them, saying 'You do not know of what spirit you are' " (Luke 9:55, according to a textual variant). However, he neither assumes the air of a victim, nor disdainfully retires from the fray, as human beings do in similar circumstances; he goes on speaking, agrees to discuss things, never refuses to explain, except when faced with manifest bad faith or hypocrisy. He goes on like this until he dies, evangelizing even on the walk to Calvary, even on the cross.

Constancy, generosity, fortitude, unction, wisdom, piety: all the gifts of the Spirit listed in Isaiah 11:1f., and an infinite number of other ones, shine in Jesus' evangelistic activity, and it is natural this should be so if it is true that "every grace" and every spiritual gift comes from him: "It was fitting that the firstfruits and the first gifts of the Holy Spirit who is imparted to the baptized should have been conferred on the manhood of the Savior, who himself bestows every grace."[1]

The Spirit therefore urges Jesus on to evangelize, but not only while remaining outside him; he follows him, helps him in the unfolding of the mission, becomes his inseparable companion. What Jesus says in promising the Spirit to the disciples at the Last Supper shows us that between him and the Paraclete there reigns perfect understanding and complete communion about the things to be proclaimed, to so great a degree that the latter can continue Jesus' proclamation, remind the disciples about him, and bring them to full understanding of him (John 14:26; 16:12).

2. *From Jesus to the Church*

We could go on describing the marvels wrought by the Holy Spirit in Jesus' evangelistic activity, but our original intention in studying what the Spirit effects in Jesus was primarily to find out what he wants to effect in us. So we must take leave of the Jesus of the Gospels and turn our eyes to the Church of today. If it is true that the Spirit prompts the Church to do the same things as he prompted her Head, Jesus, it is now for the Church, speaking in the first person, to repeat those solemn words pronounced in the synagogue at Nazareth: "The Spirit of the Lord is upon me . . . He has anointed me to bring glad tidings to the poor!"

But it is important to know at this point what those glad tidings consist of that she has been commissioned to bear: what the true content of this word *euangelion* is, in which so relevant a part of Jesus' messianic activity is summed up. Not all that Jesus himself says in the Gospels is "gospel"; the word "gospel" had, in the first instance, a restricted meaning and this we need to rediscover, since it is with a special view to proclaiming this that the Spirit is conferred.

What exactly is the good news Jesus has come to proclaim to the poor? Repeated in various forms, it is always the same: "The kingdom of God is at hand for you" (Luke 10:9; 11:20). This news is the implicit preamble to all his teaching: the kingdom of God is at hand for you, therefore love your enemies; the kingdom of God is at hand for you, therefore if your hand offends you cut it off; the kingdom of God is at hand for you, therefore do not worry about your own life but before all else seek the kingdom of God. In a word, the good news is this: the old things have passed away and the world has become a new creation, for God has come down to it as king (C. H. Dodd). Everything else hangs on this brief but great news. Jesus' "glad tidings" (*euangelion*) are the same as those proclaimed in Isaiah: "Your God reigns!" (Isa 52:7), but whereas in Isaiah it is a matter of hope and prophecy, now, with Jesus, it is a matter of fact.

3. *The gospel, or kerygma, in the apostolic Church*

With the death and resurrection of Jesus something occurs to modify the formulation, though not the substance, of these glad tidings. But let us examine the situation in the apostolic Church, so as to accommodate this new fact. All the New Testament writers assume the existence, and the knowledge on the part of their readers, of a common tradition (*paradosis*) going back to the earthly Jesus. This tradition presents two components: "preaching," or proclamation (*kerygma*) of what God has done in Jesus of Nazareth; and "teaching" (*didaché*) which presents, in contrast, ethical standards for right behavior on the part of believers. Various Pauline letters reflect this division, in that they contain a first, kerygmatic part on which depends a second part of a hortatory, or practical, character.

The preaching, or *kerygma,* is called the "gospel" (cf. Mark 1:1; Rom 15:19; Gal 1:7, etc.); the teaching, or *didaché,* on the other hand is called the "law," or the commandment, of Christ, which is generally summed up in love (cf. Gal 6:2; 1 Cor 7:25; John 15:12; 1 John 4:21). Of these two, the first — the *kerygma* or gospel — is what gives the Church her origin; the second — the law or love — which flows from the first, traces an ideal of moral life for the Church, "forms" the faith of the Church. In this sense, the Apostle draws a distinction between his work as "father" in the faith, with respect to the Corinthians, and that of the "guides" or "tutors" who have come after him, where he says, "I became your father in Christ Jesus through the gospel" (1 Cor 4:15).[2]

The faith as such therefore flows only in the presence of the *kerygma* or proclamation. The same apostle establishes this succession in the genesis of the new life and of the Church in general: first is the sending by Christ, then the proclamation; from this is born faith, and from faith, "calling on the name of the Lord," which is the beginning of the new life. And he concludes by stressing proclamation's unique importance, and quoting the words of Isaiah: "How beautiful are the feet of those who bring the good news!" (cf. Rom 10:14-15).

But, once again, what exactly is the content of this good news? We have already said that it is God's work in Jesus of Nazareth. But this definition is not enough: there is something more restricted, the germinative nucleus of all which, compared with everything else, is as the plowshare to the plow: that sword of sorts that cleaves the clod, to let the plow trace the furrow and turn the tilth. This word — for everything can in effect be reduced to one word — is actually what the New Testament calls "the sword of the Spirit" (Eph 6:17), that is to say a "word of God, living and effective, penetrating even between soul and spirit" (Heb 4:12). It is the instrument the Spirit uses to work the miracle of someone's conversion to the faith, to make someone be "born from above" (cf. John 3:3). I do not want to be the one to say this word; I leave it for Paul to say: "'The word is near you, in your mouth and in your heart,' that is, the word of faith that we preach [kerygma], for, if you confess with your mouth that Jesus is Lord and believe in your heart that God raised him from the dead, you will be saved" (Rom 10:8-9). That word is therefore the exclamation, "Jesus is Lord," uttered and accepted in the wonder of a faith *statu nascenti,* in its nascent state. The mystery of this word is such that it cannot be said "except in the Holy Spirit" (1 Cor 12:3). "As the wake of a fine vessel," as Charles Péguy would say, "becomes wider and wider until it vanishes and is lost, but starts at one point which point is the vessel herself,"[3] so the Church's preaching becomes wider and wider until an immense doctrinal edifice has been built, but begins at one point, and this point is the *kerygma:* "Jesus is Lord!" What the exclamation, "The kingdom of God has come!" was in Jesus' preaching, is now the exclamation, "Jesus is Lord!" in the preaching of the apostles. Nevertheless, between the two gospels — the one preached by Jesus and the one preached by the apostles — there is no conflict but only perfect continuity, for to say "Jesus is Lord!" is like saying that in Jesus crucified and risen the kingdom and sovereignty of God over the world has finally come to pass. The primitive Church expressed this conviction by adapting a verse of Psalm 96 and saying, "Regnavit a ligno Deus": God has begun to reign from the cross.

But we should take care not to fall into an unreal reconstruction of the way the apostles preached. After Pentecost, the apostles did not go about the world repeating the same words over and over again: "Jesus is Lord!" What they did do, when they found themselves having to preach the faith for the first time in a given environment was, rather, to go straight to the heart of the gospel by proclaiming the two facts *Jesus died* and *Jesus has risen,* and the "for why" (or, more accurately, the "for me") of these two facts: he died "for our sins"; he has risen "for our justification" (cf. 1 Cor 15:4; Rom 4:25).

Dramatizing the message, as Peter does in his speeches in the Acts, they proclaimed to the world: "You killed Jesus of Nazareth; God has raised him up, making him both Lord and Messiah" (cf. Acts 2:22-36; 3:14-19; 10:39-42). The proclamation "Jesus is Lord!" (or its equivalent in other contexts, "Jesus is the Son of God!") is nothing other than the conclusion, now implicit, now explicit, of this brief story, told in ever living, ever new form, even though substantially ever the same; and at the same time it is the sentence in which the story is summed up and made immediate for the listener. We see a perfect example of this in Philippians 2:6-11: "Christ Jesus . . . emptied himself . . . becoming obedient to death, even death on a cross. Because of this, God exalted him . . . so that every tongue should confess that Jesus Christ is Lord."

The proclamation "Jesus is Lord!" on its own does not therefore constitute the entire preaching; however, it is the soul of this preaching and, one might say, the sun that lights it up. It establishes a kind of communion with the story of Christ by means of the "particle" of the word, conjuring up the analogy of the communion effected with the Body of Christ by means of the particle of bread. In the *kerygma* "Jesus is Lord!" a mysterious transition takes place from history to "today" and to "for me." For it proclaims that the events narrated are not facts in the past, shut up in themselves, but realities still active in the present: Jesus crucified and risen is Lord here and now; he lives by the Spirit and rules over all! Coming to the faith is the sudden, astonished opening of one's eyes to this light. Recalling the moment of his conversion, Tertullian describes it as being like coming out of the huge, dark womb of ignorance and being terrified by the light of Truth.[4] It is the famous "being born again of the Spirit" or the passing "out of darkness into his wonderful light" (1 Pet 2:9; Col 1:12f.). Here the first anointing takes place, "the anointing through faith" of which the Fathers of the Church often speak.

The gift of the Holy Spirit is bound up with this moment: he it is who makes Jesus present and alive in the heart of anyone who welcomes the *kerygma;* he it is who, in baptism, infuses a new life through repentance and the forgiveness of sins (cf. Acts 2:38).

4. *A glance at the evolution of the kerygma*

To recapitulate briefly: at the very origins of the Church there existed a basic proclamation or central nucleus of the faith which, unlike the rest of what was handed down, had rousing and not formative value, as regards the faith itself; it was occasional, not systematic; assertive and not discursive. This central nucleus concerns Christ, it is a Christological creed; it does not so much stress the teachings of Jesus Christ as the events in his life and the paschal events in particular. There are two characteristics here that I feel I ought to emphasize, since it has been evolution in connection with these that has led to the situation as it is now. This central proclamation of the faith (Jesus died, Jesus has risen and is Lord) has an assertive, authoritative character, not a discursive, dialectical one. It has no need to justify itself by philosophic arguments: and accepts it or not, and that's all there is to it. However, great things depend on whether or not one accepts it: salvation, in a word. The *kerygma* is not something that can be re-arranged, since it is what re-arranges all; it cannot be established by human beings, for God himself establishes it and it is then what forms the basis of existence, since we "exist in Christ Jesus" who died and rose again for us (cf. 1 Cor 1:30). In other words, this is something different from human wisdom (*sophia*). On this topic, we need only listen to St. Paul as he develops his memorable argument with the Corinthians in defense of this characteristic of the ̇*kerygma:* "It was the will of God through the foolishness of the *kerygma* to save those who have faith. For Jews demand signs and Greeks look for wisdom, but we proclaim Christ crucified, a stumbling-block to Jews and foolishness to Gentiles, but to those who are called, Jews and Greeks alike, Christ the power of God and the wisdom of God" (1 Cor 1:21-24).

What is implied by the phrase "the Greeks look for wisdom," we know very well from subsequent debates between Christians and pagans. The pagan Celsus shows us what, in the view of unbelievers, the stumbling-block and foolishness of the *kerygma* is. For he writes indignantly: "Christians behave as do people who believe without reasoning. Some of them even refuse to give or accept reasons for what they believe, but use expressions such as 'Don't ask questions; just believe; your faith will save you . . .' The wisdom of this world is an evil, and foolishness a good thing."[5] Celsus (who here seems extraordinarily akin to so many cultured people of modern times) would basically like Christians to present their faith in dialectical form, submitting it in every respect to research and discussion, so that it can fit into the general framework, philosophically acceptable, of an effort of self-comprehension of human nature and the world (H. Schlier); it should not exact obedience, as St. Paul says, from its adherents (cf. Rom 1:5), but something more acceptable to human reason.

Naturally the Christians' refusal to offer proofs and enter into debates did not apply to the whole itinerary of the faith, but only its inception: they did not run away, even in the apostolic age, from controversy and from "giving a reason for their hope" even to the Greeks (cf. 1 Pet 3:15). However, they held that faith itself could not be generated by such controversy but had to precede it as the work of the Spirit and not of the reason, however well the latter might prepare one for it.

Ideally, the force of the attack, the *scandalum* with regard to the wisdom of the world, would have always been maintained intact. But this was not to be. The difference between *kerygma* and *sophia* (in practice, between *kerygma* and theology) gradually was smoothed away. We still find, especially in the polemics against the Gnostics, the occasional Pauline jolt: acceptance in full of the foolishness of the *kerygma*. Tertullian writes: "The Son of God was crucified; I am not ashamed to proclaim it just because there is something to be ashamed of. The Son of God died; the thing is to be believed just because it is foolishness. The Son of God was buried and rose again; the fact is certain because it is impossible."[6] But the general tendency is to affirm rather that Christianity too, in its entirety, is a wisdom, the true wisdom and the true philosophy ("our philosophy," Justin would say). People argue more and more often along these other lines: the Greeks seek wisdom; right, that's what we'll give them!

This second path was not, in itself, contrary to Paul's; the Apostle had written on the same occasion: "We do speak a wisdom to those who are mature, but not a wisdom of this age"

(1 Cor 2:6). The ambiguity arose from not sufficiently taking account of the fact that here he was talking of a wisdom "of God" (1 Cor 1:24) and not one "of this age," and therefore one not on the same footing as the systems of Plato and the other philosophers. The consequence was that, little by little, in Christian preaching we witness the disappearance of signs of the existence of a *kerygma* in the ordinary sense of proclamation "in the Spirit and power" of Christ's death and resurrection and of his present sovereignty, without other supporting argument than the existence of witnesses ("Nos testes sumus!").

The first negative development thus consists in this: that the sense of the "otherness" of the apostolic *kerygma* from every other form of exposition of the faith is diminished. The second negative development concerns another of the *kerygma*'s characteristics. Originally it was distinct from the teaching (*didaché*), as also from catechesis; these latter tend to form the faith, or to preserve its purity, while the *kerygma* tends to arouse it. The latter has, one might say, an explosive or germinative character; it is more like the seed from which the tree grows than the mature fruit ripening on the tree top, which in Christianity is constituted rather by love. The *kerygma* cannot be absolutely obtained by concentration or recapitulation, as though it were the marrow of Tradition, but stands apart from or, better, at the start of everything.

Here too the development consists in the loss of this absoluteness and otherness. Little by little, the *kerygma* begins to form part of catechesis and comes to be regarded as a kind of synthesis, or essential part, of it. The affirmations about Jesus dead and risen and now Lord, which on their own constituted the primitive creed, are now included as the second article in the Trinitarian creed, which recapitulates everything that a candidate for baptism ought to believe and profess. The original *kerygma* melts into catechesis.

All this reflects the general state of the Church after Constantine the Great. Living as they did in a Christian environment, in which everyone around was Christian or claimed to be so, the importance of the initial choice by which one "becomes" Christian is diminished all the more so that baptism is now usually administered to babies who are in no position to make such a choice for themselves. We can also say that, in a certain sense, the proclamation of faith is subjected to the phenomenon of institutionali-

47

zation: less stress is placed on the initial moment, the miracle of coming to the faith, and more on the completeness and orthodoxy of the content of the faith itself. The *fides quae* (the things to be believed) tend to carry the day against the *fides qua* (the act of faith).

5. *A return to the kerygma*

The observations I have been making on the development of the *kerygma* from its origins to the present day do not have an historical and theoretic purpose (to know how things were at the beginning), but an immediate and practical one. Paul VI, speaking in *Evangeli nuntiandi*[7] of the Holy Spirit's role in evangelization (of which he calls Him the "principal agent") expressed the wish that pastors, theologians, and laity would pay more careful attention to the nature and method of the work of the Holy Spirit in present-day evangelization. These reflections of mine are intended as a small response to this wish.

The Spirit of the Lord was on Jesus of Nazareth primarily so that he could preach the glad tidings that the kingdom of God had arrived. Today the Holy Spirit is on the Church (and on those whom the Church commissions to be evangelists) to the same end: to proclaim the glad tidings that Jesus, crucified and risen, is Lord. This, as we have said, is the real "sword of the Spirit." I have tried to bring this back to light, not for the fun of doing some archaeology but so that the sword may once more be of use to us. We can no longer do without it, for it alone can pierce the thick pall of disbelief that has settled on the world and on the heart of many a Christian. And since I have been using the imagery of the sword, I wish to make another application of it: using a sword, or a knife, or any other kind of blade with the flat rather than with the cutting edge or the point will not wound anyone. The Church's preaching is like this: if we say a thousand things, one of which is "Jesus is Lord," no one will be "cut to the heart," as we read happened when Peter proclaimed after Pentecost, "You killed Jesus of Nazareth; God has raised him up. Repent!" (cf. Acts 2:37).

It is written that "In the beginning was the *kerygma*" (M. Dibelius): in other words, the Church was born from the *kerygma* (not the *kerygma* from the Church, as Bultmann would have it!).

If it is true that our modern state is closer to that of the origins (when Christianity was at work in a pagan world, alien and hostile to it) than to the post-Constantinian situation, the call that comes to us from the experience of the primitive Church is to bring the apostolic *kerygma* back into use; for this proclaimed the faith to a pagan world, and served as nucleus for that earliest community. We must make a distinction between it and everything else, even catechesis. This basic proclamation must be presented at least once, clearly and tersely, not only to catechumens but to all Christians, given that the majority of today's faithful have never passed through the catechumenate. The proclamation of Jesus as Lord ought to have a place of honor at all the important moments of Christian life: in the baptism of adults, in Eucharistic worship, in the renewal of baptismal promises, in individual conversions, at the start of religious instruction classes, Bible-study groups and prayer meetings, in retreats, in missions to the people, and also at funerals. God seems to be raising up anew a hunger and thirst for this proclamation, which constitutes the most radical alternative to the false idols and false wisdom of the world. To those who proclaim his gospel in every city, Christ says what he said to St. Paul when the latter arrived at Corinth: "Do not be afraid. Go on speaking and do not be silent . . . for I have many people in this city" (cf. Acts 18:9f.): many people, though still hidden, who are waiting to escape from the great womb of ignorance and jump with shock at the light of Truth!

The really serious question, however, is this: how many of us are ready to proclaim this message "in the Holy Spirit," that is to say as true believers, running the risk if need be of cultural inferiority vis-à-vis the defenders of pure reason and those whose main objective is to respond to the world's expectations; how many are ready to repeat with St. Paul: My word and my message are not to be judged by my use of persuasive philosophic discourse, but by the manifestation of the Spirit and his power (cf. 1 Cor 2:4)? We cannot say "Jesus is Lord!" unless "under the action of the Holy Spirit," that is, unless we ourselves truly acknowledge this. If we say it, not "under the action of the Holy Spirit" but in sin, or disbelief, or out of habit, it remains a human saying which will not infect anyone: infection comes from contact with someone who *has* the illness, not with someone who *talks* about it. I myself have had direct experience of the spontaneously generated force that surges from the proclamation of Jesus as

Lord: on uttering these words, I have seen eyes light up, ears prick up, and something like a shiver run through my listeners — a sign of the mysterious power that these words contain and the Holy Spirit makes effective.

As at the beginning of the Church, so today what can shake the world from the torpor of unbelief and convert it to the gospel is not apologies, theological or political treatises, or endless debates, but the proclamation — simple, yes, but strong with the very strength of God — that "Jesus is Lord."

NOTES

1. St. Cyril of Jerusalem, *Catechesis* 17.9 (PG 33, 980).
2. Cf. Ch. H. Dodd, *History and the Gospel,* London 1964, chap. 2.
3. Cf. Ch. Péguy, *Le Mystère des SS. Innocents,* in *Oeuvres Poétiques Complètes,* Paris 1975, p. 697.
4. Tertullian, *Apologeticum* 39, 9 (CCL 1, p. 151).
5. Origen, *Contra Celsum* 1.9 (SCh 132, p. 98).
6. Tertullian, *De Carne Christi* 5.4 (CCL 2, p. 881).
7. Pope Paul VI, *Evangelii Nuntiandi* 75.

Chapter Four

Priestly Anointing

The Spirit urges Jesus and the Church on — to pray

In the gospel there are, in a manner of speaking, two Jesuses: the "public" Jesus who casts out demons, preaches the kingdom, works miracles, and carries on controversies, and a "private" Jesus who is almost hidden between the lines of the gospel. This latter is the praying Jesus. I say hidden between the lines, for the brush-strokes that present him to us are often short sentences, even scraps of sentences: tiny chinks that open and instantly close again. It is all too easy to overlook these scraps, and thus not be aware of this "other" Jesus: Jesus at prayer. Let us cast a glance through some of these chinks, confining ourselves to the Gospel of Luke, since he takes most pains to pinpoint the Jesus absorbed in prayer.

1. *Jesus at prayer*

Let us make a start with Jesus' baptism. Luke writes: "After Jesus too had been baptized and was praying [*proseuchomenou,* a participle], heaven was opened and the Holy Spirit descended upon him" (Luke 3:21-22). Luke appears to hold the view that it was Jesus' prayer that rent the heavens apart and caused the Holy Spirit to come down. At its very roots, the mystery of the anointing is bound up with prayer.

Let us continue our search. In chapter 5 we find: "Great crowds assembled to listen to him and to be cured of their ailments, but he would withdraw to deserted places to pray" (Luke 5:15-16). That adversative "but" is very eloquent; it creates a remarkable contrast between the crowds thronging around and Jesus' determination not to let himself be overwhelmed by them and so have to give up his dialogue with the Father.

On another occasion, "Jesus departed to the mountain to pray and he spent the night in prayer to God. When day came, he called his disciples to himself and from them he chose twelve" (Luke 6:12-13): as though by day Jesus just carried out what he had seen at night in prayer.

The transfiguration too, like the baptism, Luke sees as a mystery of Jesus' prayer-life. Why did Jesus go up the mountain that day? Not to be transfigured; this was the surprise the Spirit had in store for him, having prompted him to go: it wasn't Jesus' intention, at least not of his human consciousness. Jesus went up the mountain "to pray" and "while he was praying" his face changed in appearance and was transfigured (Luke 9:28-29). So too we discover why, immediately after his baptism, Jesus retired into the wilderness. Not to be tempted: this again was the Holy Spirit's intention who was prompting him, not Jesus' intention. Jesus went into the wilderness to pray and to fast; he went, as we should say today, to make a solitary retreat, to acquire a deeper understanding of the Father's revelation, and to prepare for his mission.

Whenever Jesus prayed, something happened to his face and his entire being and again there is merely a half-line of text to tell us so. One day Jesus was praying: watching him pray, the disciples who were around discovered for the first time what prayer really is, they realized they had never really prayed, and they say, "Lord, teach us to pray" (11:1). And so the Our Father came into the world, being we might say a living jet of Jesus' prayer passed on to the disciples. The last chink for seeing Jesus at prayer is the one illuminating the scene in Gethsemane: "Kneeling down, he prayed" (Luke 22:41).

The gospel tradition has only made a point of handing on to us information about Jesus' private prayer; but everything gives one to think that, as well as this private or personal prayer, Jesus like any other devout Israelite observed the thrice-daily fixed prayer times: at sunrise, in the afternoon during the Temple sacrifice, and at night before going to bed. If then, to all this we add the thirty years of silence, work, and prayer at Nazareth, the overall picture of Jesus that emerges is of a contemplative who every so often goes over into action, rather than of a man of action who every so often allows himself periods of contemplation.

Prayer was thus a kind of unbroken infrastructure, the continuous fabric of Jesus' life, in which all "is bathed." To Jesus' prayer life we may apply what Péguy poetically says about night (all the more aptly since prayer and night are almost always associated in Jesus' life):

> Night is the place, night is the being in which he bathes, in which he feeds, in which he creates, re-creates, builds himself up, is refreshed. Night is the place, night is the being where he rests, retreats and meditates; to which he keeps returning. . . . Night is what is continuous. . . . And the days are discontinuous; it is the days that pierce and break up the night, certainly not the nights that interrupt the day. . . . Night's silence . . . makes an august border to the day's agitations. Night is what is continuous; from it existence draws new strength: night forming one long, continuous fabric. . . ."[1]

How true this is when said of Jesus' prayer-life! It was indeed like an "august border" to all his days and works. As at the incarnation the Word issues from the eternal silence of communion with the Father, so in Jesus' preaching the word erupts from the silence of his prayers and from his conversation with the Father.

2. The Holy Spirit, soul of Jesus' prayer

Let us now try to get inside the mystery of Jesus' prayer, to discover what the content of his prayer is, what he says in those long, prayerful nights. One surprising thing has already been noted: all the prayers of Jesus attested in the four Gospels — with the sole exception of the cry uttered on the cross, which in any case is a quotation from Psalm 22:2 — have one feature in common: the use of the invocation "Father," more precisely — as is known from another source — in its Aramaic form of *Abbà*. This word, belonging to the popular tongue and originally a childhood expression, is never found in this use in Jewish prayer (J. Jeremias). It sums up the bewildering novelty of Jesus' prayer, a novelty deriving in its turn from the fact — new to the world — that the person praying is the actual Son of God. Now we know that it is the Holy Spirit who raises the cry, "Abbà!", from Jesus' heart: "At that very moment he rejoiced in the Holy Spirit and said, 'I give you praise, Father [*Abbà*], Lord of heaven and earth' " (Luke 10:21). Paul illuminatingly confirms this important discovery, for he states that when we say "Abbà!," it is in fact the Spirit of Jesus saying it inside us, thus continuing Jesus' prayer inside us believers: "As proof that you are children, God sent the Spirit of his Son into our hearts, crying out, '*Abbà, Father*'" (Gal 4:6). The Holy Spirit cannot of himself turn to the Father and cry out, "Abbà!," as we have already said, because the Spirit is not the Father's Son but only "proceeds from the Father"; he can only do so by virtue of having, at the incarnation, become the Spirit of Jesus, who is the Son of God. Every time this filial cry is heard, we ought to realize that the Holy Spirit is at work, whether in Jesus or in the Church: "Without him, whoever cries *Abbà!,* cries in vain."[2]

On that particular occasion (Luke 10:21) the Spirit raised a prayer of "exultation" in Jesus; but it was not always so. Paul says that the Spirit intercedes for the individual Christian "with inexpressible groanings" (Rom 8:26); there too, what happens subsequently in the case of the individual or the Church helps us to discover what had first happened in Jesus. It was "in the Holy Spirit" that Jesus, "in the days when he was in the flesh, offered prayers and supplications with loud cries and tears" (Heb 5:7). In other words, the Holy Spirit was with Jesus in Gethsemane, to sustain him in that supreme moment of offering his life. And again it is the Epistle to the Hebrews that reveals this deeply personal mystery of Jesus' soul: "Christ through the eternal Spirit [that is, through the Holy Spirit] offered himself unblemished to God" to cleanse our consciences from the works of death (cf. Heb 9:14). This prayer and sacrificial offering of himself to the Father reveals the third aspect of the anointing received by Jesus through the Holy Spirit: priestly unction. "It was not Christ who glorified himself in becoming high priest, but rather the One who [at his incarnation and baptism] said to him, 'You are my son'" (Heb 5:5; cf. Luke 3:22).

The priestly unction unfolds in Jesus' life, in his prayer life, but it culminates in his sacrifice on the cross. At this session however we shall concentrate only on the aspect of prayer, leaving the sacrifice of the cross for another time, since this forms part of the paschal mystery.

3. *The Spirit moves the Church to pray*

Let us now pass, as we have before, from Jesus' life to that of the Church. There were two things we observed about Jesus:

first that he prayed without ceasing, that prayer was the very fabric of his life; second, that he prayed "in the Spirit." So let us talk about these two things in the life of the Church and especially in the lives of her priests and pastors. I shall be speaking particularly about private prayer, although many of the things I say will be equally applicable to liturgical prayer and prayer in community.

The conciliar texts of Vatican II speak insistently about the importance of prayer, especially of liturgical prayer, in the lives of priests and bishops, but I should like above all to recall the passage at Acts 6:4 where Peter, at that first distribution of ministries within the Church, reserves for himself and the other apostles prayer and the proclamation of the word: "We shall devote ourselves to prayer and to the ministry of the word." Peter, or rather the Holy Spirit through his mouth, on that occasion laid down a basic principle for the Church: that a pastor may delegate everything, or nearly everything, to other people round about him, but not prayer!

Many verses in this passage in Acts about the institution of deacons remind one of the passage in Exodus describing the institution of judges. Peter repeats in the Church what Moses had done in the people of Israel. Let us listen to the passage, for it is very important:

> The next day Moses sat in judgement for the people, who waited about him from morning until evening. When his father-in-law saw all that he was doing for the people, he inquired, "What sort of thing is this that you are doing for the people? Why do you sit alone while all the people have to stand about you from morning till evening? . . . You are not acting wisely, you will surely wear yourself out, and not only yourself but also these people with you. The task is too heavy for you; you cannot do it alone. Now listen to me, and I will give you some advice, that God may be with you. Act as the people's representative before God, bringing to him whatever they have to say. Enlighten them in regard to the decisions and regulations. . . . But you should also look among all the people for able and God-fearing men. . . . Let these men render decisions for the people in all ordinary cases. More important cases they should refer to you, but all the lesser cases they can settle themselves. Thus, your burden will be lightened, since they will bear it with you. If you do this, when God gives you orders you will be able to stand the strain, and all these people will go home satisfied."

> Moses followed the advice of his father-in-law and did all that he had suggested (Exod 18:13-24).

Accepting Jethro's advice, Moses chooses for himself, out of all the possible tasks, that of "acting as the people's representative before God and bringing their problems to him." This does not prevent Moses from acting as lawgiver and continuing to be the true leader of the people; it merely establishes a priority.

In connection with "bringing the problems to God," I once heard an anecdote about Pope John XXIII which pleased me a lot. He used to tell how in the early days of his pontificate he would wake up with a start in the middle of the night, with many, many problems on his mind, each more harassing than the last, and say to himself: "I really must have a word with the Pope about that!" But then, suddenly remembering that he was the pope now, he would say: "OK, then I'll have a word with God about it!" and go back to sleep.

The decision taken by Moses arose out of something that had recently happened to the chosen people. They had only just managed to overcome the threat of being destroyed by the Amalekites. At the moment when it was a matter of life or death for the entire people and everyone was working their guts out repulsing the Amalekite attack, where was Moses their leader? He was up the mountain with his arms raised in prayer! The others strove with Amalek, he strove with God. Yet it was he who assured the victory of his people (cf. Exod 17:8-16). Amalek, Origen explains, symbolizes the hostile forces barring the way for God's people: Amalek is the devil, the world, sin.[3] When this people — and especially their pastors — pray, they are the stronger and repulse Amalek; when they do not pray (when Moses got tired and lowered his arms), Amalek is the stronger.

In the *De consideratione,* written at the invitation of Pope Eugenius III, St. Bernard applies this lesson to the life of the pastor of the Church. At a certain point he asks permission to play the role of Jethro, Moses' father-in-law, and this is what he says to the Pope:

> Do not trust too much to your present dispositions; nothing is so fixed in the soul as not to decay. . . . I am afraid that you will despair of an end to the many demands that are made upon you and will become calloused. . . . It would be much

wiser to remove yourself from these demands even for a while, than to allow yourself to be distracted by them and led, little by little, where you certainly do not want to go. Where? To a hard heart. . . . This indeed is the state to which these accursed demands can bring you if you go on as you have begun, to devote yourself totally to them, leaving no time or energy for yourself. . . . Now, since everyone possesses you, make sure that you too are among the possessors. . . . Remember this and, not always, or even often, but at least sometimes give attention to yourself. Among the many others, or at least after them, do please have recourse to yourself.''

When he speaks of ''accursed demands,'' St. Bernard is blaming all those commitments, particularly numerous in his day, which constrained a pastor of the Church and especially the pope to act as arbitrator in petty political or family quarrels and to settle ecclesiastical disputes, often turning merely on ambition or money; to be, in a word, a kind of judge in permanent session, as Moses was before taking Jethro's advice. Forcefully the saint recalls Jesus' words: ''Friend, who appointed me as your judge and arbitrator?'' (Luke 12:14), as well as those of St. Paul: ''No one who is on active service for God involves himself in the affairs of civilian life'' (2 Tim 2:4, according to the Vulgate) and he concludes by saying: ''If we were permitted to do what we should, we would always, everywhere and absolutely, prefer that quality which is of value in every way and cherish it alone, or at least above all others. And this is piety'' (cf. 1 Tim 4:8).[4]

At this point, our thoughts turn spontaneously to a vision: a *nostalgic* vision since it evokes how things were in the early days of the Church, but which I should very much like to be *prophetic* too, anticipating how things will be in the Church once more. Briefly and in general terms, the vision is of bishops' houses being primarily ''houses of prayer'' (not centers of business administration, even if only of ecclesiastical business); of parishes where the parish church can truly be called ''a house of prayer for all the people'' (cf. Mark 11:17) and, as such, will not be open, like other public buildings, only ''during working hours'' (which is when most people can't come!) but also at other hours, also at night. For people thronging our town centers of an evening, after dark, I have myself seen what a powerful attraction there can be in seeing a church open and lit up, maybe with a few people inside, praying and singing to the Lord. On one occasion of this sort, a woman confided in me that she had left home to go and commit suicide but on her way had heard singing and wandered in and found new hope from the sight of the faces of the people gathered inside.

To pray therefore. But this is not enough. Jesus taught us that prayer can be made the continuous fabric or infrastructure of the day. "Praying ceaselessly" (cf. Luke 18:1; 1 Thess 5:17), St. Augustine says, doesn't mean being constantly on our knees or standing with our arms raised to heaven. There is another kind of prayer, interior prayer, and that is desire. If our desire is continuous, our prayer will be continuous too. If we desire God and the rest he bestows, even if our tongues fall silent, we will sing and pray with our hearts. If we do not "desire," we may cry out as much as we please but as far as God is concerned we might be dumb.[5]

We need to discover and cultivate this prayer of desire or "of the heart." Here "desire" means something very deep; it is the habitual reaching for God; it is the yearning of the entire being, the longing for God. For us, prayer then becomes like a Karst river which, at times, finding one type of terrain, disappears into the ground (disappears when the activity we are pursuing absorbs us more), but which, as soon as it finds the right terrain, rises again to the surface and glides along in the sunshine (that is to say becomes conscious and explicit prayer). Even if, to begin with, the moments are rare when it rises to the surface, little by little, the spirit of prayer gathering strength within us, this "subterranean" prayer will come to the surface more and more often until it invades all available spaces in the day, until it is the background for everything, as it was for Jesus. It will be a sort of *spiritual unconscious,* at work without our knowing, that is to say without our mind's knowing. It works at night too. How many souls have experienced the truth of that sentence in the Song of Songs which says, "I sleep, but my heart wakes!" (cf. Cant 5:2); waking up at night, they realize with amazement that their heart has been praying all the time, because it is still doing so. How many souls have also experienced the truth of the psalmist's words, "I will remember you upon my couch, and through the night-watches I will meditate on you, that you are my help, and in the shadow of your wings I shout for joy" (Ps 63:7f.)!

Continuous prayer or the prayer of desire must not however make us neglect the vital need we have for a fixed time set apart for prayer, perhaps in some deserted place, like Jesus. He has told us: "When you pray, go to your inner room, close the door, and pray to your Father in secret" (Matt 6:6). There are situations in which one needs to take this advice of Jesus' very literally, for one's own room — once the door has been closed and the telephone cut off — has now become for many people, not only secular but religious too, the last refuge for prayer in this world, where they can pray without being disturbed. Without this time set apart for prayer, to aspire to "unceasing prayer" or the prayer of the heart would be self-deception.

When therefore the fixed moment comes for our prayer, we must make a clean break with what we are doing and what we are thinking about, as the first step; we must do as Jacob did that night when he went barefoot across the torrent, leaving all his dear ones and possessions on the other bank (cf. Gen 32:23f.) We have to go inside our interior castle and pull up the drawbridges. To use the words of a notable medieval work of spirituality, "you must put a 'cloud of forgetting' below you, between you and all creation," so as to be in the right state to enter "the 'cloud of unknowing' which is between you and God," that is to say in order to enter into contemplation.[6] Not easy: but we must make the effort to do it, otherwise all prayer will remain tainted and find it hard to scale the heights. It is advisable to devote the first moments of this prayer time to purifying our spirit by confessing our sins and begging pardon of God, because "nought that is sullied" can enter into contact with God (cf. Wis 7:25).

4. *Prayer renewed by the Spirit*

Jesus' prayer was certainly continuous prayer, but above all it was spiritual prayer, done "in the Holy Spirit." Thanks to the Spirit with whom he prayed, Jesus renewed human prayer. St. Paul sums up the example of prayer set by Jesus, and, in recommending it to the Ephesians, recommends it to the whole Church as well: "With all prayer and supplication, pray at every opportunity in the Spirit" (Eph 6:18). The two things are interdependent, in the sense that the Holy Spirit makes continuous prayer possible. "Once the Spirit comes to dwell in someone," we read in a great spiritual master of the seventh century, "the latter will not be able to stop praying, for the Spirit will never stop praying inside him. Thus, whether he sleeps or wakes, prayer will never be absent from that person's soul. Whether he is eating or drinking, or sleeping or working, the sweet fragrance of prayer will effortlessly breathe in his heart. Henceforth he no longer prays at fixed times, but continuously."[7] Incessant prayer therefore, but prayer "in the Spirit."

I might point out a few possible ways for renewing prayer in the Church, drawing on what we have discovered in Jesus. By raising the filial cry "Abbà!" in Jesus' heart, the Spirit put new wine, as it were, into the old wineskins of the Jewish prayer of Christ's day. Above all, Jesus restored a free, familiar, spontaneous character to a system of prayer often only half-understood, formal, and very nearly fossilized; he brought prayer back within popular reach. The Our Father, while being, so to speak, the official prayer of Jesus' disciples, was formulated in Aramaic — the spoken language — while the solemn and official prayers were recited by the Jews in Hebrew, which for them was a bit like Latin is for us. Then again, Jesus was not content with the official prayers at the three fixed times, but sometimes prayed right through the night; in other words, he did not confine himself to repeating prayers already composed and well-known, but created a prayer of his own. The Spirit that renews all things above all renews the most important of all things: prayer. This new kind of prayer, as free as the conversation of any son with his daddy (with a freedom entirely inward, not "carnal"), does not destroy official liturgical prayer but enlivens it by introducing "Spirit and life": "The hour is coming and is now here when true worshippers will worship the Father in Spirit and truth" (John 4:23).

The secret of renewing prayer, as we found in Jesus' life, is thus the Holy Spirit; he is the powerful breath that can put life back into our dried-up prayers, as he did into the dry bones of Israel (cf. Ezek 37:1f.). So we must encourage this new breath to penetrate into our private and our liturgical prayer; we must "spiritualize" our prayer. Spiritualizing our prayer means making it possible for the Spirit to pray more and more within us, so that our prayer will be ever less active and ever more passive, ever less discursive and ever more contemplative, until we reach — if God so wills — that "prayer of quiet" in which our heart is borne beside the heart of Christ and with him cries, "*Abbà, Father!*"

On the road of spiritualization, we set out from *prayer-dialogue,* in which God and we speak alternately: one speaks and the other listens; then one listens and the other speaks. From prayer-dialogue, we pass to *prayer-duet.* A duet occurs when two people say or sing the same thing together; a prayer-duet occurs when, for instance, in the Book of Revelation, "the Spirit and the bride say [to Jesus]: 'Come!' " (Rev 22:17). The prayer-duet takes place when, enlivened by the Spirit who has been poured into our hearts, we at length and lovingly repeat the simple invocation of the name of Jesus, which sums up all prayer: Jesus, Jesus, Jesus. . . . This is the prayer known to the monastic spirituality of the Orthodox Church as "the prayer of the heart," especially in its more extended form: "Jesus, Son of God, have pity on me, a sinner!"

But there is an even more spiritual prayer which we might call *prayer-monologue;* this takes place when, finding in a given situation that we do not actually know what we ought to be asking for, we allow the Spirit to pray through us. (This is why he is called "Paraclete"!) He alone "intercedes for believers in accordance with the mind of God" (Rom 8:27), being the only person who knows what it is. In practice, this prayer never fails, for in it the Holy Spirit asks for exactly what the Father himself wishes to give in the first place. But it is a prayer that cannot be taught from outside, with words; only the inner unction can cause it to be experienced. In it, our own contribution is at first limited to desiring it, saying over and over in all simplicity: "Holy Spirit, come to the aid of my weakness and intercede for me in accordance with the mind of God!" and afterwards saying, "Yes, Amen!" A yes to the darkness: "I say yes, Father, to whatever the Spirit has asked you for on my behalf! I say Amen to his prayer." This is the way the humble and the poor pray, who put their trust in God, "who surrender themselves to God's faithfulness."

These three forms of prayer need not necessarily follow one upon the other in our lives but can be interspersed at the same time, on the same day, depending on our state of mind and the promptings of grace.

In the Church and in ourselves, this praying "in the Spirit" should serve to renew one thing above all, and this is the relationship between prayer and action, "action" meaning any other thing that is not prayer. What is new is that we have to pass from *juxtaposition* to *subordination.* Juxtaposition is when first we pray and *then* we set to work (study, administration, evangelization, etc.), in our work sticking to the instructions and criteria that emerge from the work itself, from the progress of the discussion, from the established routine of our job, and so forth. This is what we all habitually do.

Juxtaposition is thus when first we pray and then we act. Subordination on the other hand is when first we pray and then we do what emerges from our prayer! The apostles and saints prayed in order to know what to do, and not merely before doing something. A profound conversion is needed. If we truly believe that God governs the Church with his Spirit and answers when we call upon him, we ought to take the prayers preceding conferences and committee meetings much more seriously; there is no rush to get down to business, so we do not get down to business unless some answer has been received by way of the Bible, or an inspiration, or a prophetic word. When discussion gets bogged down and no progress is being made, our faith makes us bold to say, "Friends, let us take a short break and see what light the Lord is willing to throw on our problem!" Sometimes it can seem as if, even after this, everything is as before and no obvious answer has welled up from our prayer; but this is not completely true. By praying, the problem has been "presented to God," so to speak handed over to him. There it is stripped of personal points of view and personal interests; whatever decision is made will be the right one before God. The greater the time devoted to praying over some problem, the less time will be needed in solving it. For Jesus, praying and acting were not two separate things; at night he often prayed to the Father and then, when day came, he did what had been decided in prayer: he chose the Twelve, he set off for Jerusalem, etc.

Here too we need "to restore the power to God": the power of deciding, the initiative, the freedom to intervene at whatever moment in the life of his Church. In other words, we need to place our trust back in God, not in ourselves. The Church is not a rowboat driven forward by the strength and skill of the arms of those who are in her, but a sailboat driven by the wind which blows it along "from above." The wind — no one knows where it comes from or where it goes to (cf. John 3:8) — is caught by the "sail" of prayer.

I should like to conclude this meditation with a prayer by St. Catherine of Siena, composed while she was in Rome, helping to sustain the Pope in his efforts to renew the Church: "O most tender love, you see within yourself your holy Church's need and the help she has to have, and you have given it to her in the form of your servant's prayers, of which you choose to make a buttress to support the wall of Holy Church. And the mercy of your Holy Spirit fills these servants of yours with blazing desires for this Church's reform.[8] May the Holy Spirit make each of us a "living stone" in the wall of prayer now being raised to buttress and protect Holy Church! Amen!

NOTES

1. Ch. Péguy, *Le porche du mystère de la deuxième vertu,* in *Oeuvres Poétiques Complètes,* Paris 1975, p. 660f.
2. St. Augustine, *Sermo* 71.18 (PL 38, 461).
3. Cf. Origen, *Homiliae in Exodum* 11.3.
4. St. Bernard, *De consideratione* 1.2-6 (PL 182, 729f.).
5. Cf. St. Augustine, *Enarrationes in Psalmos* 37.14; 86.1 (CCL 38, p. 392; CCL 39, p. 1198).
6. Cf. *The Cloud of Unknowing* chap. 5.
7. Isaac of Nineveh, *Mystic Treatises* 35 (transl. by J. Wensinck, Amsterdam 1923).
8. St. Catherine of Siena, Prayers 7.

OCEANS
Apart

by Karen Kingsbury
arge Print:

Tuesday Morning
ime to Embrace
reasury of Miracles for Women

This Large Print Book carries the
Seal of Approval of N.A.V.H.

OCEANS
Apart

Karen Kingsbury

Walker Large Print • Waterville, Maine

Published in 2005 by arrangement with Zondervan Publishing House, a division of HarperCollins Publishing Inc.

The text of this Large Print edition is unabridged. Other aspects of the book may vary from the original edition.

Set in 16 pt. Plantin by Liana M. Walker.

Printed in the United States on permanent paper.

The Library of Congress has cataloged the Thorndike Press® edition as follows:

Kingsbury, Karen.
    Oceans apart / by Karen Kingsbury.
      p. cm. — (Thorndike Press large print Christian fiction)
    ISBN 0-7862-7257-0 (lg. print : hc : alk. paper)
    ISBN 1-59415-073-7 (lg. print : sc : alk. paper)
    1. Air pilots — Fiction. 2. Air pilots' spouses — Fiction. 3. Illegitimate children — Fiction. 4. Fathers and sons — Fiction. 5. Mothers — Death — Fiction. 6. Birthfathers — Fiction. 7. Large type books. I. Title. II. Thorndike Press large print Christian fiction series.
    PS3561.I4873O28 2005
    813'.54—dc22   2004024845

OCEANS
Apart

As the Founder/CEO of NAVH, the only national health agency solely devoted to those who, although not totally blind, have an eye disease which could lead to serious visual impairment, I am pleased to recognize Thorndike Press* as one of the leading publishers in the large print field.

Founded in 1954 in San Francisco to prepare large print textbooks for partially seeing children, NAVH became the pioneer and standard setting agency in the preparation of large type.

Today, those publishers who meet our standards carry the prestigious "Seal of Approval" indicating high quality large print. We are delighted that Thorndike Press is one of the publishers whose titles meet these standards. We are also pleased to recognize the significant contribution Thorndike Press is making in this important and growing field.

Lorraine H. Marchi, L.H.D.
Founder/CEO
NAVH

* Thorndike Press encompasses the following imprints: Thorndike, Wheeler, Walker and Large Print Press.

DEDICATION

Dedicated to Donald, who continues to be my prince, my safe harbor, my best friend. You give me wings enough to fly, but keep me grounded in everything that matters. I smile when I think of our long walks and nighttime talks, the way you make me laugh after a hard day or your way of putting a layer of sensibility over any situation. You are an amazing man, Donald, gifted in so many areas, yet content to serve. I am blessed beyond words to be your wife, gifted with the joy of your presence in my life. Fifteen years have flown by in a heartbeat, and I can only pray God blesses us with so many more. I love you forever and always.

To Kelsey, my love and laughter, my silly-heart and only daughter. Can it be that you are fourteen? That you are standing on the brink of high school and cheerleading and driving and dating? You are gorgeous, sweetheart, inside and out. I cherish our together times, whether washing our faces at the same mirror or figuring out a math problem late at night. The glow in your eyes is the same one that belonged to that pixie-faced four-year-old. The only difference is this: now we don't have forever stretched out before us. Being with you is knowing intrinsically the speed of time, and my helplessness at slowing it even for a day. And so I celebrate you, Kelsey, and all we've shared, all we have yet to share as you dance closer to the front door. I love you and thank God for you, sweetheart.

To Tyler, my dreamer. How wonderful that God has blessed you with passion and purpose, a plan so big you can't help but breathe it and borrow from it and become it every day of your life. Our time in New York City was something I'll remember forever. And I'm convinced you will always know where your talent came from — whether you're singing on Broadway or playing out a scene in LA, shine for Jesus, Tyler. Shine for Jesus. And no matter what happens, if you squint through the lights, you'll see me and your dad cheering for you from the first row. I love you, Tyler. I couldn't be more proud.

To Sean, my humble leader. Watching

you among your peers, I am struck by the reality of how quickly you've worked your way into my heart. You've only been in our family for three years, and yet every child in class looks up to you. Of course, God had you in our hearts long before you came to live with us, and His plans for you continue to play out. Whether you're flying across a basketball court or reading devotions in the morning, your enthusiasm for life and your love for Jesus make you shine like a bright flame. Keep them, Sean. And know that I love you deeply.

To Josh, my gentle warrior. I'm convinced if I looked up *confidence* in the dictionary, there would be your smiling face. You have more determination than a dozen kids combined, and the belief that no matter what task is set before you, you'll not only complete it but redefine it. I'm amazed at your talents, whether in soccer, basketball, mathematics, or artwork. Don't ever forget our family verse, sweetheart. To whom much has been given, much will be expected. I can't wait to see how God uses you in the years to come. Keep Him first, Josh . . . the way you did when you joyfully went to your room and pulled out half your piggy bank savings so people in Southeast Asia would have Bibles. I love you and I'm so proud of you, honey.

To EJ, my overcomer. Before this year, you struggled some. Yet I always knew you were the first chosen one, EJ, the child God first led us to adopt. And because of that, we knew He had a plan for bringing you into our family, a plan for seeing that through to completion. Now you are blossoming, becoming the most beautiful flower in the garden. Your eyes glow with the light of Christ, and you sit a little taller each day as the compliments pour in. "EJ, what great seat work," "EJ, what great manners," "EJ, what great sports skills." I need only look at you to feel the sting of tears — and the glory of God's goodness all around. I thank Him for your willingness to see the process through, and I love you, honey. Isn't God the greatest?

To Austin, my miracle boy (or Brett Favre, as you're calling yourself these days). Can it be that you are in kindergarten already? What other six-year-old would ask for shoulder pads for his birthday? Not so you can play on a team, but so you can spend hours in the yard decked in your Packers jersey — by yourself or with your brothers — so dedicated to the thrill of sports that no team or game schedule is needed. I watch you growing and becoming, and I think back to that day six years ago, the morning when we placed you into the arms of a surgeon and prayed God would give you back to us. Your heart surgery was a miracle, but the greater miracle is the life you've lived since then. Strong, determined, refusing to settle for anything but the best. And yet . . . with all that testosterone you got from Daddy, you have a heart full of my tenderness. I can't slow the ride, Austie, but I can enjoy every minute. I love you and thank God that He allowed you to live.

And to God Almighty, the author of life, the greatest author of all, Who has — for now — blessed me with these.

ACKNOWLEDGMENTS

As always, when I write a novel many people play a crucial role in making it come together. First and foremost I must thank God for giving me the gift of story. When I write, I feel as though I'm reading, merely taking notes on the picture God puts in my head. I simply show up at my computer and download my heart. Not a minute goes by when I don't realize that this ability is completely from God.

Also, thanks to my family, especially my husband, who makes amazing sacrifices so that I can give God's best to the ministry of writing. At the same time, he's first to remind me when life slips out of balance. In that light, thanks to my mom, Anne Kingsbury, who is simply the best assistant I could ever have. You are loyal and loving and you see my heart for ministry like no one ever has. My father, Ted Kingsbury, and my sisters, Susan and Tricia, have also been a wonderful support, helping me with research projects and special assignments. Thank you for everything.

Thanks, also, to my wonderful editor, Karen Ball, who always takes my work to a higher level; and to the folks at Zondervan who team up to make a book like this one everything it is today. You are a hard-working group, and I'm privileged to be working with you.

A number of friends have also taken on other roles — prayer support, kid support, public relations, and general enthusiasm about my work with life-changing fiction. And so thanks goes to Ann Hudson, Sylvia Wallgren, Melinda and John Chapman, Bobbi and Erika Terret, Robin Jones Gunn, Rick and Robin Dillon, Cindy Weil, Randy and Vicki Graves, Richard Camp and his family, Kathy Santschi, Joan Westfall, Betty Russell, Phyllis Cummins, the Shampines (Kerry, D.J., and Brad), the teaching staff at our wonderful elementary school, the students at Don's high school, the college kids who think of our house as theirs (Thayne, Justin, Aaron, Jenna, Michele, Darren, Kara, Marc, Mark, and lots of others), and my dear friends at Christian Youth Theater. When life gets hard, I count on you and cherish the fact that you keep me cheering, even on deadline.

Of course thanks go to my agent, Rick Christian, at Alive Communications. I'm honored to work with someone so gifted.

In addition, my heartfelt thanks to pilots Eric Schoneberger and Scott Wakefield for lending their expertise to this book. It rings with authenticity because of you.

Also, a special thanks to the winner of my eBay auction that raised money for the Christian orphanage in Haiti where we adopted our three boys. You won the right to have me name a character after your son, Max. I hope you enjoy the way that turned out.

Finally, thanks to the Evans family for making the winning bid in a recent Biola University auction. The Evans family won the Forever in Fiction item, and as such were also able to have a character in this book named after them. This arrangement led to the naming of Loren Herman Evans, our pilot's father. Many of this character's traits were fictionalized for the purpose of the story. However, a few similarities exist between the fictional Loren Evans and the real man, a man dedicated to the Lord and to his family, a man who loves hand-cranked homemade ice cream and a mean game of croquet, and who pretends to be retired when he's not playing golf and traveling. You are well loved, Mr. Evans. May God bless your family's gift to Biola, and may you enjoy having your name forever in fiction.

Of Butterflies and Second Chances

I tell of hearts and souls and dances . . .
Butterflies and second chances;
Desperate ones and dreamers bound,
Seeking life from barren ground,
Who suffer on in earthly fate
The bitter pain of angry hate.
Might but they stop and here forgive
Would break the bonds
*   to breathe and live*
And find that God in goodness brings
A chance for change, the hope of wings
To rest in Him, and self to die
And so become a butterfly.

— Karen Kingsbury

ONE

Fear was an owl that rarely lighted on the branches of Kiahna Siefert's heart.

Especially in the light of day.

But it was nine o'clock on the sunniest morning of spring, and Kiahna couldn't shake the feeling — the strange gnawing in her soul, the way the skin around her neck and chest felt two sizes too small.

What is it, God . . . what are You trying to tell me?

No answer echoed back at her, so Kiahna kept busy. The passenger briefing was nearly finished, and the pilots were in their seats. She anchored herself against the service wall and found her smile, the one she used every time she flew.

Flight 45, Honolulu to Tokyo, was a nine-hour flight. With a layover in Tokyo, the roundtrip gave Kiahna eighteen flight hours. Five times a month she made the two-day turnaround, and after a decade with the airline, her pay was better than any she could get anywhere else. Out the door at seven and, with the time change, home before dinner the next day. Kiahna had earned the route after ten years with the airline, and it was perfect for one reason.

It allowed her most days to be home with Max.

"Movie today?" The man was a light traveler, briefcase and a carry-on, a regular in first class. Whatever his worn leather bag held, it took him to Japan at least once a month.

"Yes, sir. Mel Gibson's latest."

"Good." He smiled and kept moving. "Gets me over the ocean quicker."

One by one the passengers filed in, same as always. But still she couldn't shake the feeling.

It took fourteen minutes to seat the cabin, and Kiahna worked the routine. The flight was nearly full, which meant the usual readjusting to make people and bags fit comfortably in the cramped quarters. She greeted passengers, sorted out seat assignments for confused travelers, and poured a drink tray for first class.

A family with four children was seated over the wing, and already their baby was

20

crying. Kiahna found a package of crackers and coloring books for the couple's older children. With every motion she tried to sort out her feelings.

"Kiahna?"

She jumped and turned to face her partner. Stephanie was working the back part of the cabin. "We're waiting."

The announcement. She'd completely forgotten. A quick breath. "They're all in?"

"For two minutes now."

Kiahna snapped the drink tray into place on the small service counter and edged past the other woman. The announcement was hers that morning; she should have remembered. She took hold of the microphone and began the routine.

"Welcome aboard Flight 45. We're expecting a full cabin this morning, so if you have two carry-ons with you today, please store one of them in the space beneath the seat in front of you." She paused, her mouth still open.

What came next? There was more to say, something about oxygen and masks, but the words scrambled in her mind and refused to come. She stood unmoving, her heart slamming against her chest.

"Here" — Steph took hold of the microphone — "I've got it."

Kiahna's arms shook as she backed away, up against the closed front cabin door. What was wrong with her? She'd given that announcement a thousand times; she could be in a coma and say it.

Steph finished, and the copilot came on. "Flight attendants, prepare for takeoff."

They pushed their jump seats down and buckled in. Usually this was Kiahna's favorite part. A few minutes of power and thrust while the airplane barreled down the runway and lifted into the air, minutes where she wasn't needed by anyone for anything, when she could think about the day and all that lay ahead.

This time, though, was different.

All Kiahna could think about was the part of her day that lay behind, the part with Max.

At seven years old, Max was both brilliant and beautiful, a wonder boy streaking through her life like a comet at breakneck speeds. He wore red tennis shoes, and his best friend was his yellow Labrador retriever, Buddy. At school, Max had a reputation for being the fastest — and sometimes the silliest — boy on the playground. And his mouth ran faster than his legs. Kiahna liked to hold court with Max on dozens of adult topics. The death penalty — Max was against it; more money for public schools — he was for it. Max was fiercely patriotic, and at school he sometimes organized red, white, and blue days in honor of the U.S. troops in the Middle East.

But this morning he'd been quiet.

"When do you finish working?" They lived in a two-bedroom apartment, and he slipped into her room while she was still pressing her standard-issue airline navy blazer.

Kiahna studied him. "Dinnertime tomorrow, same as always."

"No, not that way." He hopped up on her bed and sat cross-legged. "When will you stay home in the daytime? Like Devon's mom or Kody's mom?"

"Max." She turned from the ironing board and leveled her gaze at him. "You know I can't do that."

"Why?" He anchored his elbows on his knees.

"Because" — she came a few steps closer and sat on the edge of the bed — "those moms have husbands who work."

"So why can't we have a husband?"

"C'mon, Max." She cocked her head and brushed her finger against the tip of

23

his nose. "We've been through this, sport."

Buddy padded into the room and sank in a heap near Max's feet. "Yeah, but . . ." Max brought his fists together and rested his chin on them. His green eyes caught a ray of morning light. "Forever?"

"For now." She crooked her arm around his neck, pulled him close, and kissed the top of his head. His dark hair felt soft and damp against her cheek, still fresh from his morning shower. "Until something better comes along."

"Like a husband?" Max lifted his face to hers. He was teasing, but beyond the sparkles in his eyes was a river of hope, a hope that ebbed and flowed, but never went away.

Kiahna smiled. She tousled the hair at the back of his head and returned to the ironing board. Max knew better than to push. A husband had never been in the picture. Not a husband and not a daddy. Kiahna couldn't trust a man with her own heart, let alone her son's. Besides, it wasn't God's plan for her to have a husband. At least that's the way she'd always felt.

Max slid onto the floor and looped his arms around Buddy's neck. The dog rewarded him with a solid swipe of his tongue across Max's cheek. "Buddy understands."

"Yes." Kiahna smiled. "Buddy always does."

A soft bell sounded, and Kiahna sucked in a quick breath. They were at ten thousand feet — time to prepare the beverage cart and make the first pass through the cabin. Steph approached her from the other side of the aisle.

"You okay?" She had one hand on her hip, her eyebrows lowered into a *V.* "What was the trip about the announcement? Never seen you freeze like that."

Kiahna stood and smoothed out the wrinkles in her navy cotton skirt. "I don't know." She gave her partner a smile. The feeling, the strange restlessness, had plagued her ever since her talk with Max. "Busy morning, I guess."

"Yeah, well" — she rolled her eyes — "you wanna talk busy? It's four o'clock, and Ron . . . you know Ron, right?"

"He moved in last month?"

"Right." Steph grabbed a piece of gum from her skirt pocket, slipped the wrapper off in a single move, and popped it into her mouth. "Anyway, he gets this call at four this morning, and it's the —"

A sudden jolt rocked the aircraft so hard Steph fell to her knees. Gasps sounded throughout the cabin, and somewhere near the wing one of the children began to cry. Kiahna fell back against the service counter and reached for a handful of soda cans that had fallen to the floor.

"What the . . ." Steph was struggling to her feet when the plane tilted hard in the other direction. The motion knocked her back to the floor. In the tenth row, a handful of screams and shouts rang out from a group of college kids, journalism students heading back home from a convention.

Turbulence.

Kiahna grabbed hold of the nearest wall and felt the blood drain from her face. The air was always choppy over the islands, especially in spring. She was about to help Steph to her feet when the copilot leaned out from the cockpit.

"We're going back." The man's upper lip was twitching. His whispered words came fast. "Something's wrong with the tail." He swallowed hard. "The whole bloody aircraft wants to nosedive."

Nosedive? Kiahna stared at him. This wasn't happening, not this morning. Not when every fiber in her being had warned

26

her something wasn't right. The copilot was gone again, and Kiahna shifted her gaze to Steph. The girl was a New Yorker, twenty-two, twenty-three tops. She was cocky and brash and had a quick tongue, but now her face was gray-white. "What . . . what do we do?"

Kiahna reached for her partner's hand and helped her to her feet. "We work the cabin. I've done an emergency before." Her voice sounded familiar, but only remotely so. "We stay calm and everything will work out fine."

"But what if we —"

"No *what-ifs*." She took the lead and headed down the aisle. "We have to work."

They weren't through first class when a strange popping sound shook the plane and propelled it downward. *It's the descent,* Kiahna said to herself. And then again for the benefit of the passengers. "We're making our descent. Cover your heads and assume a forward roll position."

Kiahna didn't dare turn around, couldn't bear to meet Steph's questioning eyes. The truth had to be written across her face: the sharp angle of the aircraft didn't feel like a normal descent pattern.

It felt like a nosedive.

Panic worked its way through the rows in a sort of sickening wave.

"Jesus, help us!" a lady shouted from row eight. She had an arm around each of her children.

"Someone *do* something!" The scream came from an area near the back of the plane, and it set off a chain reaction of loud words and frantic cries for help. No one had any doubt they were in trouble.

Still Kiahna moved forward. At each row she demonstrated the crash-landing position. Hands clasped at the back of the neck, body tucked as far forward as possible. "Assume the emergency position," she said over and over again. "Assume the emergency position."

"What happening?" An Oriental man grabbed her arm; his eyes locked on hers. "What, lady? What?"

Kiahna jerked herself free as the nose of the plane dropped again. The aircraft was almost entirely vertical.

The captain's voice — tense, but steady — filled the cabin. "Prepare for an emergency landing. I repeat, prepare for an emergency landing!"

Babies were wailing now; parents grabbed their children to keep them from falling toward the front of the plane.

"Lord, have mercy on us," a woman screamed.

The voices mingled and became a single noise, a backdrop that grew louder and then faded as Kiahna caught a glimpse of the ocean out one of the windows. In that instant time froze.

Kiahna was back at home again.

"Come on, Max. Get your backpack. We're running late!"

Max rounded the corner, Buddy at his side. "I can't find it."

"Check the coat closet."

He darted across the kitchen and toward the front door. She heard him yank the closet open. "Here it is!"

"Grab it; let's go."

The whole scene took a fraction of a second to flash across her mind, all of it routine, mundane. No subtle nuances or hesitations, nothing to indicate that this morning could be their last. Nothing but the strange pit in her stomach.

She closed her eyes . . . where was Max right now? He stayed with Ramey Aialea mornings until the school bus came, and again in the afternoon and through the night when she had a layover. The woman would see him off to school the next day and take care of him for an hour or so when school got out. Ramey was in her late sixties, a weathered grandmother in poor health who took in Max as a way of staying young. She lived just a block away and felt like family to Kiahna.

Max had been with Ramey since he was born.

That morning, as happened so often, Kiahna and Max had piled into Kiahna's old Audi and made time to Ramey's first-floor unit. Ramey and Kiahna both lived in the same modest residential section of the island, the place where apartments filled every available square inch, leaving room for only an occasional palm tree. The place where the island's food servers and hotel maids and resort staff lived.

The apartments weren't much, really. But Kiahna's complex had a fairly clean pool and a patch of gravel with a swing set. More amenities than some. That, and paradise every day of the year. It wasn't a bad place to raise a boy. A native to Honolulu, Kiahna wouldn't have lived anywhere else.

By the time she and Max arrived at Ramey's apartment, Kiahna's strange feeling had set in. She didn't want to waste time making idle talk with her old friend. Instead she stepped out of the car and met

Max near the front bumper. "Have a great day, sport."

He squinted into the sun. "Do you have to go?"

"Yes." She pecked him on the cheek. "We'll play Scrabble tomorrow night, okay?"

"It's too sunny for Scrabble."

"Okay, then basketball? Give and go, all right?" Kiahna rested her hands on her knees and kept her face at his level.

"Really?" Max's eyes held a hint of doubt. "Give and go?"

She winked at him. "As long as it's light out."

Max bit his lip. "Japan's a long way from here."

"Yes." Kiahna angled her face. Why was he talking like this? She'd flown since before he was born. "But not so bad when you go all the time."

"Yeah." He lifted one shoulder and let his gaze fall to the ground. "Sorry about this morning."

"For what?" She fell back on her heels.

"The husband stuff." He lifted his eyes to hers. "I just get sad when you're so far away all day." A few seconds passed. "What if I break my arm? Who'll help me?"

"Ramey, silly."

"She's my 'mergency contact." He pushed the toe of his tennis shoe against her leather loafers. "But I mean the hug part and the singing part. Who'd do that?"

Kiahna hesitated only a moment. This was the part of being a single mom that always made her throat swell — the idea that she couldn't be all things to Max, not while she had a full-time job.

"Well" — she framed his small face with her fingers — "*I* would."

"You'd be somewhere over the ocean." He wasn't arguing with her, only making a point. Sharing a fear she hadn't known he'd had until now.

"Even if we're oceans apart I'll always be right here." She lowered one hand and let her fingers rest on the spot just above his heart. "You know that, right, sport? Remember our song?"

A breath that was more sad than frustrated slipped from him. In a rush of arms and hands and fingers he threw himself into her embrace.

Her voice was a whisper, and she breathed it against his face as she stroked the back of his head. "Come on, sport, right?"

"Right." The word was a defeated huff, but it would have to do.

"Taco Bell tomorrow?"

"Sure."

"You can do better than that." She straightened and made a silly face, hoping she could coax a smile from him before she left. She did an exaggerated pout and mimicked him. *"Sure . . ."*

The hint of a grin broke Max's expression, and before he could stop himself, a giggle followed. "Okay, fine. Taco Bell!" He burst out the word and laughed at his own humor. "Better?"

"Much." She stooped down and kissed his cheek again. "Keep your chin up." When her face was still at his level, she looked straight through to his soul. "I love you, Max. See you tomorrow."

A faint whistling sound was coming from outside the airplane, and it snapped Kiahna from her memories. They were headed straight for the Pacific Ocean, the pilots unable to pull out of the dive. They had half a minute at best, and Kiahna was using all her strength to keep from tumbling down the aisle and slamming into the cockpit doors.

The news would have to come from Ramey . . . the news and the details that would follow. She'd written out her last

33

wishes seven years ago, days after Max's birth. And there was the letter, of course. A different one every year on Max's birthday. But even with all her preparations, she never thought it would come to this.

Don't forget what I told you, sport . . . I'm with you . . . always with you . . . as close as your heart.

For an instant she turned her thoughts toward God. She had loved the Lord all her life, loved Him even when she didn't always understand Him. If this was the end, then she would be with Him in a matter of minutes. *God . . . give us a miracle . . . or give one to Max. Please, God.*

The screaming and crying around her grew louder, then in the final moments it faded. Kiahna made a desperate attempt to right herself, to stand up so she could calm the craziness in the cabin.

They could still make it, couldn't they? The aircraft could straighten out before impact and settle safely on the surface of the ocean. The Coast Guard would be called out and they'd inflate the emergency slides and rafts. Everything would be okay and she'd tell Max all about it that night. Each seat cushion was a flotation device, right? Wasn't that what they told people every day on this flight?

I love you, Max . . . don't forget me.

Her mind jumbled, and then cleared just as quickly, until finally two thoughts remained. As the plane made impact with the water, as the fuselage splintered apart and ocean water gushed into the cabin, it was those two thoughts that became her last.

The thought of Max, and what would become of him after today.

TWO

The frantic race of another busy weekend was on from the moment Connor Evans woke up.

It was the first Saturday in April, and the girls had two birthday parties to attend. Michele put him in charge of wrapping presents and dropping their daughters off at the first party. The second was immediately after, and a neighbor would ferry the girls across town, after which Connor would pick them up.

Michele was redoing the kitchen, and sometime between drop-offs and pickups, Connor wanted to stop by Home Depot and find a riding mower for the backyard. His fall fertilizing had paid off, but now the acre of grass out back was halfway to his knee, typical of what was happening throughout Florida.

His neighbor liked to pause and hold his hand to his ear.

"Hear that, Evans?"

"What?"

"That whooshing sound." He'd point to his yard. "That's the sound of our Florida grass growing."

It seemed almost true. After West Palm Beach's record-breaking March rain, the grass was growing even faster than usual. Connor could pay someone to cut it; lots of pilots did. But what fun was that? Besides, he liked spending time in the yard. Easy, monotonous downtime. Quiet enough to give his mind the rest it needed after a week of flying commercial aircrafts.

It was 10:50 when he climbed into his silver Tundra and tapped the horn. He leaned his head out the window. "Come on, girls" — his fingers tapped out a rhythm on the steering wheel — "party starts in five minutes."

Elizabeth and Susan were ten and eight that spring, as different from each other as he and Michele had been when they first met. Elizabeth, their firstborn, was sweet-spoken and demure, a child whose favorite activities included playing tea party with her three baby dolls. Elizabeth lived in dresses and ribbons and lace, and wanted her hair curled even on play days.

Susan was supposed to be a boy from

the beginning. The ultrasound technician told them so halfway through Michele's pregnancy. "Yes sir" — the man grinned across the room at Connor — "looks like you got yourself a healthy little boy."

The boy part turned out to be Susan's umbilical cord. She was born with a lusty scream and hadn't quieted down since. Keeping Susan's hair brushed and her clothes clean was a full-time job, and with Michele already busy running a home hair salon, she had long since stopped trying.

Connor was secretly glad. If he couldn't have the son he'd always dreamed of — and Michele was adamant about not having more children — at least he had Susan. Pigtailed Susan to toss a ball with or play Ping-Pong with or take to spring training games when the major league baseball teams flocked to Florida.

Connor had been an only boy growing up. He had sisters who were younger than him, but his days were spent playing football and basketball, hanging with his teammates, and surrounding himself with guy things. College had been more of the same. Guy games and guy talk and guy silliness on evenings and weekends — right up until graduation, when he met Michele.

He cupped his hands around his mouth.

"Girls! I'm *leaving*." He sat back and released a burst of air. Nice threat, but it meant nothing. He couldn't go to the party without the girls, and he'd never been able to keep them from running late. They were Michele's daughters, after all.

Then, in a sudden blur, they flew out the door. Susan led the way, leggy and grinning, a present tucked under her arm. *Crazy girl.* Connor grinned. *She looks like a pee-wee running back, bent for the end zone.*

Elizabeth was behind her, skipping with dainty steps, a present clutched to her chest. Her hair was curled, and she smiled at him, mouthing a quick apology as they made their way to the truck. First one, then the other piled into the backseat, and the air filled with breathless giggles.

"Sorry, Daddy."

"Yeah, sorry." Susan followed Elizabeth's lead. "It's okay if we're a few minutes late."

"Let me guess." Connor stifled another smile. "Mom told you that."

"She said something else." Elizabeth dropped her chin. Her voice had that sing-song sound girls could turn on at will, and her eyes grew big — clear warning that some serious teasing was at hand.

"Yeah." Susan let loose another giggle. She covered her face with both hands.

"She said to tell you she has a *crush* on you."

More laughter, and the girls began talking at the same time. Who would be at the party? What games would they play? What presents did the birthday girl really want?

Connor let his mind drift.

Michele had a crush on him, huh? A slow smile lifted the corners of his mouth and traveled up his cheeks. His heart filled with thoughts of her, his precious Michele. Her shoulder-length dark hair piled loose on top of her head, work smock smudged and smeared, a paintbrush in her hand, telling their girls she had a crush on him.

The picture took his breath away.

He backed out of the drive and headed down Oak Street toward the parkway. At the first light he gazed at the sky, the place where he spent so much of his time. Just God and him taking one planeload of people after another into the vast open sky, and bringing them safely down. Over and over and over again.

Life on earth and life above it, everything was good. No, it was better than good. These days it was more than he'd dreamed. He had a family that played together and laughed together — a family where they actually liked each other — and a relationship with his wife that made other men openly jealous.

He turned again and pulled into the left lane.

Michele wasn't rail thin the way a lot of pilots' wives were. She wasn't heavy, either. Medium, she liked to say, with enough extra to give her a few curves. Once in a while she'd go on a diet or exercise kick, determined to lose twenty pounds. But she'd been the same size since Elizabeth was born. Most of the time she seemed content to stay that way.

Connor didn't care. He wouldn't change a thing about her. Besides, overly thin women didn't age well. Michele was vibrant and full of life, with a beauty that went beyond her pretty looks. Without question she was the brightest spot in his life.

Six years ago he'd paid a contractor to build an addition on the back of their house, a place where Michele could work magic on the hairstyles of church friends and neighbor women. The idea had paid off in every way. She was home each day for the girls and had enough energy and desire to love him long after the girls were in bed.

"We're almost there, Daddy!" Susan clapped her hands.

"Yep, two blocks." Connor glanced over his shoulder and smiled at her.

Though more rough-and-tumble than her sister, Susan was the mirror image of Michele. Michele, the woman who had made him forget his plan to not fall in love until he was twenty-five, the woman who walked into his life and in two weeks showed him more about love than he'd understood in a lifetime.

She was bright and witty, charming and sensuous. A woman who cared for him and the girls ahead of any part of her career. And running her in-house salon was definitely a career. A quiet chuckle made its way up and past his lips. He shook his head as he saw a driveway ahead anchored by pink balloons. Michele would debate anyone who thought hairstyling less than a career.

She was feisty that way. Feisty and funny and his best friend. The past few years she'd made a decent income, as well. Enough to pay for twice-a-year vacations: exotic Disney cruises with the girls or visits to exclusive dude ranches, and intimate vacations for just the two of them to places like Bora Bora and Tahiti and the South of France.

Yes, he had a crush on Michele, too. He'd have to tell her so later that evening.

"Okay, girls. Mrs. Reed will take you to the next party."

"And you'll get us after that." Elizabeth gave him a coy smile. "Right?"

"Right."

Connor pulled into a familiar driveway, the house where the party girl lived. A cluster of little girls poured from the front door of the house, jumping and waving and squealing. Elizabeth and Susan blew Connor kisses and scrambled out of the car.

He was five minutes down the road when it happened.

Stopped at a red light, he watched a burgundy sedan come up behind him in the adjacent lane. The car wasn't speeding, but it wasn't slowing down, either. Without stopping, without giving Connor any chance to intervene, the car careened through the red light and straight into the side of a white minivan.

"God . . . no . . ." His prayer came an instant too late.

The crash was horrific, louder than anything Connor could remember. A cloud of glass and metal and car pieces filled the air above the intersection and then settled across the roadway like fallout from a bomb. Connor was out of his car before the minivan came to a stop.

His assessment of the scene was second nature, the kind of thing he'd learned in the military. *Okay, Evans, locate the victims . . . identify the serious injuries . . . figure out the level of help needed.* He raced up to the burgundy sedan and peered inside. Just one person, the driver, and he looked unconscious.

But what about the minivan? Minivans held children, didn't they?

He tore across the intersection, squinting to see through the tinted windows. The impact was on the driver's side, so he went around and flung open the sliding passenger's door. Only then did he see that the woman and teenage boy inside were alive and moving around. Side-door airbags had inflated upon impact and probably saved their lives.

"You okay?" Connor had his cell phone open. He dialed 9-1-1 before the woman could answer.

"I . . . I think so." The woman rubbed her neck and began to cry. "Did he run the red?"

"Yes. Never even slowed down." He held

44

the phone to his ear and waited while it rang. "I'll check on him."

Other cars were stopping now, people getting out and milling about. As the emergency operator answered, he heard a woman behind him scream. "He's not breathing! Someone help!"

"Nine-one-one, what's your emergency?"

Connor explained the situation as he jogged toward the burgundy sedan. "One of the victims isn't breathing. Please hurry."

He snapped the phone shut and worked his way past the few people standing near the driver's door. Being a pilot didn't make him a paramedic, but he knew CPR. If the man wasn't breathing . . .

"He's dying," the woman shouted. "His chest isn't moving!"

"Excuse me!" Connor made a final shove toward the car. "Please . . ."

The screaming woman stepped back, and for the first time Connor got a clear view of the old man's face. As he did, he felt his blood drain from his face. "Dear God . . ." His voice was a whisper, and he froze. "It can't be . . ."

His father lived on the other side of the country, but for a fraction of a second he

was certain the man lying motionless behind the wheel was his dad. The woman
behind him yelled something again, and it
snapped Connor into motion.

The man wasn't his father; it wasn't possible.

Connor grabbed the man's limp wrist
and felt for his pulse. Nothing. A fine layer
of sweat broke out across the top of his
forehead. The man's face was already
turning gray, but still the resemblance to
Connor's father was striking. In quick,
jerky movements Connor slid his thumb
from one spot on the man's arm to another, and finally to his neck. Still no
pulse.

He placed the back of his hand near the
man's mouth and nose, but felt no movement of air. Everything he knew about
emergency treatment at an accident scene
told him not to move a victim. But this
man was either dying or dead. Connor
spun around and brushed back the crowd.
"We need space." Then he hoisted the man
into his arms and moved toward the sidewalk.

A few yards away an ambulance pulled
up and behind it a fire truck. The sirens
must've been sounding for a while but
Connor hadn't noticed anything but the

face of the man in his arms. A face he'd been running from for —

"Step back, please." A paramedic set down his bag, and Connor did as he was told.

Three steps away, he stood mesmerized by the scene, watching the team of paramedics work on the old man, pounding on his chest, forcing oxygen into his lungs. Ten minutes passed, then fifteen. Finally they gave up.

"Heart attack," one of them said. "Dead before the impact."

They pulled a sheet over the man's body, and everything seemed to slow down. The branches in the trees lining the streets stirred in the early afternoon breeze; one by one the onlookers returned to their cars. The drama was over; the guy was dead.

A police officer tapped Connor on the shoulder. "Move along."

Connor nodded, but his eyes were glued to the lifeless form beneath the tarp. Was this how the scene would look when his father died, some not-so-far-off day? Gone without warning, no family around even to identify his body?

He took his time heading back, and skipped Home Depot. Michele was on a stool working an off-shade of yellow onto the kitchen wall. The cordless phone was tucked between her shoulder and her cheek, and she was saying something about the school carnival in May.

"That's why we buy the tickets early, the savings is unbelievable." Pause. "Yes, I'm telling you, have her call the school office and . . ."

Connor stopped listening.

Pungent paint fumes filled the room. He took the seat at the kitchen table closest to Michele's stool and locked eyes on the back of her head. She hadn't heard him come in, but at the sound of the chair she spun around and waved her paintbrush at him. She gave him a crooked grin, rolled her eyes, and pointed to the phone.

Normally at this sort of moment, he'd find a way to rescue her, yell that he needed her or that someone was at the door. But he couldn't bring himself to do it. He smiled at her with his eyes as he sat back and waited.

"Okay, Sally, right . . . yes . . ." She glanced at him over her shoulder again. "Mm-hm, Connor's home. Okay, gotta go."

She hung up, balanced the paintbrush on the can, and took a slow step down from the stool. "Connor . . ."

"Hi." He met her eyes and saw her concern. He dropped his gaze to the floor. If only he could shake the image of the man's face, but he couldn't. Not when the resemblance was so striking.

"What is it, baby?" She came to him, touching his face as she pulled up a chair. "You look awful."

He lifted his eyes to hers again. "I just watched a guy die."

"*What?*" Her eyes grew wide and she took hold of his arm.

A slow breath filled Connor's lungs and the story spilled out. He told her about the burgundy sedan, about the deafening impact.

"The people in the minivan were fine." He lifted one shoulder and tried to sound unaffected. "But the old guy in the sedan . . . he was dead before they hit. Heart attack."

Michele searched his face, clearly looking for more.

"It wasn't the accident." Connor let his head hang, and with his free hand he massaged the muscles at the base of his neck. Not even international flights left him this tense.

"Okay." Michele slid her hand down his

arm and wove her fingers between his. "What is it?"

He looked up once more. "The guy was a ringer for my dad, Michele. He looked just like him."

She ran her tongue over her lower lip. "He wouldn't be here, would he?"

"No." Connor rested his forearms on the table. "It wasn't him. But for a minute . . ."

Silence joined them at the table and dominated the conversation. Michele released his hand and stood, studying him, an odd sadness in her gaze. Connor knew what she was going to say before she said it.

"Maybe this is God's way, a reason to call him and —"

"Don't!" He regretted the sharp word as soon as it left his mouth. A low moan escaped him, and he felt like an eighty-year-old man as he struggled to his feet. For a long time he faced her, hating himself for the fresh pain in her eyes.

She took the slightest step backwards. "You never even hear me, Connor." Tears glistened in her lower lashes. "The man's your father."

"The man's a stranger."

"Because you let him be."

"No." His voice rose a notch. "Because he wants to be."

She pressed the palm of her hand against her forehead and grabbed at her hair with her other hand. Her words were a desperate hiss. "I *hate* this."

He hated it, too. He watched her and wanted to say so, wanted to tell her how awful the whole mess made him feel. How he hated the silence and bitterness and empty, wasted years. Hated the way his own father hadn't cared enough to call any of them, not even the girls. But he could say nothing, really. He knew better than to involve Michele. Her thoughts on the issue were too simple. *He's your father,* she'd told him a hundred times in the past eight years. *Call him and tell him you love him.*

But he couldn't; and after this long, he simply wouldn't. Even if the image of the dead man in the burgundy sedan stayed with him all month.

Michele wiped her hands on her smock and used her shoulder to dab away a tear. She narrowed her eyes and stared at him, straight to the most dank, dark places of his soul. "Life is short; one of these days it'll be too late."

He worked the muscles in his jaw, then let it go. Holding out his hands, he took

51

slow, tentative steps toward her. "Ah, baby, I'm sorry." They came together in an embrace, and Connor breathed in the fragrance of her shampoo. "It's not your fault."

"But you won't call, right?"

"We've been through this." His voice fell flat. He shouldn't have told her about the accident; no matter what the dead man looked like, there would be no phone call to the West Coast. "Let it go, okay?"

Discouragement filled her eyes, but she held his gaze. "Okay."

He could hear that it wasn't, but he wouldn't push the issue. It was one thing to have no relationship with his father, but Michele . . . ? She was everything to him. He drew back and glanced at his watch.

"Errands?" The question, though it rang with sadness, was her way of saying she wouldn't dwell on the topic. They'd learned at least that much in the past eight years.

"Yep." He grabbed his truck keys from the kitchen table.

She stepped back onto the stool and faced him. "Don't be long."

"I won't." Connor grabbed a glass of water, downed it, and made his way across the kitchen. "I still need the mower."

For an instant she only looked at him, her eyes deep and thoughtful. As she turned away she said, "You need a father, too."

Her words were so soft, Connor almost didn't hear them. A hundred replies flashed in his mind, but he chose the safest one. "I love you, Michele."

With that he was out the door.

Not until he got in his truck did he realize he'd been shaking. He started the ignition. What a way to kill a Saturday. Even buying a riding mower wouldn't make him happy in light of the skeletons that had come to life that day.

As he was pulling out of the driveway he turned on the radio. Country music. That's what he needed. Garth Brooks or Kenny Chesney or Tim McGraw. Something to wash away the grimy residue of his past, to remind him his yesterdays counted for nothing. All that mattered was today. Today and tomorrow and every minute of the future he and Michele and the girls had ahead of them. It was still a brilliant spring day. Maybe an hour or two on a riding mower would right his world, after all. A song ended and the deejay came on.

"Investigation continues into yesterday's

plane crash in the Pacific. Today the FAA released a —"

Connor turned up the volume. What had the man said? A plane had crashed into the ocean?

"— report that the fuselage was found broken apart in relatively shallow ocean waters. A team of divers is looking for the cockpit's black box to determine whether pilot error was to blame. Western Island Air Flight No. 45 from Honolulu to Tokyo crashed minutes after takeoff. Witnesses said the aircraft lost speed and then nose-dived into the Pacific. One hundred eighty-eight passengers and crew were aboard the flight. Search and rescue officials fear there are no survivors."

He jerked the wheel and pulled off to the side of the road. What was *with* this day? First the guy in the burgundy sedan, and now this? A plane crash? Nearly two hundred people lost somewhere in the Pacific?

He'd never worked Western Island Airlines, so he wouldn't have known any of the crew. Even so . . . he pictured a 747 plummeting to the ground, nose first, and he shuddered. Pilot error. It had to be pilot error. Birds that big didn't fall from the sky.

His heart raced and he gritted his teeth.

Get a grip, Evans. These things happen.

A constant stream of scenarios raced through his mind. A missed switch or an incorrect setting. Yes, it had to be pilot error. He gripped the steering wheel and studied his knuckles, his hands. How horrible would it be for those same hands to be at the controls of a nose-diving aircraft? How awful not to be able to pull out of it?

Almost at the same time the statistics began shouting the truth through the hallways of his subconscious.

Come on, Evans, thirty thousand Americans fly every day . . .

Connor relaxed his grip on the steering wheel. Of course they did. Hundreds of flights took off each hour across the world without incident, day after day, week after week, month after month, and most of the time, year after year. Flying wasn't only safer than driving, it was safer than riding a bike. Safer than swimming or football or rock climbing. A person was more likely to choke to death on airline food than to die in a plane crash.

"Have mercy on them, God." As he whispered the words, his heartbeat settled into a normal rhythm. Tomorrow at the airport he would find the list of missing crew members, just in case he recognized any names, guys he'd known at West Point, maybe. But even then, he couldn't dwell on the crash.

It was one aircraft, one mistake.

At least it wasn't his airline. After so many years of flying, he knew many of the pilots and flight attendants. A loss like yesterday's crash within his own airline would definitely cost him a few friends.

As he pulled into Home Depot he dismissed thoughts about the crash and set his mind to the task at hand. Picking out a decent riding mower.

Over the next few hours he found his machine, brought it home, and took down the grass in the backyard; then he picked up the girls from the party and listened to a thirty-minute replay of the birthday girls' reactions to Elizabeth and Susan's gifts. By then Connor had forgotten everything bad about the day.

The car accident, the old man. Even the plane crash.

All he could think about was how wonderful his life was, and how much he hoped it would go on this way forever.

THREE

Something was wrong. Max knew it as soon as he came home from school.

Ramey was waiting for him at the bus stop and she had Buddy with her. At first he felt his heart get extra happy at the sight of that old dog because the two of them were bestest friends. He ran off the bus and wrapped his arm around Buddy's neck.

But halfway home from the bus stop, Max noticed a funny feeling in his stomach, the same kind of feeling he had when one time he ate an old cheese stick from his backpack. Sort of mixed up and jumpy and sickish all at once. And he knew why he felt that way.

Ramey never brought Buddy with her to the bus stop.

Buddy stayed home in his own backyard with lots of food and water, waiting for Max and his mom to come home.

"Can't he stay with me at Ramey's?" Max asked his mom over and over.

"No! You ask a hundred times each month and the answer's still no, Max. Ramey can't have dogs at her apartment."

Max wasn't sure about the hundred times. More like eighteen or nineteen. But . . . if Ramey wasn't allowed to have dogs in her apartment, how come Buddy came to the bus stop with her today? And how come he stayed for dinner and had his food bowl in the backyard?

Those were questions he thought about all evening while Ramey talked on the phone.

"Here," she told him. "Watch a movie. I'll be right in."

"Can I watch TV? TV's better than a movie because it's educational. Mommy told me that."

Ramey made a face he hadn't seen before. "No, Max. No TV. Not today. We'll watch a movie together."

"Okay."

Ramey looked strange in her eyes, the way his friend Wilton looked when he forgot his bike at the pool and someone stoled it. Scared and mad and not sure what to do. Ramey grabbed the top video from the stack and pushed it into the VCR.

58

There was no school tomorrow, so staying up late was okay. Max found his favorite spot on the fluffy purple couch, and when Buddy climbed up beside him, Ramey didn't say a thing.

She didn't join them, either.

Instead she kept her voice in a whisper and sometimes her cheeks looked wet. Was she crying? Max tried to listen to what she was saying, but most of the time the video was too loud.

He did hear a couple of things, though. "What am I supposed to do?" And "I won't say anything until there's proof."

The movie was *All Dogs Go to Heaven*, and Max watched it with the side of his face against Buddy's. Every few minutes Max checked to make sure Buddy was watching it, but halfway through the movie the dog fell asleep. And Ramey stayed on the phone the whole time.

When the movie was over, Ramey put on another show. *Peter Pan, Part II*. She brought Max a meat sandwich and milk to eat in the TV room. Max's funny feeling got worse. Ramey *never* let him eat in the TV room.

Finally, when the second movie was over, Max walked up to Ramey and tapped her on the shoulder. She was still on the phone. Her eyes had little black lines running under them.

"Yes, Max? Do you need another movie?" She used her whisper voice.

"No." Max whispered back. "I need my mom. See?" He pointed out the window. "See how it's dark out there, Ramey? That's when my mommy's supposed to call, only what if she can't call because you're on the phone?"

Ramey stared at him, and little bits of water spilled into her eyes. She did a big sniff. "Max, we'll talk about that in a minute."

He pushed out his bottom lip and walked with slow feet back to Buddy. "Hey, Buddy, wake up." Max gave him a light shake near his old red collar. "Wake up, boy."

Buddy lifted one eyelid, then the other. Max put his face up close against Buddy's nose and waited until the dog licked his cheek. Then Max put his fingers on either side of Buddy's wet nose. "I'm telling you, Buddy . . . something's funny here."

The dog tilted his head to the side and gave Max another lick.

Just then Ramey came up to him. She looked old and tired, and her face was reddish. "Max, your mom can't call you tonight."

A scared feeling came into Max. A goldfish feeling. One time he and his mom watched a show about people who ate live goldfish.

"I bet they wiggle around in those tummies for a long time," Max had told her.

That's how he felt now. Like maybe ten or eleven goldfish were wiggling in his stomach. He let go of Buddy and stood up straight and tall. The way his mommy liked him to stand. "How come?"

"Because something's come up, and she can't call, that's why."

The goldfish wriggled around some more. "Why?"

"I don't know, Max. We just have to wait." Ramey came and sat down on the edge of the sofa in front of where he was standing. Then she hugged him the way she did once when his turtle died.

Max stood stiff and scared. "Is she going to call me tomorrow? Before she flies?"

"I hope so." Ramey's voice sounded disappointed. Like she didn't really think his mom would call then, either.

Max pulled back and sat down. All of a sudden he didn't want to think about getting a phone call from his mom. Buddy jumped off the couch and lay down on the floor in front of him. Max patted his head. "Good boy, Buddy. It's okay."

Ramey let Max sleep on the couch that night, him on the top and Buddy on the floor beneath. But no TV; definitely no TV. In the morning Ramey came to him and reached out for his hand. He liked Ramey a lot because she was sort of like family. But he didn't like holding hands with her. Her hands were roughish. Plus, she wasn't his mom.

"Max, I have something to tell you."

He sat up and rubbed his eyes because sleep was still in him. Ramey sat next to him, and he noticed her eyelids were thick. The way his teacher's eyelids looked when kids in Room 8 gave her flowers. *Allergy*, teacher called it. Maybe Ramey had allergy, too.

A long breath came out of Ramey. "Your mom isn't coming home, Max."

He sat up a little straighter. "What?" Why would she say that? Ramey was wrong. "Only two days away. She promised."

Ramey moved her head with little shakes. "No, Max. Something happened. Your mommy isn't coming home ever again. Not ever."

The goldfish feeling was back, but this time he was mad, too. Very mad. "*No*, Ramey!" Next to him Buddy did a little bark. "Don't say that. She's coming home today. Before dinner!"

Teardrops started coming down Ramey's cheeks. She sat on the couch and put her hands over her face. "Help me do this!"

Max wasn't sure what to say. Buddy was sitting up now, watching Ramey the same way Max was. Max didn't want to be angry, but every time he let go of the mad, a scared feeling came. A big scared feeling that made him want to run out the door and straight home.

Finally Ramey lowered her hands. "Come here, Max."

He didn't want to do it, but he had to. Gentlemen obeyed grown-ups. His mother taught him that. His feet dragged across the carpet until he was standing near Ramey's knees.

She took hold of his shoulders and looked straight at his eyes. "Max . . . your mom is dead." A crying sound came from Ramey. "Jesus . . . Jesus took her to heaven to live with him."

Max jerked back hard and fast and shook his head. Ramey never lied to him before, never. But his mom wasn't dead.

She kissed him good-bye yesterday morning and he saw for himself. She wasn't dead; she was alive. Very, very alive. "No, Ramey . . . you're wrong." He backed up and ran quick into the bathroom and shut the door. Then he pressed his back against it so no one could get inside.

His breathing was fast and hard like when he raced Jimmy Jackson at recess. He squeezed his eyes shut and told his brain to think fast. Why would Ramey say that thing? His mommy was fine, she wasn't sick or old or anything. Jesus didn't take her to heaven. She was in Tokyo, that's all. Same as always.

His breathing got slower. She would call any minute.

Then a very awful idea popped into his heart and made his eyes sting. What if something bad happened to her airplane? Like maybe the wings fell off, or a door blew open? Or the pilot landed in the water? One time he asked her about airplane doors. "If someone opens the door, what happens?"

"You can't open the door when the plane's flying, Max. It isn't possible."

"But if someone did, couldn't you fall out?"

"I guess." She did a little laugh at him. "But that won't happen. Airplanes are super safe, okay?"

He asked her a few more times, but she always told him the same thing. Planes were safe. Wings didn't fall off, doors didn't blow open, and pilots never landed in the water. Never.

A knock came against the door and Max felt it push against his back.

"Max . . . open up. Please." Ramey wasn't crying anymore, but scared was in her voice. Scared and nervous and not sure what to do.

Now that the idea was in his head, he couldn't make it go away. What if something bad *did* happen to his mom's airplane? What if she didn't know it could happen, but it could? He stepped away from the door and opened it slow and careful. Then he peeked out at Ramey and he was all of a sudden afraid to ask.

His mom's words whispered in his heart. *Be brave, Max . . . whenever you're afraid be brave.* He did a swallow and straightened his shoulders. "Ramey, did . . . did something bad happen to her airplane?"

She did a little nod with her head. "Yes, Max. Something real bad."

His eyes got stingers in them again, and

his throat stuck together the way it did when he ate pancakes too fast. "Did the wings fall off?"

"No." Ramey opened the door a little bit more, and Buddy stuck his nose through the space. "It landed in the water, Max." Ramey's cheeks had wet on them again. "It never made it to Tokyo."

It never made it? A broken feeling grabbed Max's heart, and his knees felt rubbery. "They landed in water?"

"Yes, Max." Ramey made a crying sound again. She pulled him close and hugged him to her big, gray dress. "I'm so sorry, honey."

"Mommy said airplanes never land in water." He pushed back and looked at her again.

"They usually don't. But this time, well . . . something must've happened. Max . . . she didn't make it, honey."

"But Mommy knows how to swim, Ramey. Maybe she's swimming back to the island."

Ramey looked up and made her eyes shut tight. Then she said, "Please . . . I can't do this."

Max tugged on her sleeve. "Is she swimming, Ramey? Is she?" Max couldn't take a breath until Ramey answered him. "We could help her; it's not too late."

"No." Ramey's body made a shaking move and for a long time she didn't talk. "She's dead, Max. Everyone on the plane died."

"But maybe she isn't dead . . . maybe she's in there and she needs someone to help her out." He started to run for the front door, but Ramey caught him.

"She's not in the ocean anymore, Max." Her face was wet, and the skin around her eyes was even thicker than before. "She's in heaven. With Jesus."

Max couldn't run or move or even breathe. His mom was dead? Her plane landed in the ocean, and now she was in heaven? His legs crumpled under, and he fell to his hands and knees. "No, Ramey! She can't go. Not without me . . ."

His eyes got blurry and tears started coming down his face. More tears than he'd ever had in all his life. How could Mommy be gone? Who would read to him and hug him and love him now? Who would make him blueberry pancakes for breakfast and get him dressed in the morning and take him to the park for roller-skate lessons? Who would sing him his special song about *I love you, Max, the most, I love to make you toast?*

Buddy came up beside him and licked his face.

"Go away, Buddy."

The dog stepped back and lay down. He had sad in his eyes, and Max felt bad for yelling at him. Buddy must've known about Mommy's plane landing in the water. But why couldn't someone get her out of the plane and bring her home? "Mom!" His voice was loud and scared, so wherever she was she might hear it. Even all the way to heaven.

Ramey put her arm around him and sat him on the couch. She sat beside him and hugged him for a long time. They cried and cried together, and the more Max thought about it, the more true it felt.

His mommy was dead. She really was.

He knew, because a hole was in his heart now. A big hole where his mommy used to be. His whole self must've been filled with tears because they spilled out from his eyes without stopping. For Ramey, too. And he couldn't understand that, because it was *his* mom who died, that's why. After a long time, Ramey told him, "Let's pray."

Pray wasn't something Ramey did, but he and Mommy did it all the time. Ramey prayed before they ate sometimes, but that was all. She didn't know the other things about God, like that He lived in heaven, Max was pretty sure about that. But now God wasn't the only one there, because his mommy had joined Him. Max wiped his hands across his cheeks.

All he needed was a map and he could go there, too. Maybe Ramey could look it up on the Internet. But until then, God would have to tell his mommy how he was feeling. He knew about praying, but he wasn't sure about messages. "Could God give Mommy a message for me?"

"Yes, Max." Ramey bit her lip and her chin got jiggly. "If there's a God, somehow He'll tell your mom."

"Is there a God?" Max wanted to be sure. He always thought so; Mommy always told him so. But he didn't want to give Him a message if He wasn't real.

"God . . ." Ramey's eyes were closed again. Her voice was extra quiet. "Where are you?" Ramey's head bent down. Crying came over her for a minute and then she looked up and did a couple nods. "Yes, Max. There is a God. Even on a day like this."

"Okay, then." Max folded his hands together the way he and his mommy always did. But sad filled his mouth and he couldn't talk. *Mommy . . . Mommy, where are you? Come back to me, please* . . . The words stayed in his mouth. A missing feeling came all through him. He didn't just miss her in his heart and in his head, but his arms missed her and his hands and his feet. Because after today he wouldn't hug her or swing hands with her or walk beside her. Not ever again.

"Max?" Ramey put her hand over his two smaller ones. "Want me to say it?"

"No, thank you." He wanted God to hear the message straight from him. He did a little sniff. "God, hi, it's Max." He moved a little in his seat because he had never asked God to give a message before. "Ramey says my mommy's with You now, so can You tell her something for me?" He waited, in case God wanted to say something back. When he heard no words, he started again. "Tell her I'm sorry I wasn't there when her plane landed in the water, because I would've helped her out. Me and her coulda swimmed to the island, and she wouldn't have to live in heaven."

The missing feeling got worse, and he remembered his mom's face.

Be brave, Max . . . be brave.

Max sat a little straighter. "But I guess now it's too late, so will You tell her something else, God, please? Tell her I'm being

70

good for Ramey and that Buddy says hi." Buddy made a little whiny sound. "And tell her to sing me our special song, 'I Love You, Max, the Most,' tonight before she goes to bed." He wasn't sure how to finish. "Thank You, God. I'll think of more stuff later."

It wasn't until that night when he and Buddy were in bed that Max realized something. If the plane would've landed on the ground like it was supposed to, his mom would've been home by now. She'd be in his room, sitting on his bed and singing him his song.

But if God gave her the message, then maybe she was singing it right now. He thought about that for a minute. Maybe she was waiting for him to sing it with her. His throat felt like a frog was in it, so he did a loud cough.

Buddy looked up, and his ears got pointy.

"It's okay, boy." Max patted Buddy's head and gave it a light push back down toward the bed. "Go to sleep."

Buddy made a soft breath on Max's arm, and a tired sound rattled in his neck. Then he dropped down his head like a good dog. That's when Max began to hum just a little. Finally the words came, too. The words to their special song. He circled his

71

arm around Buddy's neck and sang them soft as a buzzing fly.

"I love you, Max, the most, I love to make you toast. When oceans we're apart . . . you're always in my heart."

The humming part didn't sound the same without his mom, but it made the hole in Max's heart feel smaller. Even if his hum was in a whisper voice. Because if his mom was singing their song somewhere in heaven, then they were together sort of. The song had hand motions, which meant he could sing it with his voice and his words and his hands, the way he and Mommy always sang it.

First his hands over his heart, then one hand open like a pretend bread, and one hand brushing back and forth like a pretend butter knife, the way his mom made him toast each morning. Then big arms for the ocean, and last, hands back over his heart.

He started again, but his eyes felt watery, so he didn't do the hand motions. They were only fun when he and his mommy were in the same room. It wasn't the same if she was in heaven.

"I love you, Max, the most . . . I love to make you toast. When oceans we're apart —"

Just then he stopped because he remembered a P.S. for God. Mommy told him about P.S. It's when you write a note and add something at the very end, something 'portant you forgot.

"God?" He whispered. His throat was sticky, and the hole in his heart was big again. Bigger than before. "God, if You're there, it's me, Max."

Buddy stretched out against him and did a huffy sound. His nose was cold and wet against Max's arm.

"God, I forgot a P.S." Max blinked in the dark room and ran his fingers into Buddy's warm fur. Buddy had been next to him all day because Buddy missed Mommy, too, that's why. Ramey was nice, but Buddy was all the family Max had left now. He heard Ramey say that to someone on the phone during lunch. "Please, God, tell my mom I'm going to talk to Ramey tomorrow about heaven. Because I'm not sure how to get there, God. But if Mommy's going to live there, I want to live there, too. Really soon, okay?"

When Max finally fell asleep with his arm around Buddy, he dreamed about airplanes landing in water and a place called heaven where they could all be together. Him and Mommy and Buddy. The way a family should be.

Forever and ever and ever.

FOUR

Ramey couldn't stop the flow of memories. They came to her constantly, bits and pieces of Kiahna's life, information that Ramey had to rely on now that Kiahna was gone.

Just weeks before Max was born, Kiahna sat Ramey down and told her what to do if one day she didn't come home.

"Let's talk about death." Kiahna rested her hands on her extended abdomen and leveled her gaze at Ramey.

"Stop." Ramey had brushed her off, not sure Kiahna was serious. "This is your season of life. Don't talk like that; you scare me."

But Kiahna didn't let up. "Ramey, I mean it. If anything ever happens to me, you need to know what to do."

Ramey looked at the young woman for a moment and finally nodded. "Okay. Tell me."

The plan was simple. Kiahna had

written a brief will and a note for her un-born son. The two documents were being kept by an attorney on the island, someone Kiahna had paid to handle things in an emergency.

"What about the boy's father?"

Kiahna's expression shut down like a bank at closing time. "No. You must not ask about him."

Ramey never asked again. Whoever the man was, he'd hurt Kiahna deeply. The girl was beautiful inside and out, half Irish, half Hawaiian, leggy with tan skin, pale green eyes, and a heart deeper than the waters off Honolulu. But the only men al-lowed access to that heart were God and Max. Always Max.

Ramey used to dream about finding Max's father and shaking him, asking him if he knew what he was missing by leaving Kiahna pregnant and alone. Max was an amazing boy, a child filled with awe and wonder, very much in need of a father.

At first, when Max was a baby, Ramey would ask Kiahna whether she was meeting anyone worth dating. "Every time I think of that boy I see a father in his fu-ture," Ramey would say. "With all those businessmen and pilots you work with, one of them must be worth smiling at."

Kiahna's features would take on a far-away look. She would give a few subtle shakes of her head, and that was as far as the conversation went. By the time Max was three, Kiahna told her it wasn't a daddy the boy needed. It was a Father. A heavenly Father. Kiahna grew up in a church, but that year her faith became doubly important because of Max. She wanted him to know everything about living a life for God.

But when Kiahna tried to share her faith, Ramey bristled. "It's all a fantasy, Kiahna. It's okay for you, but keep it to yourself."

"I won't ask you about God, if you don't ask me about men."

Ramey planted her hands on her hips. "Deal."

Every now and then, though, Ramey found a way to bring the forbidden subject up to Kiahna.

"Look, I have God and Max." She'd give Ramey a shrug and a sweet smile. "That's enough for now."

Ramey got the point, but that didn't stop her from mentioning a single man down at the grocery store, or another one out by the pool. Kiahna's response was always the same. There would be no men in her life except for her son.

A handful of years passed, and Ramey's own two children moved to the mainland and rarely made it back for visits. Ramey still had a heart full of love, so she opened a day care in her home. Six children came every day after school, but Max was the only one who sometimes spent the night. When he turned five, Ramey was too ill and too tired to care for so many children. She kept only Max, and she realized something about the boy.

He felt like her own.

Now she was sixty-eight with heart disease, diabetes, poor circulation, and failing eyesight. With Kiahna gone, whatever Max's future held Ramey wanted very much to be part of it. But she couldn't be the only part. Max was an active child, a boy who learned from Kiahna on the sidewalk outside their apartment how to throw a spiral pass, one who raced his mother down the beach and took bike rides with her on lesser-known island trails.

Ramey's body simply didn't have that much left to give.

So it was, first thing Monday morning, three days after the tragedy, Ramey was on the phone with Kiahna's attorney, hoping against hope that whatever financial plan the documents held for Max, they also contained some type of physical plan.

Ramey wasn't sure what she was hoping for. That Kiahna had a long-lost sister maybe, or an aunt or uncle. Someone who cared enough to step in and be a family for Max. The receptionist at the attorney's office had her on hold, but that didn't bother Ramey. She would've waited all day if it meant helping Max. Poor baby. He and Buddy had been practically attached at the ankle since Saturday morning, and several times she'd found Max sitting at the foot of his bed, knees drawn up, face buried in his arms.

Sobbing and calling in quiet desperation for his mama.

Today was the first morning Ramey woke up dry-eyed, but she had no doubt there'd be more sadness before the day was done. She held the receiver close to her ear.

"Hello, this is Marv Ogle."

Ramey steadied herself. Never . . . never had she thought she'd have to make this call. Back when Max was born it had seemed impossible that Kiahna would ever be anything but the boy's mom, young and alive and driven by faith. "Hello, Mr. Ogle. Kiahna Seifert is a client of yours, I believe."

"Kiahna?" The man's voice softened. "Yes . . . she's a client."

"Well . . ." Ramey swallowed. She had the feeling Kiahna had been more than a client to this man. Perhaps she had even been a friend. "I have some bad news, Mr. Ogle." She closed her eyes for a moment. "Kiahna was killed in Friday's plane crash. She . . . she was a flight attendant."

A moment passed while the man recovered. "Are you sure?"

"Yes."

The attorney moaned, and his voice cracked when he spoke again. "I was worried. I heard about the crash and looked for a victim list, but the papers haven't printed it yet."

"No." Ramey blinked back a fresh wetness in her eyes. "They're still notifying next of kin."

"You're absolutely sure?" He sighed long and slow, the way people did in hospitals and funeral parlors. "I thought she flew the Los Angeles route."

"Before Max was born." Ramey stared at her hands and saw they were shaking. "It's been Honolulu to Tokyo ever since."

Another quiet moan. "My dear Kiahna." The attorney said her name as though by itself it might have contained a thousand memories. "This was her worst fear."

"Yes, sir."

"Kiahna was like a second daughter to me."

"Oh." Ramey understood. She felt the same way. "I didn't know."

The man's voice drifted. "She and my daughter were best friends through junior high, closer than sisters. Marlee . . . she fell in with a bad crowd and when high school came around, she and Kiahna didn't spend much time together. Even then Kiahna was a friend. A sweet girl who lived out her faith every day. She . . . she would drive to parties and pull my daughter out. Then she'd come by the next morning to talk a little sense into her. She did everything possible to save my daughter from the life she'd fallen into."

The man grunted as though he was trying to gain composure. "Marlee died of alcohol poisoning the summer before her senior year. At the funeral, Kiahna hugged my wife and me and told us we were like parents to her. That if we ever wanted time with our second daughter, she'd be there."

A single teardrop pushed its way from the corner of Ramey's right eye and a warm stream of tears followed. She couldn't think of a response.

The man sucked in a quick breath. "We hadn't seen her in a while, but she came by a few months ago. Brought my wife flowers and chatted while Max ran around out back." He paused. "She loved that boy more than life."

"Yes. Yes, she did." Ramey wanted to keep sharing lovely memories of Kiahna, but the matter at hand was pressing. "Mr. Ogle, you have Kiahna's will, is that right?"

"It is." He sounded suddenly tired in light of the obvious reason for the phone call. "Two envelopes — one with her last will and testament. One with a letter for Max."

"The one she wrote before he was born?" Ramey gripped the phone a bit tighter. "She told me about it."

"No. She brought by a new one every year around Max's birthday. So the file would be current."

Ramey's heart sank a bit in her chest. The physical ache within her doubled. Why . . . why would God — if there was a God — take Kiahna when she loved her little boy so? When she was all the child had? She squeezed her eyes shut. "Mr. Ogle, Max is in my care. We need to know Kiahna's intentions." A lump formed in Ramey's throat. "The sooner the better."

Ramey heard the sound of pages flipping. "This afternoon at two o'clock, how does that look for you?"

She glanced through her sliding glass door. Max was on the small back patio, lying on the cement, his head resting on Buddy. He was in no condition to go to school, and depending on what Kiahna's letter told them, he might not return. Whatever Max's future held, a resolution was needed. She brought her thumb and forefinger to her face and massaged her temples. "Two is perfect."

The attorney hesitated. "Will Max be there?"

"Yes. He . . . he has nowhere else to go, Mr. Ogle."

"I understand." Again the man's pain resonated across the phone lines. "But some of what I'll be reading to you is very sensitive. We'll need at least some time alone. Without the boy."

A dozen thoughts competed for Ramey's attention. Kiahna's documents held something sensitive? What was it, and why hadn't she shared the information earlier? Ramey's throat grew tight again, and she heard herself begin to wheeze. An asthma attack. She'd need her inhaler within a few minutes or she'd be in trouble. She gave the attorney directions to her apartment. "Mr. Ogle" — she coughed twice — "I'll have Max play inside. We can talk on the patio."

They hung up, and Ramey found her medication. Three puffs and her airways were clear again. For now, anyway. Her doctors had told her that her health was deteriorating, succumbing to the many ailments that plagued her. Asthma was only one of them, and each was a reminder that Max had no one.

Short of becoming a ward of the state, whatever plan Kiahna spelled out in her will wouldn't be one of many options for the child.

It would be his only hope.

FIVE

Tuesday was Michele Evans's favorite day.

Though a new schedule came out each month, the airline had been giving Connor a series of short flights that started Tuesday at two o'clock in the afternoon, home again Wednesday night, out Thursday by seven in the morning, and home late Friday. The schedule allowed him weekends at home — time for yard work and backyard projects and outings with the girls.

But most of all it gave him his Tuesday mornings with Michele.

A routine had developed, one she looked forward to all week. Each Tuesday they'd get up with the girls, share hot pancakes and sausage, take Elizabeth and Susan to Lakewood Elementary School, and return home by eight-thirty. At that point they'd unplug the telephone, climb back into bed, and share the next three hours pretending time didn't matter.

A mini-vacation in the midst of a mundane week.

On Tuesdays they could be intimate without fear of the girls needing them, they could talk about the past week without interruption, and once in a while they even had time for a dip in the hot tub.

Already this Tuesday morning had been fantastic. Sunshine warm enough to leave the windows open, lovemaking that would keep a smile on both their faces at least until Connor came home Wednesday night, and a conversation that was only just getting started.

"So what exactly happened at the fair? Tell me about Elizabeth's science project." Connor rolled onto his side and studied Michele. She was propped up on two pillows, flat on her back and still beneath the covers. Her knees were pulled up, and as she grinned at him she felt a decade younger than her thirty-nine years.

"Okay" — she angled herself onto her side so they were facing each other — "remember the idea? Prove which kind of junk food ants liked best?"

"Right." He slid a few inches closer and ran his fingertips through her bangs.

"We put out ant-size piles of Oreo cookies and Butterfingers, chocolate cake and marshmallows." She raised her eyebrow at him. "Guess what happened?"

"Butterfingers?" His voice was low, soothing. The way it often was hours into their Tuesday mornings.

"Nope. They hated all of it. Elizabeth brushed strawberry jam on the cardboard so the ants would get stuck, but as of yesterday, she didn't have a single ant."

"Maybe they don't like strawberry jam?"

She grabbed a pillow and gave him a soft whack across the face. "Stop."

This was her favorite part, the moments of laughter and silliness. In some way, these times made their marriage strong, kept her more in love with Connor Evans every year. If they could play together this way, they would always be okay.

The conversation drifted from the kids to the house and finally to her hair clients.

"Renee Wagner came in yesterday."

Renee was married to a pilot who worked for Connor's airline. The two couples had been close five years ago, but over time the men took on different schedules. Renee's husband, Joe, worked international flights, so his hours almost never coincided with Connor's. Renee spent most of her hair appointment crying.

Connor stroked the day-old growth on

his chin. "I haven't seen Joe in months."

Michele sat up and leaned against the headboard. "Then you don't know?"

"Know what?" Connor's eyes told her he had no idea.

A sigh slipped from Michele's throat. "They separated two weeks ago."

Connor pushed himself into a sitting position, never taking his eyes from hers. "You're kidding? Renee and Joe?"

"She was pretty broken up. I figured you would have heard at work."

He raked his fingers through his hair and shook his head. "Guys don't talk about that stuff. Not unless you're sharing a cockpit, and even then . . ."

"I guess he met someone overseas. Europe somewhere."

"Oh, man."

For the slightest instant, Michele thought she saw something in Connor's eyes. An odd flicker that was there, then gone. She didn't dwell on it. Both of them knew the score. Affairs weren't uncommon for pilots.

"I don't get it." Michele drew her legs closer to her chest. "Renee's one of the most beautiful women I know. Two little boys, and a house in the Heights." Her voice dropped some, and she searched her husband's eyes. "How could he, Connor?"

A tired sound came from him. "Simple." Connor held her eyes. "Too much time on the road."

"You're on the road and you're faithful."

"That's different." A smile filled out Connor's face once more. He caught her face in his hands and drew her close for a lingering kiss. "I've got the best marriage in the world, and the best wife, too."

Michele rubbed her nose against his — but the mood wasn't quite what it had been. "You have, right?"

Connor drew back and studied her eyes. "Have what?"

"Been faithful?" She'd never asked before, never needed to. She had no reason to ask it now, but after what happened to Renee, her heart wanted reassurance.

"Ah, Michele." He brought his hand up alongside her face and brushed her cheekbone with his thumb. "Do you have to ask?"

"No, it's just . . ."

"Baby, listen." His expression changed and suddenly she felt he was looking straight to the deepest part of her soul. "I've never loved anyone but you. Not ever."

Something in her heart relaxed, a part

88

that for some reason had been holding its breath. "I just thought . . ." She gave him a sad smile. "After talking to Renee, I don't know. She thought everything was okay, too. I guess every now and then it's good to hear it from you."

"Michele." He let his forehead fall against hers. "You have nothing to worry about. Not now . . . not ever."

"Good." She framed his jaw with her fingertips. "Sorry for asking."

Connor glanced at the alarm clock on her bedside table. "Almost noon. I better shower." He leaned in and planted one last kiss on her cheek. Then in a single fluid movement he pushed himself off the bed and headed for the bathroom.

"Wait . . ." Michele slid to the edge of the mattress.

Connor stopped and looked back at her. "What?"

"What about the Bible? Every Tuesday, remember?"

"Right." Connor frowned. "I completely forgot."

"Me, too."

He glanced at the clock on their bedside table. "Can we start next week?"

"Sure." Michele hid her disappointment. For months they'd been meaning to get back to reading Scripture, praying together. But always time seemed to get away from them.

Connor stretched and flashed her a crooked grin. "We'll do it next week for sure . . . I promise, okay?"

"Okay." The disappointment faded. Michele studied Connor, dressed only in a pair of shorts, and was struck again by the strength of his body, the way he cared for himself. Connor Evans was a man who had once single-handedly pulled his plane out of a death spin. He liked to say he appreciated his wingmen as much as his copilots, but he never allowed himself to rely on either. And when it came to his workouts, they were an hour a day, three days a week, whatever city or hotel he happened to be in.

"My body's a tool," he'd said a hundred times. "I'm only as good as my level of physical fitness."

Michele smiled. Every aspect of her husband's life involved some type of perfection. Perfection in the cockpit, perfection at the gym, perfection in the way he doted on their girls. Even perfection in their marriage.

Michele watched him walk away until he closed the bathroom door. Only then did she realize how quickly he'd changed subjects. One minute they'd been talking about affairs and faithfulness. The next he was heading for the shower. She froze, replaying their conversation in her mind. Maybe the switch hadn't been so sudden. After all, he showered at this time every Tuesday morning, and he was nothing if not punctual. And praying and reading the Bible together would become routine too — if they could find a way to get back to it.

From inside the bathroom, she heard Connor turn on the shower, but instead of heading downstairs to make him a sandwich, she sat there, unmoving. At the center of her heart, something didn't feel right. Was it something Connor had said, the tone of his voice, maybe? Or was it simply her sorrow for Renee? A chill made its way down her arms. How would it feel to be Renee Wagner? Michele remembered something Renee said once, a year ago.

"I don't have to worry about Joe." She gave Michele an easy smile. "Some guys have cheating in their blood, but not Joe. He can't even tell when a woman's hitting on him. The last thing he'd do is have an affair."

Michele let the words play again in her

mind. She could see herself nodding along, agreeing with her friend. Yes, Connor was the same type of man. The kind who could turn heads as he strode down an airport hallway, and never look anywhere but straight ahead. Good guys, safe guys. The kind that didn't cheat on their wives.

But one lonely night across the ocean in Rome, Joe tossed the rulebook out the window. An affair, one lousy affair, and now what? Eighteen years of marriage . . . the family they'd spent a lifetime building . . . all of it gone.

So why were Joe and Renee's troubles bothering her now? Joe and Connor were different men, weren't they? For one thing, Joe didn't have Connor's faith. Even though they didn't attend church as often as they once had, even though they couldn't make time to pray together, God was the staying power in her husband's life.

Right?

Michele stared at the closed bathroom door and a strong breeze rattled the blinds. She jumped at the sound and rose to her feet.

Enough.

She needed to get downstairs and make Connor lunch before he left. Worrying was nothing but a waste of time. What had happened to Renee would never happen to her, never. Connor was not a man given to impulsive moments, unplanned emotion. He was far too self-controlled, too sure of what he wanted from life and his future and his relationship with her and the girls. Too perfect to let himself make a mistake like that.

Not even overseas on the loneliest night of his life.

The shower had been running for five minutes before Connor's heart settled into a normal beat. What would have made Michele ask a question like that?

Had he always been faithful?

She'd never brought that up before. Never.

Water streamed down Connor's chest and arms. Had she seen anything in his re-action? A hesitation or twitch of some kind? His face must've gone pale as he scrambled for the right words. Even now he had no idea how he'd come up with a cool, quick answer.

Connor worked the shampoo through his hair and nudged the hot water knob higher, hotter. Space. That's what he needed now, space between the troubles with Joe and Renee — and the conversation with Michele. By the time he was out of the shower and dressed, Michele would forget the whole thing, and the topic of his faithfulness wouldn't come up again. Not ever. Michele was everything to him now, and never . . . never would he let himself do the thing Joe had done.

That was a lesson he'd already learned.

Suds ran down his face and chest, and the clean smell of bar soap filled the warm wet air. He loved Michele more than ever. Or maybe he'd always loved her this much. That awful night eight years ago was so far back down the road, most of the time Connor could convince himself he'd never been there at all. He was a good guy. Out of a hundred opportunities to fall, he'd been almost perfect.

Ninety-nine times perfect.

And that one time had been nothing more than crazy circumstances and strange twists of fate. Even then he hadn't been bored with Michele or wanted another woman. Michele was everything to him. As the hot water pounded his shoulder blades, Connor let the shower fill his senses and take him back, back to the days when he and Michele first met.

SIX

High school romances didn't mean a thing to Connor. He was a decent football player and a starter on the basketball team, one of the socially elite who had no trouble finding a date. But Connor rarely let things get serious with any of them, not in a physical or emotional way. He dated girls one weekend and forgot about them the next. His father drilled into him the importance of studying, of setting a goal and going after it. From the beginning his goal was clear.

He would be a pilot.

After graduating he earned an appointment to West Point. In his senior year, months away from being made an officer and earning his wings, he made time for some relaxation. That's why he agreed to go to a barbecue with a group of guys from school. Connor wasn't given to reckless drinking or drug use, not so much because he was afraid of how it would make him feel, but because he was afraid of his father.

"Always be on top of your game, Son," he would say. "Keep away from the stupid things other boys do. That goes for women, too. Don't let anything take away your edge."

And Connor hadn't. Not drugs or drinking, and especially not women. Not that there had ever been a shortage. Women liked West Point students, especially seniors, and they'd made themselves available to Connor since his freshman year. His lanky, muscled body and clean-cut dark hair always turned heads, though Connor had come to think of his looks as something of a curse. Because his father was right. If he got mixed up with a girl too soon, his dedication toward becoming an officer, earning his wings, and getting in the skies would be compromised. And he wasn't about to let that happen.

But by his senior year, a barbecue seemed harmless enough.

It was at Paul Overgaard's house. Paul was also a senior, probably Connor's best friend at West Point. The two had rooms across the hall from each other, and despite the gravity of their classload, and the goal of making officer, they shared an easy sense of humor.

Paul's family lived close by, but Connor had never been to his friend's house until now. From the beginning of the party, he was certain he'd made the right choice by coming. Paul's parents' house was a palace. The backyard was spacious with a massive swimming pool and in the distance, a sand volleyball court.

He was glad he'd worn his swim shorts and a T-shirt, and as soon as introductions were over, the guys headed out to the sand pit for a three-game volleyball tournament. The competition felt wonderful — it was good to do something other than flight training and class work.

At the end of the set, his team came up losers, but Connor didn't care. The stress of upcoming finals was gone, and he ambled with the guys toward the smell of fresh-cooked hamburgers. He made up his plate, grabbed a seat with Paul and a few of his buddies, and took his first bite.

That's when he saw her.

Like a vision, she strolled out through the sliding doors. She was long legged, with a figure that made him set the burger back down on the plate. She had pale brown eyes and dark hair that fell in waves around her face and shoulders. Her laughter rang out across the patio, and when she smiled, the sun looked dim in comparison.

"What's the matter?" Paul poked him in the shoulder and followed his gaze toward the group that had just entered the back-yard area. "Connor, come on. Don't be stupid."

He swallowed his bite and shook his head. "Man, she's the most beautiful girl I've ever seen."

"Don't you know?" Paul laughed and leaned back in his chair. "That's my kid sister. I've got two of them. That one's a junior at the state school an hour away." He shot her a look over his shoulder. "They're already out on break."

"Why didn't you tell me about her?"

"You never asked."

"Okay." Connor nodded, but he was in a trance. "That's fair enough." He paused, studying her. "She's home for the summer?"

"Yes." Paul chuckled. "You can go back to eating."

"Does she have a boyfriend?" Connor's eyes were still locked on Paul's sister. "Tell me she doesn't have a boyfriend."

"You have a month left, remember?"

Paul gave him a kick under the table. "You told me to remind you if you ever got like this."

"That was different." He grabbed a napkin and wiped his mouth. "Introduce me."

At that moment, the girl turned and found Paul. Still talking to the friends around her, she made her way to their table and gripped her brother's shoulders from behind. But already her eyes had found Connor's. "Hey, big brother, how's school?"

Paul looked up and grinned at her. "One month left."

"What about your friend?" She motioned at Connor with her chin. Her eyes held a teasing that made it clear she was intrigued.

"Connor?"

"Okay, yes." She angled her face and her smile looked more shy than before. "What's Connor's story?"

"I've got it." Connor shot a look at Paul. Then he stood and held out his hand. "I don't think we've met. I'm Connor Evans." He could feel his eyes dancing, teasing her the way she'd been teasing him. "My story is the same as your brother's. Senior at West Point, graduating officer in a month."

"I see." She took his hand and gave it the slightest squeeze. "Nice to meet you, Connor. I'm Michele."

They were together the rest of the evening. Over the next four weeks, Connor drew on all his discipline and saw her only twice. The evening of their graduation and wing ceremony, Connor and his family joined Paul's family at the reception.

When the commotion died down some, Connor found Michele. "It's stuffy in here."

She smiled. "Yeah, all those pilot egos crammed into one room."

"Touché." He grinned at her. "Let's take a walk outside. The pond's just a few minutes away."

She took his hand and when they reached the pond, he turned and drew her close. "Michele, I've thought about you every day since we met."

Her eyes fell to the ground, and a blush spread across her cheeks. "I wasn't sure."

"I would've called you every day, but I had finals and graduation and . . ." He searched her face. "Well, now I have the whole summer ahead of me." His voice fell a notch. "Let me take you out, Michele. Please."

Connor realized as he stood there, brush

and tree groves surrounding them, that she was the first girl he'd sought after. Every other time the girl had done the seeking. He held his breath, waiting for her answer.

"Okay, but don't fall in love with me."

She was grinning, teasing him the way she'd done back at the barbecue. He took a step back, his hands on her shoulders. "How come?"

"Because I could never be with a pilot."

"Really?" He raised a single eyebrow. "Too much like your brother, huh?"

"No." Her smile fell away. "Because I'm scared to death to fly. I couldn't stand to fall in love with someone who spent half his life in the skies."

With feather-soft care, Connor eased his hands up her neck and on either side of her face. "Well, then . . ." He wanted to kiss her with everything in him, but he held back. "We'll have to change that, won't we?"

For the next two months they were rarely apart. The attraction was there for both of them, but Connor didn't let her see how intense his feelings for her had become. Before the summer was up, he got permission to borrow a friend's Cessna. He got her to the airfield by telling her he was taking her out to eat, giving her a chance to watch takeoffs and landings and see that they weren't so frightening.

Instead, when they climbed out of his jeep, he reached into the back and pulled out two helmets, one for him and one for her.

"Connor . . ." Her face went slack, and her mouth hung open. "What are you doing?"

"Helping you conquer your fears." He smiled and took her hand. And to his surprise, she took his in return.

They flew for an hour that night, circling over the area and doing basic maneuvers that caused Michele to gasp out loud. She was seated behind him, and several times she reached out and grabbed his shoulders. "Connor!"

Her voice was muffled in the helmet, but even from the front seat he could hear the panic in her voice fade. A minute later, she'd laugh, her hold on him looser than before. When they were back on the ground, he waited until they were in the parking lot near his jeep again before he asked her what she thought.

"You won't believe it." She giggled, her cheeks ruddy from the exhilaration of the flight. "It was amazing, Connor. I'd go up again in a minute." She gave him an impulsive hug. "You took away my greatest fear."

"Good." He leaned his back against the door of his car and eased her close to him. Then, for the first time, he kissed her. The slow, lingering sort of kiss that bared everything he felt for her, the kind he'd never given any woman before or since.

"Why?" When she pulled away, she was breathless, her eyes colored with passion. "Why good?"

"Because I broke your rule, Michele." He framed her face with tender hands and kissed her again. This time he looked straight to her soul and said the words he remembered clearly to this day. "I fell in love with you. And I know I'll spend half my time in the air, so I had no choice —"

She kissed him this time, grinning all the while. "No choice but to teach me to love being up there, just like you do."

The memories stayed with Connor long after his shower. As he made his way to the airport, they played in his mind, keeping him company and assuring him that Michele's question was innocent enough.

Married people asked that of each other now and then, didn't they? *Honey, have you been faithful? Have you ever cheated on me? Am I the only one you've ever loved?* His answer had satisfied her. And, thankfully, he'd been right — she hadn't brought it up again.

Still . . .

Connor shuddered. He pulled his suitcase and flight kit behind him, a sleek black unit emblazoned near the top with the airline's fashionable insignia. He'd been briefed on the upcoming flight, a two-hour hop from West Palm Beach to Atlanta, followed by three short flights across the Midwest, and an overnight in Dallas. His copilot that day was a man he'd flown with before, a young guy hired a year ago.

Young and idealistic and dedicated to his family.

The way Connor was when he first started flying. The way he still felt.

He checked his watch and stepped into a men's room three gates from his own. He had an extra fifteen minutes, time to make sure his uniform was pressed the way he liked it. The conversation with Michele had gone longer than usual, and he'd been in a rush since he left the house.

Three men were washing their hands, and Connor waited until they were gone before stepping in front of the mirror.

He already missed her, missed the proud

way she held her chin, and the teasing sparkle in her brown eyes. Michele was not one of the needy, insecure housewives so many pilot friends married. She was a free spirit, a woman who carried a sense of independence that drove him crazy with desire. No matter how long they lived he would never quite catch her, never see her without seeing the challenge she'd been to him back when they first met.

No, he couldn't get enough of her, even after nearly fourteen years. Their Tuesday mornings were constant proof. He loved that time each week with his wife. Loved the way she often initiated their lovemaking, and the way their arms and legs tangled together, making it impossible to tell where one of them ended and the other began. If that morning he'd missed some of his usual routine, he'd live with the fact.

Alone time with Michele was worth every minute.

The bathroom was filling up with passengers again, and Connor made one last tuck of his uniform. He had ten minutes before he had to be at the gate, and halfway through the door he remembered something.

The plane crash.

He'd never seen a passenger list, and

105

though this was his first day back since the accident, he'd heard none of the other pilots or staff talking about it. He probably didn't know anyone on the plane. But he never read about an aircraft going down without wondering who was on board. Too many years in the air to not at least check.

The nearest counter had a woman working it and no one in line. He went to her and gave her a polite nod. "Hey."

"Hello, Captain."

Connor didn't know her, but she had a familiar face. "Have you seen the passenger list from the Western plane crash this past weekend?"

"Yes." The woman thought for a moment. She was older, fifty-two, fifty-three, a former flight attendant, no doubt. "Over at Gate Eleven."

Connor nodded his thanks and worked his way back into the flow of traffic along the concourse. Eleven was two gates past the one where his plane was parked. He grinned at himself. His plane. Michele liked to tease him about the way he took ownership of every aircraft he ever flew.

The thing was, he had to take ownership. It was why he flew so well, not by mere instrumentation and formulated turns, but safer and more instinctively. By the seat of his pants, she liked to say. And she was right. But that same flying was why he'd always come home to Michele — especially after the Gulf War.

He picked up his pace and focused hard on the action at Gate Eleven. The attendants were intently working two lines for a flight due out in twenty-five minutes. He came up alongside the counter and waited until one of them noticed him.

"Captain, what can we do for you?"

"I understand you have the passenger list?" He kept his voice low, so the passengers wouldn't hear him. "The one from this past weekend's Western crash?"

The attendant returned her eyes to the customer at her counter, reached into a drawer, and pulled out a folded newspaper. With only a quick glance, she handed it to him and flashed him a sad smile. "You can keep it. None of us knew the pilots or crew."

He took the paper from her. "I'm checking the same thing."

She returned to her line of passengers, and Connor moved to a spot near the windows, removed from the crowds. There he unrolled the newspaper. It was already opened to the passenger list.

Jared Browning, pilot; Steve McCauffey,

copilot; Angela Wielding, flight attendant; Kiahna Siefert —

Kiahna Siefert?

His heart thudded hard, then stopped. He stared at her name, taking it in one letter at a time. That was her last name, wasn't it? Siefert? The Kiahna part he was sure about. No matter how hard he'd tried to forget it, every now and then, in the early morning hours before dawn, her name would come.

Kiahna.

With a jolt, his heartbeat resumed, twice as fast as before. How many years had it been? Almost eight, right? He'd met her that awful summer, back in 1996 when his entire world was upside down. And even then they'd known each other only a few hours, the time it took for a massive storm to make its way across Hawaii and farther out into the Pacific.

Just long enough for her face to be indelibly written across the canvas of his mind, his heart. She was breathtaking. A Hawaiian girl with deep green eyes, light skin, and a hundred dreams about her future. For an hour she had seemed the answer to every problem that stood against him.

And now she was dead.

Passengers came and went a few feet

from him, but Connor was frozen in place, his heart still pounding. His eyes remained locked on her name, willing it to disappear from the awful list. But no matter how hard he stared at it, the words wouldn't go away.

Kiahna Siefert.

Yes, it was her. Of course it was. She'd switched airlines, but she'd stayed in Honolulu, where she was raised. And what else? Had she married or studied medicine the way she'd dreamed? Had she raised the family she'd spoken so openly about?

A dark and buried memory flashed in his mind: him and Kiahna early on the evening they'd met. Because of the storm, hotel space was limited, and somehow their paths had crossed. A few hours in the lobby and then . . .

He closed his eyes, willing the memory to disappear. Instead it grew more vivid, her words as clear as they'd been that night. She talked about her hopes and dreams, and he shared his frustration over being stationed in Los Angeles, his fears about the FAA investigation. He even told her about his father.

The only thing he didn't tell her was —

"This is the first boarding call for Flight 1205 to Atlanta."

Even two gates away he heard the announcement. They were waiting for him. He blinked and in a sudden, swift movement rolled the paper, tucked it beneath his arm, and headed for his plane. Before he reached the Jetway he crushed the newspaper into a tight wad and popped it into the first trash can. As he boarded the aircraft and took his place in the cockpit, he had a sudden awful thought. One so bad he would never have admitted it to anyone.

If the article was correct, then the single darkest secret in his life was no longer a threat. Never again would he wake up breathless at three in the morning as he'd done four or five times a year, every year since. No longer would he backtrack through the alleys of his mind, desperate for a way to cover his bases, to make sure Michele and the girls never, never learned about his layover in Honolulu the summer of 1996.

Connor had kept the information to himself, never told another soul about it. But the possibility always existed, as long as Kiahna was alive, that somehow the truth would get to Michele.

Now . . . that possibility had drowned right there in the ocean.

Kiahna was dead; his wife would never find out.

Connor felt himself relax. He adjusted his tie and tugged on the brim of his hat. It wasn't his fault her plane had gone down. Rather it was one of those strange and rare occurrences, the freak one-in-a-million air disaster that hit the industry every few years. His copilot was saying something, running through some of the checks on gauges and computerized systems.

He exhaled and realized he'd been holding his breath. Once more he read over the flight plan, but he couldn't concentrate. He was too busy hating himself. Because at a time when he should have felt sorrow and remorse for the green-eyed island girl who'd lost her life, he felt only one thing.

Complete and utter relief.

SEVEN

The doorbell rang at five minutes before two.

Ramey watched Max, how his eyebrows lifted and a spark came to life in his expression as though maybe, just maybe, his mother had come home. Maybe she'd found a way to swim off the doomed airplane and make her way back to the island, after all.

But even with his little-boy hopes, the glimmer lasted only a moment. "Who is it, Ramey?"

She considered lying to him, telling him it was a passing salesperson or a personal friend. Anything to keep Max from knowing that days after his mother's death he was about to be dealt a hand that would decide his future. But in the end she decided against it. The boy knew the attorney. No point raising his suspicions about the visit.

112

Once more, the doorbell rang.

"Ramey?"

The boy's voice brought her back to the moment. She said, "It's Mr. Ogle, you remember him, right?"

Max's eyes were wide and vacant. "Yes."

She headed for the apartment's small foyer, watching Max the entire time. "He wanted to make sure you were okay."

Max nodded, and his chin quivered. He stood straight and still, waiting.

Ramey opened the door and stepped back. The attorney was a man in his fifties, pleasant and distinguished with black slacks and a white short-sleeve dress shirt. Standard island business fare. He introduced himself and then stepped past Ramey toward Max.

The moment their eyes met, the attorney dropped to one knee and held out his arms. "Max . . ."

The child hesitated. Then in a rush he ran to the man and clung to him. His back shook and his words were short and choppy, almost impossible to understand in light of his sudden wave of emotion. "Mommy's . . . plane . . . landed in the water."

Mr. Ogle stroked Max's back. "I know, pal. I know."

"She couldn't get out."

"I'm sorry." The attorney held Max for a long time, until the boy's sobs subsided. Then he drew back and studied Max's face. "I need to talk to Ramey, okay?"

"Okay."

Max looked at Buddy and that was sign enough. The dog was on his feet at Max's side, and the two went outside.

When Ramey and the attorney were alone, she struggled to find her voice. "Should we sit down?"

"I think so." His eyes held hers, unwavering. He nodded to the sofa. "It won't take long."

Ramey glanced at Max as she followed Mr. Ogle. The boy had dropped to the cement patio and had his arm around Buddy's neck again. Her eyes stung, and she blinked hard to stop the tears. At least the boy had Buddy. She took the spot at the other end of the sofa so that one seat cushion separated them.

"Kiahna's instructions were very clear." Mr. Ogle pulled out a two-page document and a white sealed envelope from a file and spread them on the space between them. Less writing covered the top page, and the attorney held it up. "This one is a will, Kiahna's last testament. The first part is fairly straightforward. It leaves Max all her worldly belongings — a few thousand dollars in savings and whatever material goods she's collected. And her life insurance, of course.

"The second part is somewhat unusual." He leaned back and exhaled. The tension in the room doubled. "It's a request, something that wouldn't be legally binding, really. But it was her wish all the same."

Ramey folded her hands, waiting.

"I'll read it." Mr. Ogle held the paper closer and did a small cough. " 'In the event of my death prior to Max's eighteenth birthday, it is my desire that before he is turned over to state custody, he spend two weeks with his father.' "

"His *father?*" Ramey's breath caught in her throat. The man Kiahna had refused to talk about, the one whose identity and whereabouts remained a complete mystery? She forced herself to listen.

"Yes." His eyes found his place on the document. "The letter goes on, 'The man is a married pilot who was living in Los Angeles eight years ago. I am providing you with all the information I have; it should be enough to find him.' "

A knowing filled Ramey's heart. No wonder Kiahna hadn't wanted to talk about him. Max's father was a married man, which meant . . . what? That his time with Kiahna had been only a one-night stand? Or worse, that he had led her on, made promises to her, and then left her alone with Max?

Either way the situation was sad, and somewhere in the center of her being, Ramey's heart began to hurt.

Mr. Ogle kept reading. " 'If you find him, and if he's willing to agree to the two-week visit, tell him that at the end of that time he'll have to make a decision about Max.' As you know, Kiahna didn't list the father on Max's birth certificate, so the man will have to decide whether to adopt Max and tell him the truth, or send him home to be placed for adoption by the state."

Ramey tried to imagine the reaction the man might have to the news. For that matter, whether he'd even consider such a request after so many years.

The attorney was almost finished. Kiahna's letter went on to provide the man's name, the name of the airline he flew for, and two phone numbers. One for the airline where the man worked, the other for the apartment where he had lived back when they spent their one night together.

"That's it? One night?"

"Apparently." The attorney pursed his lips. "Makes me wonder if he even knows about Max."

Ramey thought about that. Kiahna had been pregnant when she made the will, and since part of her request included telling the man about Max, chances were he had no idea he'd fathered a son with Kiahna. None at all.

Mr. Ogle set the paper down and looked at Ramey. "The apartment will be useless. Too long ago." He narrowed his eyes. "The airline's our best chance."

For a moment neither of them said anything. Then, for the first time since the attorney began speaking, Ramey thought of something other than the information in Kiahna's will.

"What about Max?"

The attorney reached for the sealed white envelope and held it up. "She wrote him a letter. The directions on the envelope say that it can't be opened until Max is present." He paused. "She wanted him to hear it first."

For a crazy instant, Ramey wanted to tell the attorney to take the letter and leave. Kiahna couldn't possibly have wanted Max, just days after her death, to travel from the island and spend time with a stranger! But she waited only a heartbeat before she stood. Kiahna and Max were as close as any mother and son Ramey had ever seen. Whatever the letter held, it was exactly what Kiahna wanted to say. She sniffed and looked at Mr. Ogle. "I'll get him."

Max was remembering a special butterfly day between him and his mom.

Butterfly days happened once a month because butterflies helped you remember that life was good. At least that's what Mommy always told him. She would pack him a peanut butter banana sandwich and a juice pack and they would set out.

You had to get in your car and drive a long time, more than just the time it took to go to the store for milk or hot dog relish or marshmallows. Usually they sang songs, and after five songs or six if they were quick ones, the street would end and become bumpy and slippery. That's when his mom would reach her hand back through the seats and hold his fingers.

The bushes and trees were thick back there, and after another song the trees made a wall along the road so that it didn't feel like a road at all. More like a secret path. Then, after he counted three coconut trees and two mailboxes, they would stop. Through the trees was a grass place and a bench.

"Okay, Max," Mommy would tell him. "We're here."

That's when she'd grab hold of the lunch bag, and they'd climb out of the car, careful not to get scratched by the trees and bushes. His mom would smile at him and they'd hold hands over to the bench. Max would move his feet very quiet because the butterflies didn't like a lot of loud shuffling feet, that's why.

Once they reached the bench, his mommy would turn to him and do a wink. Then she'd shush him real quiet, just in case he forgot about the butterflies.

They would sit down and his mommy would put her arm around him and hug him close. "Now we wait."

After about as long as two TV commercials, the butterflies would come. Two or three butterfly friends, and then whole entire butterfly families. Their wings were sunny yellow and pumpkin orange and chocolate brown and darkest black, and every time Max saw them come and bounce around in the close sky above them he thought the same thing.

Butterflies were God's bestest artwork.

His teacher told him once that artwork was when little boys colored inside the lines. God definitely colored inside the lines with butterflies. Pretty soon the butterfly families would become a butterfly village all bouncing and lifting and falling over him and his mommy.

She would lean close to his ear and whisper, "Know what I love about butterflies, Max?"

"What?"

"They prove that God gives second chances."

"Why?" Max knew the answer, but he liked to hear her say the words.

"Because a butterfly spends most of its life as a caterpillar, scooting along on the ground, barely getting by. When a caterpillar sees a butterfly he thinks how wonderful it would be to fly."

"And then one day he gets tired."

"Very tired. He builds a little room, curls up inside, and takes a nap. Deep in his heart he wonders if maybe that's all. Maybe life is over."

"But one day . . ." Max always smiled here, because this was his favoritest part of the story.

"One day the caterpillar wakes up, and

God has done an amazing thing. The caterpillar shakes off the little room and feels something on his back. This time when he goes a bit down the tree branch he doesn't scoot like before."

"He flies!" Max would look back at the butterflies.

"That's right." His mommy's voice would get sort of scratchy at this part of the story. "And one day, Max, you and I aren't going to scoot anymore, either. Because God loves us even more than He loves the butterflies."

"Right."

"So butterflies make us remember, don't they, Max?"

"Yep."

"That life is good no matter what. Because just like the caterpillar, the best days are ahead of us, and then . . ."

"And then we'll have wings just like the butterflies."

That's when they'd wait a little bit with no words. And after that Mommy would pick up the lunch bag and give them each a sandwich. Some of the butterflies would go away because of the crinkly bag, but it didn't matter because Max understood. Butterflies couldn't stay in just one place.

That's why they had wings.

Max stopped remembering and looked at Buddy. He was asleep, his furry legs stretched out both ways. Max looked up to the sky and wondered. Maybe this was what Mommy meant by one day they'd have wings. Maybe this was the part of her life where God was giving her a second chance, just like the butterfly.

If that was true, then maybe she could bounce and rise and fall over to Ramey's back patio. Because the hurting feeling inside him was worse than before. But then . . . he didn't want her to be a butterfly, not really. Because butterflies couldn't laugh or hug or sit next to you and hold your hand. They couldn't sing you a special song.

Behind him, a door made a noise and he did a fast breath. Because all of a sudden he remembered about the talking inside. And the special meeting with Mr. Ogle.

"Max." It was Ramey. "We need you to come in for a minute."

He turned around and stood up at the same time. Ramey's voice was tired, the way it had been that day when Mommy's plane landed in the water. "Why?"

"Because Mr. Ogle has to read you something."

She held her hands out to him and he came to her, hugging her big legs close because sadness was so strong it wanted to make him fall on the floor. "What's he going to read?"

"A letter from your mom."

Max raised his eyes at Ramey. "From my mom? From heaven?"

Water came across Ramey's eyes. "No, Max. A special letter she wrote you earlier this year."

"How come . . ." Max rubbed his eyes because he didn't want to cry again. "How come she didn't give it to me before?"

"Because she wrote this in case . . . in case . . ."

"In case her plane landed in the water one day?"

"Yes." Ramey did a long breath. "In case of that."

Max couldn't figure out the feeling in his tummy. It was sad because his mommy was gone, but happy, too. Because the letter was a piece of her she left behind. A piece just for him. And that made him feel special.

He took Ramey's hand and led the way into the apartment. Mr. Ogle told him to sit in the middle between him and Ramey. Then he said the same thing Ramey had said about his mommy leaving him a letter. Max nodded and tried to have patience. His mommy always said patience was good.

Finally Mr. Ogle opened a piece of paper and began reading.

" 'Dear Max, if you're hearing this, then . . . I've already gone home to be with Jesus.' " Mr. Ogle stopped and bit his lip. " 'Before I go on, you need to know something: I'm safe in heaven now. No matter what else, I want you to know that; I'm okay. And, Max, you're going to be okay, too.' "

Max sucked in his cheeks so he could stay strong on the inside. But two tears spilled onto his face before he could stop them. He rubbed his cheeks hard and looked at Mr. Ogle so he'd keep reading.

" 'Deep in your heart I'm certain you wonder about your father. If you're old enough, then you know that even though you don't have a daddy, Jesus is your Father. But, Max, I want you to know you have a human father somewhere out there. He is a man I loved very much, but only for a short time. He couldn't stay here on the island, Max, because he had to go home.' "

Mr. Ogle looked at Ramey. That gave Max a chance to put his hand over his heart and feel how the beat there had gotten fast and jumpy. Very jumpy. His father was out there somewhere? Why hadn't his mom told him that before? Mr. Ogle did a choking sound and looked back at the piece of paper.

" 'Home was so important to your father, Max, that when God gave you to me, I never told him. Never once. Because he had his home across the ocean, and we had our home here, on the island. I don't know if you'll ever find your father, Max. But I wanted you to know he was somewhere out there, and that he doesn't know about you.

" 'Also, Ramey is going to help you find a special friend of mine, a man who lives on the mainland. If Jesus takes me to heaven, and if Ramey can find my special friend, I want you to spend a few weeks with him. This might be hard, Max, but it means a lot to me. It's what I want you to do. Really and truly.

" 'I know you love the island where we live, and our special places where we go for talks. But this trip will be good for you; I believe that with all my heart. My friend has a nice wife and two little girls about

125

your age. If it happens, then God wanted it to happen, Max. If it doesn't, then God didn't plan for you to meet my friend.

" 'It's funny, Max, as I write this I feel sure that you'll never hear it. Because I want to be here with you forever and always. But if not, if something happens, and Jesus brings me home to live with Him, then the things I'm telling you in this letter are very important.

" 'Be a good boy, Max. Whatever you do, remember to be strong and brave, and to love Jesus. When you're sad, remember our song, because it will always be the truest thing I could tell you. And remember that even if you never find your father on earth, your Father in heaven is watching over you. And if God lets me, I'll be watching you, too. Cheering you on when you're up to bat in baseball, pulling for you when you have a spelling test, and believing in you always. Believing that you'll do your best to grow into a young man who will make me proud of you. Even from as far away as heaven.' "

That part stuck in Max's heart like peanut butter. His shoulders began to shake and more tears came. It wasn't right to hear his mommy's words with Mr. Ogle's voice, that's why. And because if she were only here one more day he could hug her and tell her yes. Yes, he would always do his bestest work for her even when he was a grown-up man.

Ramey patted his knee. "You okay?"

He wanted to say no, but then he wouldn't hear the rest of the letter. So he quick moved his head up and down and used his shirtsleeve to wipe the wet on his cheeks. He looked at Mr. Ogle. "Finish, please."

"Okay." That's when he noticed Mr. Ogle had wet eyes, too. The man took a slow breath and looked at the paper once more. " 'And here's the best part, Max. Remember our special butterfly days? I'm finally getting my second chance, sport. And one day not so far from now we'll be together again, and we won't scoot around like caterpillars on the ground. We'll fly. Well, that's all. I love you, Max, the most. Forever and ever, Mommy.' "

EIGHT

Connor was coming home.

That thought kept Michele moving through the day, and now that she was almost finished with her last client, she could hardly wait to see him. At just past four o'clock she grabbed her tallest can of Shaper hairspray and applied it in short bursts around the woman's hair. Five minutes later the client was on her way.

Michele was just catching her breath when she heard the door behind her creak open. Before she could turn around she felt his hands on her waist, his breath against her skin. "Hi."

A warmth radiated out from her heart, the way it always did when he came home. She turned in his arms so that they were facing each other and slid her hands up around his neck. "Hi, yourself."

"I have an idea." He grinned and searched her eyes, but before he could say

128

anything more, she brought her lips to his and kissed him. The kind of slow kiss they hadn't ever stopped sharing.

When they pulled apart to catch their breath, she brushed her nose against his. "You always have an idea."

"Yes" — he gave her another brief kiss — "but that's why you married me."

She leaned back and lowered her chin, flirting with him the way she'd done since the first time he took her flying the summer after his college graduation. "Is that what you think?"

"Well . . ." His eyes told her how much he'd missed her. "That and a few other reasons."

They came together again and she rested her head on his shoulder. "Maybe we should hear about your *idea* later." Once more she drew back and this time she could feel the way her eyes danced. "You have four phone messages, a broken window in Susan's room, and the girls will be starving in an hour." She poked a finger into first one of his sides, then the other. He'd been ticklish as long as she'd known him, and her playing always seemed to strip him of the strain of his job.

"Not *that* kind of idea." He chuckled as he squirmed in her arms and caught her hands with his own. "Let's have a picnic. Over at Langley Park by the beach."

"A picnic?" Michele tilted her head. "Hmmm. Not bad. We could pick up some chicken and skip the cleanup."

"Exactly." He was moving closer to her again, working his hands up her back and drawing her into his arms. "Of course the other idea could be even better . . ."

Connor wiped his hands on his napkin, and eased his legs out from beneath the table. Then he turned to face Elizabeth and Susan. The girls were staging races on the beach, and Michele was acting as the official. He crossed his arms and felt the corners of his mouth work their way up his face.

The picnic had been a hit.

It was warm, not quite eighty, and this April was one of the nicest he could remember. He let his eyes wander from the girls to the expanse of ocean beyond them. Beautiful, blue water that could have been a beach in Cancun or somewhere on the Mediterranean. How was it possible that everything had worked out so well? Back during those awful days in Los Angeles he'd been convinced life could never be good again.

130

But nothing about that time had been his fault. Life had simply formed a conspiracy against him, and in the course of a few months he figured out a way to deal with it.

But here . . . now . . . he was one of the lucky ones. He had it all, and life was bound to keep getting better.

He stood and stretched. Then without waiting another moment he loped over to the place where Michele was about to signal the start of another race. "Wait a minute, count me in."

Susan and Elizabeth ran to him and grabbed his hands. "Race us, Daddy . . . come on, race us." Their voices sounded almost the same as they pulled at him and jumped up and down on the sugary white sand.

"Okay." He winked at Michele. "But be easy on me. Your old man isn't what he used to be."

The girls giggled and lined up on either side of him.

Michele lowered her voice and leaned first toward Susan, and then Elizabeth. "Beat him good, girls." Then she grinned at Connor. "On your mark, get set . . . go!"

Connor intended to let the girls win, but he ran anyway, so they'd think he was trying. He was fifteen feet out when his left foot caught on a string of seaweed. He reached down to free himself, but before he could, he fell smack onto the ground. Without his hands free, his face planted flat against the sand.

Michele was laughing before he had a chance to sit up.

"Daddy!" The girls were at his side. Elizabeth knelt near him, her curls falling in a cascade over her shoulder. She helped him to a sitting position. "Are you okay?"

Susan stayed on her feet, covering her mouth so he wouldn't see her laughing. "Daddy . . ." A few short bursts of laughter broke free. "You look like a sea creature."

"I feel like one." Connor chuckled as he reached down and pulled the wrap of seaweed from his foot. Sand was in his mouth and he leaned over and spit some of it out. His arms and legs were also covered with sand, and his knees were skinned where they'd taken the brunt of his fall. The picture of competence and dignity.

Michele was at his side now. Her entire body shook from the quiet laughter simmering inside her. "Susan's right." She laughed out loud this time. "Your face . . ."

Connor felt his cheeks and chin and forehead. Sure enough. He'd picked up an entire mask of sand. His chuckle joined those of his family, and all four of them fell to the ground laughing.

Almost a minute passed, when Connor gave a flick to Susan's ponytail. "You still didn't win the race, you know."

Elizabeth and Susan looked at each other, and in a flash they were up and tearing down the beach to the makeshift finish line — a trash can twenty-five yards away. Connor brought his legs up and leaned forward. He could feel Michele near his side as they watched Susan raise a victory hand.

"I won!" Her voice mixed with the sound of the distant surf and faded in the wind.

They watched Elizabeth give her sister a high five. The two girls wandered toward the shore and began looking for seashells. The tide was out, and the sand was covered with a hundred different types.

"We have the best kids in the world." He leaned against Michele, his eyes still on the girls.

"Yes." Michele let her head fall against his. "And they have the best daddy." She gave him a light elbow in the ribs. "Even if he does look like a sea creature."

They laughed and the ring of it mingled

with the hush of the gentle waves. A breeze had picked up and the air smelled of early summer and salt water. Connor reached out and took Michele's hand in his. "Okay . . . so tell me about my phone messages."

Her voice was relaxed and easy, content after their evening together. "The dentist had a cancellation and wants to see you at nine tomorrow for your checkup."

"On a Saturday?"

"It's new. The guy puts in four hours every Saturday."

"Wow. Okay . . . got that. What else?"

A flock of seagulls swooped low over the water just beyond them and their cries competed with the sound of the waves. Michele ran her thumb along the side of his hand. "The guy from the bank wants to set up a meeting, something about rates and refinancing. And the lawn mower part you ordered is in."

Connor nodded. "Very serious messages." He turned and kissed her cheek, then locked his eyes on the girls once more. They were moving closer, working their way up the beach, their hands full of sand dollars and clamshells. This close to the water, he liked keeping them in his view. His tone was a teasing one when he continued. "Yes, those are major messages, all right. I can see where the world might've stopped if I didn't hear about those."

"Now . . . the dentist was pretty important, you have to admit."

He glanced at Michele again and remembered something. "Didn't you say I had four of them?"

She nodded. "Wasn't that four?"

"Three. The dentist, the bank, and the hardware store."

Michele thought for a moment, and then her face lit up. "I remember." Her smile faded some. "It was a strange one. I have no idea what they want or why they called."

"Who was it?" Connor's eyes were still on the girls. The sun was setting behind them, spraying pink and blue across the eastern sky.

"An attorney." She hesitated. "Marv somebody. Said he was from Honolulu."

Connor felt his body go stiff. He pulled away from Michele so she wouldn't notice. *Calm, Connor . . . be calm.* He couldn't draw a deep breath. "Honolulu?"

"Strange, huh?" Michele slipped her legs beneath her and doodled a series of circles in the sand. "Probably one of the lawsuits you have to testify for."

"Yes. Probably." Connor took a long breath and held it. That had to be it. What other explanation was there? He had no connection to anyone in Honolulu, not now. Not since the plane crash. But attorneys . . . they held offices all around the country, didn't they? Of course they'd be stationed in Honolulu. Why not?

"What do you think it's about?" Michele looked at him and he caught the innocence in her eyes. She had no doubts, no suspicions. Only a passing interest at why an attorney from Hawaii would call him at home.

Like lightning, Connor's mind began to flash with possibilities. It wasn't uncommon for pilots to be called into court. And over the years he'd been used by the airline as a professional witness, someone who would articulate the company's policies and standards if a passenger sued for one reason or another. Too much turbulence, too rough a landing, too much pepper in the onboard meal. It could have been a hundred reasons.

He swallowed hard and uttered a dry laugh. "Who knows. These days people sue over anything."

"And you're the expert because you've

testified a dozen times on these cases."

"I guess." His voice no longer sounded like his own. With everything in him, he wanted to believe that the reason for the call had something to do with a lawsuit. But the timing was too strange, too close, to the recent crash. He stopped himself from saying anything more.

Michele gave a soft huff. "Why you, Connor? Couldn't they use someone current, someone who flies into Hawaii now? You haven't been there in years."

"Right." Connor massaged his throat and managed a smile. "But once you're on the list of expert witnesses for the company, they keep using you."

It was true. Attorneys working for the airline called Connor three or four times a year looking for him to testify on its behalf. But never had they called from Hawaii. In fact, other than once when a Chicago attorney had contacted him, they consistently called out of Atlanta, the airline's home base.

Chills flashed down Connor's arms and the length of his spine. If the attorney in Honolulu wasn't with the airline, then who was he? And why, just days after the air disaster, was he calling him at home?

The thought kept him distracted

throughout the night, and regardless of the ideas he'd had when he first came home that afternoon, Connor let Michele head off to bed alone. When the house was quiet he crept into the office and signed onto the Internet. There, for the next three hours, he searched the Web for every detail he could find about the crash. Who was Kiahna Siefert, anyway, and what connection could he, Connor Evans, possibly have had to the tragedy?

By three o'clock that morning, Connor was convinced that the answer was simple. There was no connection. He hadn't spoken to Kiahna since that long-ago summer night, and he knew nothing about either the airline or the flight in question. The fear he felt was nothing more than an overactive imagination and a forgotten bit of guilt, resurrected by the crash.

First thing Monday at work, he would call the attorney back. Until then he would put the entire matter out of his mind. Obviously his fears were unfounded. Once he was convinced of these things, once he was certain no connection existed between the phone call and his time with Kiahna, Connor climbed into bed next to Michele.

The strange message all but forgotten, he was asleep instantly.

NINE

Connor had fifteen minutes before he had to report to the gate.

He moved at a snappy pace, his single piece of luggage rolling along behind him, smooth and efficient. The pilot's lounge was a few gates from the one he'd be flying out of, but he didn't want to make the call from there. He strode across the concourse to an empty gate across from his.

The area was quiet, and he took a seat next to the sheet of glass windows. He flipped out his cell phone and reached into his pocket for the long-distance number. He studied the scrap of paper and felt his stomach tighten.

Marv Ogle.

The attorney's name meant nothing to him, and neither did the phone number. But here, in the light of day, the reasons he'd dreamed up to explain the message no longer seemed airtight. For half a second, he thought about praying, but he changed his mind.

Prayer was for difficult situations, right? Trials or emergencies or major life decisions. No need to bother God with something like this. He clenched his jaw and tapped out the number sequence. Even with the typically poor airport reception, the call went through without hesitation.

"Ogle and Browning," a voice on the other end said.

"Marv Ogle, please."

"Who's calling?"

Connor felt his heart skip a beat. "Connor Evans. Returning his call."

"Just a moment."

A tinny version of something slow and instrumental played in the background, and Connor glanced at his watch. Thirteen minutes before he had to report. He was about to hang up and try again after he landed in Atlanta, when he heard a click.

"Hello . . . Marv Ogle, can I help you?"

"Yes." His throat was suddenly tight. "Mr. Ogle, I'm Connor Evans. You left me a message a few days ago."

The pause that followed lasted a lifetime and an instant all at once. When the man on the other end finally spoke, Connor's shoulders relaxed. At least after this he wouldn't have to wonder.

"Mr. Evans, I'm afraid I have some very sad news for you."

Connor held his breath.

The attorney continued, his voice a notch more somber than before. "As you're probably aware, Western Island Air Flight 45 crashed last week and left no survivors." He hesitated. "I represent the estate of Kiahna Siefert, a friend of yours, I believe. I'm afraid she was on the flight."

A pounding started in Connor's head. How could Kiahna's death involve him in any way? Had she left a list for him to contact everyone she'd ever known? He closed his eyes and found his voice. "Yes, I . . . well, we hadn't spoken in several years."

"I'm aware of that."

Connor wanted to shout at the man. *Get to the point!* He could do nothing for Kiahna or her estate now. He pinched the bridge of his nose and forced himself to sound appropriately saddened. "I saw her name on a passenger list. I'm . . . sorry about what happened to her."

"Yes . . . well, that's only part of the reason why I called."

He wanted to exhale, but his airways were paralyzed. "I don't understand.

Kiahna and I . . . we had no ties at the time of her death."

"Actually, you have one, Mr. Evans. A seven-year-old boy named Max Riley."

Connor's eyes flew open. What? A boy named Max Riley? He stared out at a handful of aircraft parked at various angles across the airport's apron. A seven-year-old boy? How would a child involve him and Kiahna? She had no children that he'd known about.

Unless the boy wasn't only Kiahna's, but . . .

His brain swirled and in less time than it took his heart rate to double, everything around him stood still. He considered snapping the phone shut. Walking away and pretending he'd never heard the man's last words.

But he'd heard them. He'd heard them and with everything in him he knew he was neither dreaming nor the victim of some sort of prank.

A seven-year-old boy?

The floor dropped away, and Connor felt himself begin to freefall. Faster and faster into an abyss that couldn't possibly have a bottom. The math was not difficult. Seven years old? He'd been with Kiahna the summer of 1996.

There could be only one reason attorney Marv Ogle was calling him now.

"Mr. Evans, are you there?"

He squeezed his eyes shut and shielded them with his hand. "Yes . . . I'm sorry. How . . . how does this involve me, Mr. Ogle?"

Another pause. "The boy is your son."

So there it was. With five short words, the man threw a spear at Connor that caught him in the chest and tore open his heart. A spear that burst his nicely fashioned reality and ripped a hole in all the justifications he'd ever made about that long-ago night. He had a son? A son he'd never known about nor heard of until this moment?

"Mr. Evans," the attorney went on, "Kiahna left very specific instructions for the boy, and part of those included contacting you." The attorney paused again. "The child has no one. Kiahna wanted you to consider taking him for two weeks, getting to know him before he was made a ward of the court."

His head pounded harder with every word. He had a son? A seven-year-old boy named Max Riley? If he was the child's father, why hadn't Kiahna told him sooner, as soon as she'd found out she was preg-

143

nant? And now . . . now she wanted the boy to stay with him for two weeks? What about Michele and Elizabeth and Susan? What about the way their lives were going so well, exactly as he'd planned for them to go?

But with every question fighting for position in his mind, only one demanded his immediate attention.

He had a son?

After all these years, there was a boy in Honolulu who was his very own?

The truth twisted his heart and made a logjam of his words. He knit his brow together, concentrating until the clog broke apart and his words began to come again. "How . . . how do you know, Mr. Ogle? She never told me."

"I've known Kiahna since she was in high school, Mr. Evans." The attorney sighed in a way that rattled Connor's nerves even further. "She was a good girl; she didn't sleep around. After . . . after she found out she was pregnant, she told my wife and me what happened. The whole story."

Nausea welled up in Connor. With every sentence the weight of the millstone around his neck grew.

"We told her to contact you, but she

wouldn't. Never told a single person your name or how she'd met you. Just that you'd been together."

"How . . ." Connor didn't recognize his voice. He had five minutes to report to the gate, and he was barely able to think, let alone move. "How did you find me?"

"When Max was born, she brought me an envelope. Inside were two documents — a will, and a letter for Max. She replaced the letter every year on Max's birthday. But the will stayed the same. In it she named you and the airline you work for. She asked that we do everything we could to find you . . . before her son be given over to the state."

"Is he mine? Legally?"

"No. Your name isn't on his birth certificate."

"Oh." Connor was buying time, trying to fit this new information into his framework of reality. "She wanted me to adopt the boy?"

"Not that either. At least not at first." The man's tone was kind, not accusing. "She wants him to visit you for two weeks. During that time he would be told only that you were a friend of his mother's. When the trial period is over, you would have a choice."

145

"A choice?" Connor's hands shook. Sweat drops rolled down either side of his face.

"Yes. You could send him back and never contact him again. Or tell him the truth and keep him forever."

The nausea grew worse. All his life he'd prided himself for his quick reactions, his ability to confidently tackle any problem he'd ever faced. He had run bombing missions in the Gulf War and pulled himself out of a death spin when his tail was hit by enemy fire. Twice he'd made emergency landings that had caused the airline to rewrite that part of the handbook. Connor could count his mistakes on one hand.

But this?

This was so far out of his league he couldn't remember how to breathe, let alone think up a way to unravel the ball of knots he'd just been tossed. For the first time in his life, he had no idea what to do next, no clue what to say. The news was still detonating in his soul, taking no prisoners as it worked its way through his consciousness and into the reality of his world.

"Mr. Evans . . . I realize this is probably somewhat of a shock. Do you have any thoughts on Kiahna's request?"

Thoughts? Yes . . . he had thoughts, but

146

what were they? Across the concourse he heard the first boarding announcement for his flight. He opened his eyes and let them dart around the empty gate area that surrounded him. As though maybe the answer lay somewhere out in the open.

"I . . ." — he chewed on the inside of his lip — "can I have a week to . . . to talk to my wife?"

"Of course." The man's voice was sympathetic. "But I'll need to know, Mr. Evans." He made another loud exhale. "Max is staying with his baby-sitter, but she's not well. If he's going to be put up for adoption, we should set the procedure in motion as soon as possible. Homes for seven-year-old boys are not easily found."

At mention of the child, anxiety tightened the knots even more. He still seemed to be falling, still couldn't stop the spinning in his head, but even so he couldn't hang up without asking one last question. "What's the boy like?"

"He's . . ." The attorney's voice cracked.

In that instant Connor knew. Everything the man had said was true. He'd known Kiahna all her life, and he knew the boy, as well. This phone call was probably as difficult for him as it had been for Connor.

"I'm sorry." The man coughed.

147

"He's . . . he's a very special boy, Mr. Evans. He's striking looking, tall and well built for his age. He loves baseball and football. He has his mother's tanned skin and green eyes, and a face that must come from someone in your family. He laughs and loves easily. He and Kiahna seemed to . . . well, they seemed to share one heart, really."

Connor closed his eyes. He could almost see the boy, the way he must've looked throwing a ball or walking alongside Kiahna. Because after all these years, he still had not forgotten what she looked like. If he had his mother's eyes, the boy would stand out in a crowd of a thousand seven-year-olds.

The second announcement came over the PA system.

"Look . . ." Connor glanced at his watch. He needed to switch gears, become the professional pilot once more. Not the broken man he'd been that awful summer. "Give me a week. I'll call you as soon as I know."

They ended the call, and Connor blocked everything he'd just learned from his mind. As he jogged to the gate, not one detail was allowed time in the foreground of his mind. Not one.

He checked in, took his place in the cockpit, and went through the motions of preparing for the flight. Concentration was a must in any piloting situation, and this one would be no different. Connor gave the matter at hand his full attention, making appropriate conversation with his copilot, and taking the plane full of passengers through a textbook takeoff.

Not until he was up at thirty-three thousand feet, disconnected from everything that awaited him on the ground below, did he let down his guard and then, like the rush of airspace that surrounded his plane, the memories came. Vivid and in full color, they came, and in light of the news the attorney had shared with him that morning, he could do nothing but let them.

TEN

There'd been reasons for his fall.

But they had little to do with the bizarre circumstances of that stormy August night when all Hawaiian air traffic was grounded for three full days. Rather, they involved the five months prior, at least that's how Connor saw it.

He pressed back into the seat of his cockpit and stared at the vast stretch of blue before him. No, if he was honest, the problems started a year before that, in the days after Michele's mother woke up one morning vomiting, and wound up dead two hours later of a brain aneurysm.

Connor had been flying a little more than three years by then, and competition for schedules and hours was tight. But after her mother died, Michele — who was five months pregnant with Susan — slipped into a depression that frightened him. She spent entire days in bed, doing nothing more than feeding and clothing Elizabeth, who was almost two at the time.

One afternoon when he came home from work, he found Michele asleep on the sofa, their daughter toddling around the kitchen alone. He knelt near his wife, frightened that somehow she, too, had died.

"Michele!" He shook her, and when she stirred, relief flooded his heart. "Michele . . . how long have you been sleeping?"

The scene happened again three times in the next two weeks, until finally Connor was forced to make a decision. His wife wasn't dead, but she might as well have been. She was no longer capable of taking care of herself, let alone little Elizabeth. He contacted the airline the next morning and requested two weeks off, with a shortened schedule after that.

Michele's improvements were immediate.

They found a baby-sitter who could come in while they attended counseling together. And after a two-month dose of antidepressants, and the prayers of their friends at church, Michele was herself again.

But by then the damage at work was

done. Connor had fallen to the bottom of the seniority chart, and after Susan was born in November, he was assigned a temporary move to Los Angeles.

The memory broke apart and he tightened his grip on the controls. He'd thought about that assignment a thousand times since the night with Kiahna. If only it hadn't been temporary. If the airline had been willing to move his entire family to Los Angeles, then at least he would've had more time with Michele.

The transfer was effective in March, but from the beginning they both knew it could last months. Which meant Michele and the girls would stay in Florida, while he set up a company-funded, furnished apartment in Los Angeles.

"I'll be home at least once every week," he told Michele.

And he was at first. But after a while, the commute was hardly practical. Twice-a-week flights from Los Angeles to Hawaii with a layover in Honolulu left him exhausted, struggling to find the energy to go on.

Michele became friends with Renee Wagner, and since both of them were often home alone, they helped each other. Knowing that Michele had a friend made it easier to sometimes let as many as three weeks go by without a visit home.

Then in May, the unthinkable happened.

Connor was bringing a 737 into Los Angeles International Airport when the tower gave him orders to land on one of the western runways. The request was unusual — every other time he'd been instructed to land from the east. But something else made it strange. As far as Connor could tell, another jet a few miles south of him was headed for the same runway.

Even now, Connor remembered the fear. LAX was one of the busiest airports in the world. Every pilot knew how possible it was for an air traffic controller to make a mistake.

He made the request without giving it further thought. "Flight Four Zero Three requesting change of runways, over."

Silence filled the airways, and Connor glanced out the right side of his cockpit. The neighboring aircraft was closer now, narrowing the distance that separated them. Normally, he would've made a second attempt at the request, but time had run out. If he was going to avoid a possible collision, he needed to make a northern angle and land on one of the adjacent runways.

"Hey." It was his copilot. The man sat straighter in his seat, his voice tense. "What're you doing?"

Connor felt sweat on his brow. He snapped at the man, "We've got company." He nodded his head toward the first runway. "Another aircraft coming in." His eyes narrowed. "I had to make the change."

"But you didn't get —"

"I did what I had to." He glared at the man. "I know what I'm doing."

He was partway through making the move when he tried again. "Flight Four Zero Three, requesting change of runways, over."

"Name your reason, Four Zero Three."

"Congestion coming in on the assigned runway, over."

The pause that followed was Connor's first sign that something was wrong. When the controller's voice came over the air again, his tone was frustrated, almost panicked. "We're picking you up moving away from the designated runway, is that correct?"

"Yes. My first request went unanswered, so I made the decision to avoid a ground collision."

"That decision isn't yours to make, Captain." The controller gave a huff loud enough for any incoming flight to hear it over the radio. Then he cleared Connor's flight for a landing on the other runway.

Long before he landed the plane that day, Connor knew he was in trouble. Representatives from the FAA ushered him into an initial inquiry the moment he was at the gate. At the end of the brief meeting, a red-faced man in his fifties stared at Connor and shook his head.

"This type of defiance is unacceptable, Captain Evans." He tapped his pencil on the sheet of notes he'd taken. "I'll be recommending a formal FAA investigation first thing in the morning."

The demotion came before his next flight.

He was informed that until the investigation was completed, he would fly as a copilot only. Michele was frightened by the change, worried Connor would be stationed in LA longer. For the next month, every time he and Michele spoke, things felt strained between them. Tense. As though they'd become strangers.

Finally, in June that year, Connor made a decision. He would purchase a small regional airport near their home in West Palm Beach and he'd forget commercial aviation for good. The FAA could figure out their investigation without him.

The airport had been on the market for nearly a year, and after his transfer to Los Angeles, Connor checked on the price every month or so. It had dropped from nearly a million dollars to $550,000. With a hundred thousand down, he could have payments that would easily be covered by the small plane owners who used the air-field.

Finding the hundred down was the problem, but not one Connor couldn't see past.

Connor's father, Loren Herman Evans, had been more than an ace pilot in his day. Long before he hung up his wings, he and Connor's mother invested heavily in real estate. It wasn't so much what they bought, as where. They purchased open land and rental houses in an area of New Jersey thirty minutes outside of Manhattan.

By the time his father retired and sold their real estate holdings, the value of each piece had gone from tens of thousands to hundreds of thousands. When it was all sold and counted out, his parents netted nearly two million dollars.

Pilots were a different breed, and though

Connor had never had an intimate relationship with his father, they shared a mutual respect and admiration for each other. There was no one Connor would rather shoot a round of golf with, but hugs were stiff and rare, declarations of love all but nonexistent.

His parents settled on a ranch in Cambria, California, not far from San Luis Obispo and the Pacific coast. His dad was healthy and hearty, a man whose gray hair and piercing blue eyes only made him more attractive as the years passed. For a while he dabbled in stocks, but he showed a continual penchant for buying high and selling low. Finally Loren Evans relaxed and left his money alone.

Once a year in the spring he organized a family vacation for Connor and Connor's three sisters and their families, and over time the lot of them came to expect glitches in the itinerary. One year their hotel reservation ran out three days before their outbound flights. Another time they were forced to bring cots into each of the rooms to make up for his booking three rooms instead of six.

In the summer, Connor and Michele would meet up with his father at the Cambria ranch, where he cranked up a bucket of homemade strawberry ice cream and convinced the group to play a round of croquet. At some point in the visit the conversation would turn to the paperwork towers in his father's office.

"Hire someone, Dad," Connor would say. "You shouldn't have to live like that."

But always his father's answer was the same. "I like it this way. I know exactly where everything is."

His answer was typical pilot speak. Always in control; never admitting error or defeat. It took utter confidence to take hundreds of people into the air every day, so Connor understood. He was the same way, after all. Still, sometimes Connor wondered how his father had ever been organized enough to fly commercial airplanes.

In the end, their visits were pleasant enough, and Connor did more than respect his father when they were together. He enjoyed him.

So when the idea for the regional airport came up, Connor used his two-day break to drive north to Cambria and talk to his father. He felt certain of the outcome. What would a hundred thousand dollars be to his father? Besides, the man had always been generous, giving to charities and

158

scholarship funds. Why would this time be any different? By then, Connor's mother was dead and his father had already suffered one heart attack. It wouldn't be long before at least part of the money was his anyway.

Connor waited until they were seated at a table on his father's back veranda, overlooking acres of rolling green hills and oak trees.

"Dad, I'm thinking about leaving commercial aviation."

His father looked up, but said nothing. The lines on his forehead froze, and his expression turned to stone.

Connor gulped back his sudden doubts and launched into an explanation of the airport and his ideas about running it. "The place could handle twice the air traffic it has now. With a little advertising and promotion, profits could double in two years."

Silence hung in the air for a beat. "You know my feelings on finishing a job. Work now, invest now. Make a hobby out of a regional airfield later, when everything else is finished."

"Dad." Tension sprouted between them. "I'm a man, and if I don't want to wait for retirement to change careers, I don't have to."

"Fine." His father's gaze was unwavering. "Why are you here, then?"

Connor was convinced his father already knew the answer, but he plodded ahead. At that point, only a confident request would earn his father's favor. "I'd like a loan against my inheritance, Dad. Either that, or I'd like you to consider going in on the airport with me."

His father looked hard at him for a moment and then chuckled. "You're kidding, right?"

A rush of heat filled Connor's cheeks. "No, Dad. I need the money. I've already made up my mind. The airline has me stationed across the country from Michele, and the FAA investigation is —" Suddenly he stopped short.

He watched his father's eyes narrow and grow angry, disapproving. "What investigation?"

Connor gave his father a short version of the story, heavily weighted in his favor. But still the old man sat unmoving, his arms crossed. Connor finished with, "So that's why I want out. It isn't worth it. Michele and I are fighting all the time, and the girls won't even know me. I need to get back to Florida."

"You need to obey the rules." He gave an

abrupt shake of his head and smacked his lips. As if Connor had buzzed the control tower or done a 360 loop with a plane full of passengers. "That's always been your trouble, Son. You think your opinion is all that counts." He hesitated. "Stay in the air and you'll never be sorry."

Connor's control dissipated like early morning clouds over Phoenix. For the next hour, he and his father debated — sometimes in loud voices — Connor's request for the money and his father's staunch refusal to write Connor a check.

The last thing Connor said before he left was this: "If you won't help me, I can't possibly call you my father."

His dad stood up and followed him to the door. He wasn't ready to give in, but he was clearly concerned by Connor's statement. The elevation of his tone made that much clear. "Don't be childish."

"Look, Dad . . ." Connor spun around and met his dad's gaze head-on. Anger filled his heart, anger that had been building toward the man for decades, anger about his expectations and lack of expressed love. All of it came to a head. "I always wondered how you really felt about me." Connor bit the inside of his lip. "Now I know. You think I'm cocky and arrogant, irresponsible." A chuckle that was more angry than funny came up from him. "I'll tell you what. Until you change your mind about the money, our relationship is over." He took another few steps toward the door. "I'll be waiting."

He hoped his father would reach out and grab his shoulder, tell him not to be crazy, that it was all a misunderstanding and yes, they could talk about the loan, or at least they could talk about their relationship. After analyzing that moment for so many years, Connor was convinced the argument that day wasn't about the money. At least not on his part.

It was about seeking his father's approval. The airport and the loan to fund the purchase was only the means by which Connor sought it. But the combination of the man's attitude and his callous statements convinced Connor that the relationship had suffered a heart attack that afternoon.

After that confrontation, Connor felt like a lost boy, confused and out of sorts. At times that week, he wondered if he'd become a different person altogether. He was no longer satisfied with being a commercial pilot. He suddenly no longer had a father — or a passionate interest in his wife.

And whatever his waning feelings toward Michele, she felt even less excited about him. The loss of her mother and her frustration with his living in Los Angeles had brought back her depression. The few times they were together each month, Connor found himself afraid the wife he loved might never return. Gone was the woman who looked into his eyes, hearing not only his words but his heart. Instead Michele's expression seemed distant. Dead.

Often she handed Susan to him the moment he walked in the door. "Here, she needs a new diaper. I'm going back to bed." Then without another word, she'd turn and head for their bedroom.

Their bond badly frayed, Connor avoided coming home.

All of these feelings weighed on him that fateful Thursday in August 1996. He'd already had a one-night layover in Honolulu, and that morning he checked out of his hotel. But because of the storm, his early afternoon flight was delayed first one hour, then two. By the afternoon the tropical storm grew to hurricane levels and took up residence just off the islands.

Winds were too strong to fly in, so while Tropical Storm Henry did its slow dance around the Hawaiian Islands, Connor and

163

hundreds of pilots, flight attendants, and passengers sat grounded. Hotel rooms were gone in less than an hour, full with both the outgoing and incoming tourists. Some people gladly roomed with strangers. Whatever it took to find a safe place to stay.

He saw Kiahna for the first time Thursday night, when the storm was building at a rapid rate. From the beginning, something about the young woman reminded Connor of Michele. The way she angled her head, or the light in her eyes when she talked to the waiter. Not the flirty, forced look some flight attendants had with men, but something deeper. A sensitivity, maybe.

She was pretty enough — light tan island skin, and vivid green eyes. But even so he wasn't interested. Intrigued, yes. Curious about the way she reminded him of Michele, but nothing more. Their tables were adjacent, close enough that he was aware they had ordered the same thing. When the waiter returned to the kitchen, her eyes met his and held. What would it hurt? He had plenty of time to kill. Besides, he wanted to know exactly how much like Michele the woman was. So Connor spoke first.

"You live here?"

"Yes." An odd sadness haunted her eyes, but she smiled. "My flight's delayed. And with the storm, we might not fly at all." She leaned back and studied him. "You're a pilot?"

Connor nodded. "Finished my layover. Supposed to fly out a few hours ago. The new time is in two hours."

"Me, too." She glanced out the nearest window. "But I'm not counting on it. This one could hit pretty hard."

Their conversation continued. Questions from Connor about the island, and questions from her about the airline he worked for. Before their meals were delivered, they joined tables, and he told her about his plans to own a regional airport. When dinner was over, she anchored her slim elbows on the table, linked her fingers, and rested her chin.

"You know what I like about you?"

The candid way she spoke caught him by surprise. She was so like Michele. The Michele he'd fallen in love with. "What?"

"You're a doer; I can tell. You'll do whatever you set your mind to, and somehow you'll make it work out."

In the hundred times since, whenever Connor would analyze that scene looking for escape routes, he was certain that comment was the turning point. Back then, Michele was forever telling him he wasn't doing enough. Not enough to find a way out of Los Angeles, not enough to help with the kids, and not enough to keep her happy. But without knowing him, the island girl saw something in him Michele no longer saw.

He was a doer.

The rest of the memory was smudged black and charcoal, streaked with dirty oranges and yellows. He'd tried to get away from her, hadn't he? Hotels and bed-and-breakfasts, even the airport pilot lounge, none of them had been open. And he tried at least what, three times to tell her he was married? Tried to find a way out of the strange circumstances that somehow conspired to bring them together.

But it was no use. His convictions about faith and morality and marriage were no match for the way things played out that night, or the temptations that presented themselves in the next twenty-four hours.

Not in light of her comment.

As time passed, the FAA investigation ended in Connor's favor, with a warning for him to follow control tower instructions. Flying became fun again, and with the help of prayer and medication, Michele found her way out of depression. Before the end of that awful year, he was even stationed back in Florida.

But he would never be the same again.

Because his feelings for his father had all but died. And the secret of what happened that stormy night was locked permanently in the darkest closet of his heart.

In a place where Michele would never find it.

Next to him, his copilot mumbled something, and the sound of it caught Connor's attention.

He let the memory go. Besides, who had time for remembering? He had a plane to land, and a future that suddenly demanded his every waking minute. Somewhere in Honolulu he had a son, a boy who maybe even looked like him, a child who needed a home.

He realized something then, something as painful as it was stark and true. He could call Marv Ogle back and tell him no, and none of them would ever be the wiser. Max would never know his father rejected him, and Michele . . . Michele would never know a thing about that awful summer night.

The muscles in his jaw tightened. How could he tell her a thing like this, that nearly eight years ago he'd had an affair and never found a way to tell her? He sighed and the sound of it filled the cockpit. Beside him, his copilot glanced over.

"You okay?"

"Yeah." Connor's answer was quick. "Fine."

The words tasted bitter and deceitful, because the truth was only just starting to work its way through him. No matter what pain his decision would cost Michele and the girls, he could think of no way around it. He hated himself for what he was about to do, what was about to happen to his life, his home, his family. But now that he knew about Max, now that he understood that somewhere in Honolulu lived a boy that was his own flesh and blood, his mind was already made up.

Regardless of Michele's response, or the lies they'd have to tell the girls at first, the answer was obvious. He could argue with himself, refuse the possibility, even deny it existed. But still the boy would come. No matter what he might want to tell himself about putting Michele's feelings first, or leaving well enough alone, the boy would come.

Connor couldn't live with his curiosity otherwise.

The visit would last only two weeks, a trial run, to satisfy Connor's questions even though the very act of doing so would scar Michele and the girls for life. But if he was honest with himself, Connor would admit he was already looking past the trial run with Max, and on into the slightest hint of a possibility. The possibility of a future with the boy.

A future that in the past few hours had changed to include a son he'd not yet met.

Which was why his throat felt thick, and he had to work to fight the overwhelming urge to hate himself. Because no matter how much pain he was about to inflict on his family, he would do it willingly, all so he could take a chance at being the boy's father. All so maybe, just maybe, he might have the one thing he'd wanted all his life.

A son to call his own.

ELEVEN

The date was Connor's idea, and it improved everything about Michele's day.

He called her before his last flight and asked her to find a sitter for the girls. "Meet me at the beach, at our spot."

She was finishing a haircut, and the sound of his voice was a balm to her soul. She sank into her desk chair and dropped her voice to a whisper. "What's the occasion?"

"I miss you; we need time alone."

His answer kept Michele guessing for the rest of the afternoon. Nothing in his tone suggested the talk would be anything serious, but maybe he'd decided to contact his father. Maybe after seeing the car accident the other day he'd realized that life was too short. His father couldn't possibly have long to live, his heart being damaged as it was.

Or maybe it was something else.

Maybe he'd gotten a promotion at work and now he'd be flying international flights again. International flights brought a pilot more hours, which in turn meant more money. Only the most senior pilots had the option of flying international. Though Connor had flown them when he was younger, after the FAA investigation he'd had to work his way back to the place where he was now.

By the time Michele handed off instructions to the sitter, kissed Elizabeth and Susan, and headed for the car, she was almost certain that was it. It had to be. And knowing Connor, he was probably wondering if that type of promotion would actually be good for his family.

Of course he wanted to talk.

She pulled onto the main highway and pictured their spot.

The place was three miles north of the beach where they liked to take the girls. It had more grass, with a beach too narrow for most tourists. A fallen log not far from the sand worked as a bench, and every few months she and Connor made their way to the spot for time alone.

Michele turned her car onto the frontage road. She was almost there now, and her heart beat harder at the thought of his news. Whatever it was. Yes, he'd left only the day before, but life at home had been crazier than usual — missed hair appointments, late clients, and a permanent wave that practically burned the hair off the head of a seventy-two-year-old woman from the school's volunteer library staff.

All morning Elizabeth and Susan fought over which of them owned a certain blouse, each certain that it belonged to her. When Michele told them to work it out, they ripped the shirt in two, and were relegated to their bedrooms as soon as they returned from school.

An hour of quiet intimacy with Connor was just what she needed.

The talks they had at their beach spot were crucial for her, maybe even more than for Connor. It was at their quiet spot that they used to pray together, back before life grew so full and busy. But even without prayer, here she didn't bury her emotions the way she so often did. Passion and depth were a part of her, the same way they were a part of Connor. But it was easier to breeze through the day confident in her work and her time with the girls, listening to her clients pour their hearts out while she did little but interject an occasional yes or no.

Her heart took time to draw out, and Connor was excellent at doing that. He'd start with lighthearted, silly one-liners, and like a therapist or a magician, he'd pull from her a detailed report of her innermost feelings. Whether she'd wanted to share them or not. The thing of it was, she'd spent her life before Connor being independent, not needing anyone but herself and her God.

But Connor . . . Connor she needed. It had been that way from the beginning, and every year she relied on him more, found herself more in love with him. It wasn't the same crazy, starry-eyed love they'd shared after college. Rather it was something deeper, something that blended love and friendship and complete, utter vulnerability.

The combination was intoxicating. Michele rarely let her mind wander, as she had a few days ago, down the path of what-ifs. Because deep within her, in a place only he was allowed to see, she didn't think she'd survive if anything ever happened to him.

She pulled into the parking lot and headed for their familiar spot. Connor's car was there, and already she could feel the layers slipping away. From the place where she parked she saw him, saw his back to her as he stared out at the Atlantic Ocean.

For a fraction of an instant she wondered if something was wrong. His posture wasn't quite right, not as tall and proud. More defeated, somehow. But she dismissed the thought as soon as it came. Connor didn't call her out here to tell her bad news. What bad news could he possibly have?

She took light steps, and managed to sneak up behind him without gaining his attention. When she was a few inches away, she eased her fingers over his shoulders and loosely around his neck. "Hey . . ."

He turned just enough to see her. "Hi." His smile looked forced, and again she swallowed back a surge of doubt. "Thanks for coming."

"I needed it."

"Rough day?"

"Very." She walked around the log and took her place beside him. "Bad hair for Thelma Lynn, a torn blouse for Elizabeth and Susan." She angled her face and caught his gaze. "But this was a good idea."

Connor searched her face, then looked back out to sea and a sad sort of moan came from deep within him. Michele could barely hear it above the sound of the surf, but it touched a nerve in her soul all the same.

"Michele, we need to talk."

"Okay." She ignored his tone and kept hers light. "I'm here."

He hung his head and with his right hand, he rubbed the base of his neck. When he looked up, he sucked in a full breath and found her eyes again. "Remember that call the other day, the one from the attorney in Hawaii?"

"Yes." Michele reminded herself to smile. "They want you in Honolulu for a week to testify, and you're taking me along." She let loose a bit of stiff laughter. "Right?"

"I wish." Not even a hint of humor shone back at her from his eyes. He took her hand in his and worked his fingers between hers. Without looking away, he exhaled through his nose and gave a single shake of his head. "What I'm about to say is the hardest thing I've ever told you. I want you to know that."

A lightheaded feeling came over Michele and made her dizzy. She gripped the edge of the log with her right hand and felt her guard go up. What was he talking about,

175

the hardest thing he'd ever told her? She gave a slight nod of her head. "The hardest thing, Connor . . . what do you mean?"

He turned so that he was facing her and brought his other hand to circle around the one he was still holding. "The attorney was representing the estate of a woman named Kiahna Siefert. She was a flight attendant killed in the Western Island Air crash the other day in Honolulu."

Michele felt a twinge in her feet — she had the sudden urge to run. Why would an attorney for a dead flight attendant want anything to do with her husband? Did Connor know the woman? If so, why hadn't he ever mentioned her?

And why was this the hardest thing he'd ever told her?

She stared at the path to the beach and wondered how long it would take her to jerk her hand free and run to the surf. She could jump into the waves and swim until she was too tired to move another inch, and when she looked back at the beach Connor would be gone. It would all be a dream, and she would wake up beside him, free from worry or concerns about an attorney or a dead flight attendant or anything that might even remotely involve her and Connor.

Instead she tightened her grip on the edge of the log and found the strength to speak the single question burning a hole in her heart. "Did . . . did you know her?"

"Yes." Again Connor held her gaze, but this time she was sure she saw regret layered across his expression. "For a short time."

She dug her nails into the wood and made a weak attempt to pull her other hand free from his. He didn't let go. Anger joined the host of emotions wreaking havoc on her insides. "Get to the point, Connor."

"I'm sorry." He looked at the water once more and gave a slow shake of his head. "The attorney tells me Kiahna left behind a son, a seven-year-old boy." Connor's voice fell, and Michele had to strain to hear it above her pounding heart. He turned to her again, and this time his eyes were colored with an even deeper regret, a regret she hadn't known he was capable of.

He looked straight up for a moment, and then back at her. "The boy is mine, Michele. I didn't know about him until yesterday."

"Y–yours?" She stared at him, her throat so tight the word barely squeezed through. She pulled her hand from his and crossed her arms hard against her stomach. Shock slapped her around and left her speechless, unable to even imagine what might come next.

If the child was Connor's, then . . .

He'd had an affair.

He'd been with another woman and never told her about it. Even when she'd thought everything was perfect between them. Pain seized her chest and she knew instinctively what it was. A piece of her was dying. The part that had trusted Connor without hesitation was suddenly gasping for air, losing its heartbeat, unable to exist in light of the news.

What had she done wrong? She grabbed at the details floating in her mind and ordered them to line up. If the boy was seven, then Connor was with his mother what . . . eight years ago? So what was it, her depression? The trouble she'd had with losing her mother? She could hardly help those things.

She'd been pregnant back then, hadn't she? Pregnant with Susan. So, maybe he hadn't been attracted to her. Maybe she wasn't thin enough for him.

And who could blame him?

"It was my weight, right? I wasn't thin enough."

"No!" He shot her a look that mixed shock with growing shades of desperation. "Of course not." He rested his forearms on his knees and stared at the sand and grass beneath them. "It was one time, Michele, I swear. One night when we were grounded in Honolulu during a storm."

Michele closed her eyes and in a rush the things he was saying became real. It was true; he'd had an affair with a flight attendant. Michele held her breath and in the devastated places of her soul, a desperate prayer began to form.

God . . . I'm dying. I can't breathe . . . help me.

Daughter, I am here with you . . . I will never leave you nor forsake you. Never . . .

She sat up a bit straighter. Where had the voice come from? It was the faintest whisper, but then . . . it wasn't a whisper at all. More of a soft breath inside her soul. She had believed in God all her life, but never had she felt anything like this, this certainty that God Himself had spoken to her.

He would never leave her nor forsake her? Weren't those words in the Bible somewhere? The thought gave her the strength to open her eyes and consider once more the things Connor had said.

In the distance a couple walked by, hand in hand, their voices blending with the breeze and the sound of the water on the sand. Michele turned to Connor and stared at him. He had his hands over his face, but he was still staring at the ground through the cracks in his fingers.

Michele gritted her teeth, hating him for doing this to her, to both of them. Hating him and desperate not to lose him all at the same time. How *dare* he call her out here to say something so devastating? She wanted to slap him and scream at him, fall into his arms and run for her life, but she was frozen, unable to do anything but focus on breathing. Black dots danced before her eyes, and she held her breath, determined not to give in to them, not to pass out from the blow.

It struck her that while Connor was staring at the ground, she couldn't think of anything to do but look at him. She couldn't scream or laugh or run or cry. That type of pain would come later, for sure. But now it was all she could do to navigate the broken pieces of her life. She whispered the words that wouldn't go away. "How could you?"

Without looking up, Connor opened his mouth. "Everything was so crazy that summer, Michele . . . I never meant for it to happen."

She had to keep from covering her ears and spewing something awful at him. Instead she forced herself to analyze the situation. If the boy was seven, then yes, the affair had happened in the summer of 1996, the year Connor was stationed in Los Angeles and everything about their lives seemed to be falling apart. She'd always believed that she was the reason he'd found his way back, the reason he'd been able to continue on as a pilot and put the mess with the FAA investigation behind him.

Now, in a single moment, all of that certainty was gone.

"Connor . . ." She had no strength for the questions that lined up and demanded her attention. But first — no matter what it cost her — she needed the rest of the story, the part about the boy. "What did the attorney say?"

Her husband made a slow move to straighten himself. The confident, cocksure man who never let life get the better of him was defeated for the first time as far back as she could remember. His shoulders looked small, his face drawn and wrinkled around the eyes, as though exposing the secrets of his past had aged him ten years in as many minutes.

He dragged his fists hard and rough across his cheeks, and gave another brief look at the sky before turning to her. The air eased from his lungs and he seemed to shrink some more. "His mother left instructions that if anything ever happened to her, the attorney was supposed to find me."

"Why?" How dare this other woman want her son to meet Connor . . . after so many years. "Why would she want him to call you?"

His eyes searched hers. "She wanted Max to spend two weeks with me . . . with us. He wouldn't know I was his father, Michele. It would only be a chance to connect. Then . . ." He paused and pursed his lips. "Then if things worked out, maybe he would come here."

She was on her feet. "Here? With us?"

"Yes." The word was so soft, so hesitant, Michele almost missed it.

Her mind raced, and she took two steps toward the water, spun, and walked back to Connor. "You told him no, right? We couldn't do that, Connor, none of us. Not me or you or the girls. Tell me you told him no."

Connor only looked at her, his eyes begging her to understand. When he said nothing, she knew. Not only had her husband had an affair and fathered a child, but now, instead of moving on, he wanted the boy to become part of their family. The idea was unthinkable, the information more than she could process.

Without saying another word, she turned and headed down the beach.

"Michele!"

His tone sounded weak, hopeless, and she neither stopped nor turned around. She walked to the place where the surf lapped against the shore and veered right. Then she ran as hard and fast as she could, harder than she'd ever run in her life until she was certain she'd placed a mile between her and Connor.

There, alone on the beach, she dropped to the sand and let the flood of hurt come.

How *could* he? How could he destroy her with not one, but two bombs in a single conversation? She was still trying to believe he'd cheated on her, still trying to reckon with the idea that all those years ago he'd slept with another woman. But the idea of bringing that woman's child into their home?

Connor had to be crazy to consider it.

What would the girls think? Daddy had a *special friend,* and now her son was going to move in with them? They'd see through that story before they were in middle school, and then what? Would they hate him for being unfaithful, hate him for taking them to church all those years, all the while living a lie?

She didn't know how long she sat there, letting the ocean breeze play against her wet cheeks. With every passing minute, her options became more painful, if less complicated. Connor had given her no choice, really. He wasn't looking for her approval in the matter. He was telling her what he wanted to do.

Otherwise he never would've brought it up.

He'd kept the news of his affair silent for nearly a decade. Surely he could've taken the details of it to his grave without her knowing the truth. Here, now, only one reason existed for his saying anything.

He wanted the boy, wanted a chance to have the son she'd never given him.

"*Why,* God?" She shouted the words at the ocean. "Why weren't we enough?"

Connor would force her to agree to the plan, because what were her options? Tell him no, and have him quietly resent her

184

forever? That would never do, but then neither would bringing that child into their home. How long could he live with them before she went crazy from the constant reminder of Connor's unfaithfulness?

The truth of that burned within her, but it left her no choice. Whatever happened from here, the boy would have to come. If she refused Connor the chance to see the child, he'd hold it against her for the rest of her life.

And if he came . . .

Michele stood and walked back to Connor. She felt like a zombie, a member of the walking dead. He was still there, sitting on the log, waiting for her. When she was close enough for him to hear her, she crossed her arms and locked eyes with him. "Bring him, Connor."

She hated the momentary flicker of hope that flashed in his eyes. The look was gone as quickly as it had come, replaced with a more appropriate guilt and regret. "Michele . . ."

"I'm serious. Bring him."

For a long while Connor said nothing. Then he looked at her, searching her eyes. "Really?"

"Yes. Bring him here for two weeks." Her voice had taken on a different quality in the past hour, though she couldn't quite figure what it was. Before she changed her mind, she continued. "We'll tell the girls he's the son of one of your friends."

She held his eyes a moment longer, then turned and made her way to the car. She pulled out of the parking spot and left him sitting on the log, still facing the ocean. That was fine with her. He could drive home by himself and think about how he'd been willing to destroy her, ruin all they shared, for a boy he'd never even met.

She was halfway home when she found a way to define the difference in her voice. Whereas before it sang with joy and hope and possibility whenever she was with Connor, now it sounded dry, mechanical. It was a tone that was bound to get worse as time went on, as the boy came to stay with them, and she was forced to see in his face a woman who had lured Connor into sleeping with her.

She felt sick at the thought of seeing him.

"God . . . I can't do this."

No reassuring thoughts flitted through her head this time, and again she was struck by her voice. Because she recognized the sound. She'd heard it that long-ago morning when her mother called to report that she was feeling sick.

"Honey, I think I need a doctor," her mother had said. And the sound of her voice was almost exactly the same as the sound in her own voice now. Dry and broken and terrified.

The sound of someone dying.

TWELVE

Again, Connor made the call from a quiet chair at a deserted airport gate.

He was transferred to Mr. Ogle's office, and when the man didn't answer, Connor left him a message. "Call me as soon as possible."

An hour remained before he needed to report to his gate, and he had nothing else to do. So he sat back, clutched his cell phone, and thought about his life. In less than twelve hours it had become a nightmare.

Michele hadn't said anything more than necessary, functional things since hearing the news. "Pass the salt, please," or "Here's your laundry." Their Tuesday morning time was spent with her in the utility room organizing the cupboards. It felt like a lifetime ago that he'd promised they would pray together, read the Bible together. The girls had noticed last night, of course. Each of them came to him several times with their concerns.

"What's wrong with Mommy?"

And from Elizabeth, their oldest, "Are you and Mommy in a fight?"

He did his best to calm their fears, explaining that Mommy and Daddy had a lot on their minds, but no, they weren't in a fight. It was true. Michele didn't seem up for a fight. She hadn't asked about Kiahna or how he'd met her or how important their time together had been. Almost as if she'd rather let their relationship die a sudden death than know the details of that August night, and fight him over what had happened.

Connor tightened the grip on his phone. No matter what direction things went from here, he would never forget the look on Michele's face when he told her the news. She'd always talked about how much she trusted him, and recently how what had happened to Renee and Joe would never happen to the two of them.

But he hadn't known until that evening on the beach exactly how much she'd believed in him. He watched the truth become clear in her heart as the initial shock wore off and the facts became part of her. The doubt in her eyes since then was enough to bring him to his knees.

Not literally, of course.

This wasn't the type of thing he was going to run to their pastor over, not the type of thing he'd go to the men's minister to confess. It happened eight years ago, after all. Eight years. He'd been perfect since then, faithful, honest, everything Michele and the girls needed. Even now, in the wake of the trauma his announcement had caused Michele, they had no issues to resolve, no conflict to work through. Her heart was bruised, yes, but as long as she could separate the past from the present, Michele would eventually forgive him for something that had happened so long ago.

Counseling would be a waste of time at this point. Unless Michele couldn't learn to trust him again. Then he'd call the pastor for sure.

But not yet. For now, the situation was simple. They would take the boy in for two weeks and make a decision after that.

He hated how the truth had hurt Michele, regretted the confusion it was causing his girls, but the affair hadn't been his fault. He hadn't planned it, after all. It simply happened. The result of a kind of accumulated pressure unlike anything he'd ever experienced. He'd never loved

Kiahna. Never even fallen for her. It had just been one of those things, one of those awful situations that happen.

Yes, he'd made a wrong choice, but that was in the past. Too far in the past for Michele to doubt him today.

But she did. No question about it. Doubt filled her eyes the way hope and joy and love had filled them just a few days earlier.

The phone in his hands vibrated and he jumped. In one motion, he flipped it open and pulled up the antenna. "Hello?"

"Mr. Evans, this is Marv Ogle, the attorney in Honolulu."

"Yes, Mr. Ogle." Connor felt his chest tighten. "My wife and I have made a decision about Kiahna's boy." He paused. After his next statement, there would be no turning back. "We'd like Max to come visit for two weeks, the way Kiahna requested in her will."

"Very well." The man's voice filled with a kind of uncertain relief. "Today is Tuesday. When shall we fly him out?"

Connor already had an answer, not that he'd discussed it with Michele. When he'd tried the night before, she held up one hand and shook her head. "This is your thing, Connor. Do what you want."

Now he slid to the edge of his seat and clenched his jaw. "How 'bout Friday evening?"

"Friday evening." The attorney paused and the sound of shuffling papers filtered through the phone lines. "Very well, that should work."

"Can we . . . talk about the guidelines, the story we'll tell him?"

"Certainly. Kiahna assumed you wouldn't want to tell the boy you were his father. Not at first, anyway."

"Right." Connor felt his heart beat harder against his uniform. It was really going to happen; in a few days he would meet his son for the first time, come face to face with the sins of his past. Shame colored his tone. "What will you tell him?"

"Just what Kiahna said in her letter, that you were a friend of hers, and that it meant a lot to her that Max spend a few weeks with you."

"Okay." Connor swallowed. His palms were sweaty, and the list of questions he'd prepared suddenly slipped his mind.

"Max knows he has a father, Mr. Evans. Kiahna told him in her letter that perhaps one day he would find his biological dad and have a relationship with him. Then again, perhaps not. Either way, he believes he has a father in God." The attorney paused. "Faith is very important to Max."

Faith?

Guilt washed over Connor as he considered that. He was supposed to be a man of faith. But since 1996 his relationship with God hadn't amounted to much more than a few appearances at church each month and the constant intention to get back to praying, back to reading the Bible. Back to connecting with God. Instead he'd rarely found time, and in the absence of a relationship with the Lord, Connor had done his best to work things out on his own.

But Max . . .

Apparently Max believed in a way that made people notice.

"What . . . what else?" Connor was stalling, buying time until his thoughts cleared.

"He loves a cold can of Coke, especially the little bit that gets stuck on the inside rim of the can. His favorite food is whipped cream and blueberry pancakes, and on stormy nights he's afraid of the dark. He likes trees because they point up to heaven, snowmen because they seem real, and any kind of animal. He's the fastest boy on his baseball team, and he loves listening to Jana Alayra's music."

"Jana Alayra?"

"She sings Christian songs, stuff for kids. When her CD's playing in the house, he sings along at the top of his lungs."

"He's a singer, too, huh?"

"Not really." The attorney chuckled. "He's tone deaf, but he loves it all the same. And seeing him sing songs about not veering from the path that's right is as beautiful as anything I've ever heard."

An idea struck Connor. Mr. Ogle loved Kiahna's son like his own. It was something he hadn't asked the man, but better that he do so now, before the boy came for the visit. "Mr. Ogle, have you and your wife considered adopting Max?"

The pause at the other end frightened Connor in a way that was irrational. "We've known Max all his life, Mr. Evans, but we're old enough to be his grandparents. I'm afraid we wouldn't be much good to a boy as active as Max. The same is true for Ramey."

"Ramey. The baby-sitter?"

"Yes. Ramey would take him, but the doctors have said she has a year or two at best. Heart disease is winning the battle for her energy, and caring for Max would only make her disease less manageable."

"I see." So there it was. He alone was the answer for the boy. The responsibility was almost as overwhelming as the possibility. "Anything else?"

"Hmmm . . ." The attorney thought for a moment. "Oh, yes. I almost forgot about Buddy. Max's best friend is his Labrador retriever, Buddy. The two were inseparable before Kiahna's death, and now . . . well, the dog hasn't left his side ever since."

"Meaning . . ."

"Meaning would you mind if Buddy came with him for the visit? He's completely house-trained, and in warm weather you can keep him outside around the clock. I think it would be helpful for Max."

Connor didn't doubt it. But he and Michele had long since agreed that dogs belonged on wide open farms. Fencing one up in a neighborhood lot was cruel, and often resulted in the kind of incessant barking that turned neighbors into enemies. Besides, Michele had never liked the idea of owning pets. Too much mess and upkeep. The girls were content with their Barbies and goldfish.

He took a moment to imagine what Michele would say if he came home and told her that Max was coming with his dog. A shudder worked its way down his spine, and he cleared his throat. "Uh, no. I'm afraid we can't have the dog. Is there anywhere he can stay?"

Disappointment rang from the attorney's voice. "I discussed that with Ramey, the boy's baby-sitter. She offered to keep Buddy if you were unwilling."

Unwilling. The word poked darts at his conscience, but he could do nothing about it. Bringing Max home would be shock enough, without bringing the dog, too. "I'm sorry, Mr. Ogle. The news has been hard enough on my wife."

"Of course."

"It's only two weeks."

"I understand."

But would Max? How was the boy supposed to feel, yanked from his home and his dog and everything he knew about life and sent to live with a family he'd never met? The question sent an undercurrent of doubt across Connor's resolve.

The attorney launched into some of the details. He was online now, surfing the Internet and finding flights that would work. The most likely one was outbound on the airline Connor flew for. He promised to take care of the reservation, and the conversation stalled.

Mr. Ogle changed directions. "You understand Kiahna's intentions in requesting this visit, is that correct, Mr. Evans?"

"Yes." Connor's stomach tightened. "It's a trial. If we . . . if it works out, we would keep him."

"Exactly. Kiahna didn't list you on the boy's birth certificate. So even though you're his biological father, you and your wife would need to go through the courts to make his adoption legal." The man paused. "And if you don't want him, Kiahna wishes for you never to contact the boy again."

Connor had assumed as much, but he hadn't been sure until now. He felt the stakes of the boy's visit triple. "I'm not sure which way it will go. Not yet anyway."

"Would you like to know my thoughts?" The hint of a smile sounded in the attorney's voice.

"Okay . . ."

"You'll keep him."

Connor tightened his grip on the phone. The idea seemed impossible at this point. "How can you be so sure?"

"Because I know Max, Mr. Evans. It's simple, really. Max is an easy boy to love."

The conversation ended, but Connor sat stone still, replaying the attorney's words in his head. His son sounded like a fantastic kid, but what if he came to visit and hated Florida? What if all he wanted was to catch the next plane back to Hawaii so he could be with this Ramey woman and the Ogles and his best friend, Buddy?

Of course that was only half the battle they faced.

The real issue was how Michele and the girls would take to his presence in their family. Timing for Max's visit would be perfect. The boy would arrive Friday, just in time for the family's annual camping trip, a time when the kids took a few days off school and they enjoyed their favorite lake without the usual crowds. Connor had asked Michele if she wanted him to wait and have the boy visit the following week, when the vacation was over, but she said no.

"We might as well get used to him, Connor. Whether he comes on the vacation or not, he'll be with us. There's no getting around it."

While her answer wasn't exactly positive, she hadn't refused.

The more Connor thought about the plan, the better it seemed. They'd made reservations almost a year earlier for their favorite spot, a shady campground just off

Lake Okeechobee. The boat docks were fifty yards away in one direction, the beach fifty yards the other way. Connor had serviced the jet skis and gone over the camping equipment days ago.

He had no doubt that once the boy got past feeling homesick, he would like their family. And if he was as lovable as Mr. Ogle thought him to be, then they would all love him in return.

Even Michele.

THIRTEEN

The phone call came later that day.

Max was at school, and Ramey learned the news just before lunchtime. Max was going to Florida to spend two weeks with the man who had fathered him. Not that Max would know. The man was only willing to take the boy for two weeks, and Buddy wasn't welcome for even that long.

Ramey settled into her chair near the television.

No question, it wasn't fair. But then that was the way of life, wasn't it? How fair was it that she was sick, that even if she wanted Max she couldn't care for him in her condition? She glanced down at the floor near her chair, where Buddy lay curled in a ball. At least she could take care of Buddy. He was a good dog, and she would be there for him when he missed Max.

Earlier that day she'd gone to Kiahna's apartment and sorted through some of her belongings. A moving company was coming to take her furniture to storage until Marv Ogle could decide what to do with it. Ramey had offered to pull together a few bags of clothes for Max and whatever items might be too precious to place in storage.

She found the journal in a nightstand beside Kiahna's bed.

Inside was a detailed accounting of her time with Max's father, as well as her reasons for standing by her faith in the years since. Dozens of entries were devoted to Max, and Ramey's eyes were blurred before she placed the clothbound book in a bag and moved on.

An hour later she had packed everything of any sentimental value. Max's baby book, two photo albums, a box of his schoolwork, and Kiahna's Bible. Mr. Ogle had offered to come by and collect the heavy clothes bags when he was finished with work. But the other items, Ramey brought home herself.

The small bag sat near the patio door, and Ramey struggled to her feet. Maybe something in Kiahna's journal would help her know how to break the news about the trip to Max. She opened the book and thumbed through it.

Her eye connected with an entry dated November 12, 1996. Ramey worked the numbers in her mind and realized Kiahna would've been maybe three months pregnant. A twinge of guilt hit her as she stared at the date. Maybe Kiahna wouldn't have wanted anyone but Max to see her journal. But then, this was different. Kiahna would've wanted her to read the journal if it could shed any light on the way she'd felt about Max's father.

She took a deep breath and found the beginning of the entry.

The doctor says the baby is growing fine, but he knows nothing of my heart, how much I wish I could call Connor and tell him the truth. But I won't, not now or ever. I promised God and myself. If things had been different, Connor and I would've fallen in love slow and proper, married and lived a hundred years together. But he was already spoken for, already committed to a family he loved.

God's ways were clearer to me after Connor. Of course God didn't want us to be together that night because, despite the way we shared our hearts, we should have waited. Then I would've known about his wife, his family. Instead I gave in to my emotions, and now the shame of what we did will stay with me a lifetime.

No, nothing will change my mind about calling him, not even the precious baby growing within me.

When this child is older, maybe he'll seek Connor out for himself. I'll explain that yes, I loved his father — if only for a short time. But what we did by coming together that August was wrong, and I will beg God's forgiveness every day of my life as long as I live. Even so, that doesn't change the way I felt about Connor. Or how determined I am to keep the truth about our baby to myself.

One day, though, one day it could happen. If my God and Father takes me home before my child is full grown, it'll be up to Connor. Because if that happens I'll want my baby to find him.

I pray that if that happens, that God will be merciful in bringing forgiveness to Connor's family. Forgiveness for me and Connor and anyone else who was hurt by what happened that stormy night.

Ramey blinked and a single tear fell on the

page just beneath where Kiahna's entry ended. So she had loved the man, after all. The young woman's words were exactly what Ramey had hoped to find. Connor wasn't a man she hated, or someone who had hurt her. He was a man already spoken for.

No wonder Kiahna had never fallen in love again. She took her love for Max's father with her to the grave, as determined to leave him alone as she'd been the day she'd written that journal entry.

Ramey closed the book and stared out at the simple patio beyond her sliding glass door. Nearly all her life she'd shied away from prayer and talk of God. But now, in light of Kiahna's journal entry, she felt obligated to ask Him for a little help. Just in case He was real and actually could hear her.

"God . . ." At the whispered word, she glanced around the room, as though perhaps a flash of light might race through it. She let her eyes settle on the ceiling. After a moment of silence she felt safe enough to continue. "God, if You're up there, then You've got Kiahna now, and . . . well . . ." Her words stuck in her throat and she brought her fingertips to her eyebrows. This wasn't a time to cry, not when she had business with God.

She waited for the lump in her throat to

ease some. "If You've got Kiahna, then You know how much we miss her. And You know how hard things are for Max." She did a short cough and swallowed back the sadness in her voice. "From the sounds of it, Kiahna made a mistake with Max's father. But, God . . . I know how sorry she was. She died sorry, I'm sure of it. And now, well, now Max is in a heap of trouble, because what man would want to find out about a son he never knew he had, a son who might ruin his marriage or his whole family."

Her hands fell back to her lap and she soothed her thumb over the worn cloth cover of Kiahna's journal. "What I'm saying, God, is Max needs a little help here. If You want the boy to live with this . . . this Connor man, then You're going to need to work a miracle. A forgiveness miracle, God. Otherwise none of this will work out, and Max will wind up —"

The sadness came then, and Ramey could do nothing to stop it. Because if God didn't work a forgiveness miracle for all of them, then Max would become a ward of the state. And there was no telling what would happen to him after that.

Ramey leaned over and snatched a tissue from the box on the coffee table. She dabbed her eyes and blew her nose and ordered herself to get a grip. If God was still listening, she needed to finish her prayer. For Max's sake.

"So, God, please . . . do this thing for Max. And if You do, I promise You something . . ." Ramey hesitated. She hadn't planned on making any promises to God, but her words were flowing without a filter. "I promise I'll believe in You, God. If You let Connor and his family forgive each other, if You let Max find a place with them, I'll believe in You for the rest of my life."

When Max came home from school, Ramey piled him and Buddy and a picnic dinner into her beat-up station wagon.

"What about my homework?" Max bit his lip. He seemed unsure about the trip. But then he'd been unsure about most of life since his mother's death. The only time he looked at peace was when he was reading the Bible his mother gave him the year before, or when he sat with Buddy out on the patio.

Ramey sighed and motioned Max to come closer. "Buddy loves the beach, right?"

"Right."

"So let's do homework later. Let's spend a few hours on the sand. You can play with

Buddy, and then we'll have a picnic and talk a little."

Red flags flashed in Max's eyes. "Talk about what?"

"About life, Max, okay? About life." Ramey turned for the door. "Come on. Buddy needs to get out."

Max set his backpack down and followed her.

They were set up at the beach half an hour later with an early picnic dinner of peanut butter and banana sandwiches and red fruit punch. When they were finished eating, Max and Buddy ran down the beach to chase seagulls.

Ramey brought a bag with her and pulled out a notebook. The idea had been forming in her mind since earlier, after reading Kiahna's journal. If Max was going to spend two weeks with this Connor Evans man and his wife, then several things seemed certain. First, if Kiahna had loved the man in so short a time, Ramey had no doubt that he'd cared for her in return. That meant that no matter what grief the news about Max caused him, Connor would feel for the boy. Max had that effect on people; his father would be no exception.

The problem was bound to be with Connor's wife.

Ramey thought back to the days before her own husband died. How badly would her world have been shaken if he'd come home one day with that kind of news? That he had a son in another state, with a woman he'd slept with while they were married?

She watched Max run through the surf, Buddy close at his heels. It wouldn't matter if the child was wonderful. The blow would've been enough to knock her off her foundation. Maybe even tear their marriage apart.

The idea came to her after the prayer, after she begged God — if He was listening — to make a forgiveness miracle for Connor's family. Maybe she could do something to help, give a message to the man's wife about what God might want in this situation.

She opened the notebook and found a clean sheet of lined paper. Then, with another glance at Max, she began to write.

To Mrs. Evans:

Hello. My name is Ramey, and you don't know me. I've been Max's baby-sitter for all of his life. Whenever his mother was out of town on a flight, the boy was with me. During that

*time I haven't been much of a believer.
In fact, I haven't believed in God at
all, really.*

*But now as I watch Max, as I think
about the months and years he has
ahead, I want to believe, ma'am. With
all my heart I want to believe.*

*Marv Ogle tells me that you and
your husband are Christians, the
same way Kiahna was a Christian.
I've read through some of Kiahna's
journal so I might understand Max's
situation better, and what I found has
given me the beginning of belief.
Enough so that I've asked God for a
forgiveness miracle for Max.*

*You see, ma'am, I might not be very
educated, but I know it will take a
forgiveness miracle for life to work
out the way Kiahna and even, I think,
God wants it to work out.*

She kept writing, detailing for the
woman a Scripture she'd found on the inside cover of Kiahna's journal. It was a
verse that seemed strong, somehow, in a
way Ramey had never felt before. She
ended the letter as best she could. Then
she folded it and placed it in an envelope.
Across the front she wrote, *For Mrs. Evans.*

Before Max left she would stick it in his Bible and remind him to give it to the woman. Then she wrote Max a short note. She would stick both letters and a picture of Kiahna and Buddy in Max's Bible. That way he'd remember what was in his heart even when he was so far away from home.

She looked up and scanned the beach for the boy and his dog. The sun was dropping in the sky, and Max and Buddy had tired out. They sat together near the shore, Max digging his toes into the sand, looking out at the ocean, one arm flung around Buddy's neck.

What could he be thinking? Ramey bit her lip. If she did nothing else for Max in all her life, she would stay happy that night. Sadness would only tell Max that whatever lay ahead could be even more painful than the days he'd already survived.

She cupped her hands around her mouth. "Max . . ."

He turned his head in her direction. His eyes looked more at peace than they had earlier. "Yes, Ramey?"

She swallowed hard. After this conversation his future would be set in motion, one way or another. "Can I talk to you, bucko?"

His mouth hung open, as if her question

scared him. But he stood and began walking, Buddy beside him. When they reached Ramey, they both dropped to the ground in front of her. Max looked up, his eyes searching hers. "Is this about Mommy's friend?"

So the boy remembered. He'd probably been thinking about spending two weeks with a stranger ever since hearing his mother's letter. Ramey lifted her chin. *No tears . . . no tears . . .* "Yes, Max. It's about that." She reached out and used her thumb to brush a lock of hair off from Max's forehead.

The boy's eyes grew wide. "What about it?"

"Well" — Ramey looked to the deep places of the child's heart — "Mr. Ogle found your mom's friend, and he wants to see you. He lives in Florida with his family. You'll be gone for two weeks." She hesitated. "I wanted you to know."

Max's chin quivered some and anger flashed in his eyes. He put his arm around Buddy. "I don't want to go. I want to stay here with you."

Ramey had never been overly affectionate with the boy. She had never needed to be; Kiahna had showered him with more than enough love. But Kiahna was gone forever, and as Max's shoulders began to shake, she reached out to him. He stood and came to her, falling against her and burying his tan, little-boy face in the soft part of her shoulder. "Don't make me go, please, Ramey."

"Max . . . shhh. It's okay." She soothed her hand against his back, and beside them Buddy rose to his feet and whimpered. "Your mom wants you to do this, remember?"

He drew back, his eyes searching hers. "But she was wrong, Ramey. She thought I would want to go, but I don't. Not ever." He took three quick breaths and rubbed his cheeks. "Do I have to, even if I don't want to?"

Ramey's heart hurt and she made a mental note to take additional nitroglycerin that night before going to bed. Stress like this wasn't good for her. She cocked her head to the side and managed a sad smile. "Yes, Max. You have to go. You leave Friday."

His mouth hung open, and his eyes filled with hurt, as though somehow she'd betrayed him by letting Mr. Ogle and his mother's friend make plans without his approval. He gave a few slow shakes of his head and then he gulped back another wave of sobs. "Is . . . is Buddy coming with me?"

Ramey moved her hands to his shoulders and hoped with everything in her that Max would understand, that he would move past the pain he was feeling to a point where he would be open to whatever God might do in the coming weeks. If God had heard her prayer.

"No, Max." She chewed on her lip for a few seconds. "Buddy will stay with me."

For a moment, Max didn't move. He stared first at Ramey, then at Buddy. "No . . . that isn't *fair*, Ramey." His voice rose and he pulled away from her. "No!" Then he turned and ran, hard and fast, toward the surf.

Buddy seemed confused by the boy's outburst. He stood, looked at Ramey, and wagged his tail. Then he followed after Max. Ramey watched the boy reach the water and shade his eyes.

"No, Mommy!" He shouted the words out over the water. "Don't make me go, not without Buddy!"

This time Ramey could do nothing to stop her tears. They escaped from her heart and made a silent stream down her face. It dawned on her that she needed to ask God for one more part to the forgiveness miracle. Because before Max could ever learn to like the man in Florida — or any part of his family for that matter — he would have to do something he'd never had to do before.

He would have to forgive the mother he loved more than life.

FOURTEEN

Ocean water was getting Max's shorts wet, but he was too mad to care.

He lowered his voice, and this time the words he spoke to his mommy were whispered. From his heart to hers. "Why . . . why should I go?"

The ocean made a *whooshing* sound, and Max had the strongest feeling. If only he could swim across the ocean and find her plane, maybe she wasn't really dead at all. Maybe she was sitting on top of it, waiting for someone to find her. He could be the one, couldn't he? He could find her and sit up there beside her and ask her why she wanted him to take a trip to Florida, wherever that was. Especially when all he wanted to do was stay with Buddy and Ramey.

He dropped to the sand and felt a little bit of wave fill into his shorts pockets. Buddy leaned close to him and licked his face. "She could be alive, don't you think, Buddy?" Max turned his nose to the dog and accepted another swipe across his cheek. "Yeah. Me, too."

A long huff came from inside him, from his heart, maybe. He looked back out at the water, and all of a sudden he remembered what Ramey had told him the day he found out about his mother's plane.

She's dead, Max. No one on the plane lived . . . no one on the plane lived . . . no one on the plane lived.

New tears covered over his eyes and made the ocean blurry. His whispery words were more scratchy than before. "But . . . what if she was the onlyest one?" Buddy made a little whining sound, and Max rubbed him behind his ear.

This time he looked up to the sky, the place where God lived. "Is she really gone, Jesus? Is she with You? Or is she on the plane, waiting for me to help her?"

Most of the time God didn't actually talk back to him. Not with words. But once in a while he could sort of feel what God was saying. He shut his eyes and waited. And just then it came. A feeling that was happy and sad all at the same time, because Ramey was right, that's why. His mommy wasn't on the plane at all, not anymore. She was up in heaven with Jesus.

But what was he supposed to do with the mad in his heart? Mommy should've known he wouldn't want to leave the island to stay with some friend of hers. He wanted to be here, near the water where the two of them had played as far back as remembering could go. Near their apartment and Ramey's apartment and Buddy.

He stretched out his legs, opened his eyes, and let the water come over him. The ocean had a thing called tides; that's what his mommy taught him. When the tide was out, the sand was extra big. But when it came in, it moved real slow up the beach until most of the sand was underwater.

The tide was coming in now, but Max didn't care. Waves could come to his waist and he wouldn't move, because he needed to understand. He squinted his eyes up at the sky again. "God . . . I don't want to go to Florida." He lifted his arm and wiped at his cheek with his shoulder. "But I don't want to be mad at Mommy either."

A sense came in him then. A sense was when you knew something even though no one had said it. Mommy told him that good senses came from God, and that when they happened, Max better listen to them in case God was trying to tell him something. This time the sense was that Mommy had a reason for asking him to see her friend.

A reason?

Max had never thought of it that way. But when he turned it around in his brain, the sense seemed pretty smart. His mommy always had a reason for telling him something. She wanted him to wipe his shoes on the mat after playing at the beach, but that had a reason. So he wouldn't make the carpet dirty. He had to wash his hands before he ate, and that had a reason, too. So he wouldn't eat germs with his food.

Yes, maybe the sense inside him was right. Mommy had a reason for the Florida trip. All he had to do was not be mad at her so he could pay attention to what the reason was. The sense got stronger. If he went to Florida, if he used his best manners and didn't complain too much, he would know the reason why his mommy wanted him to go. One day God would make the reason extra clear to him.

Max ran his hand along Buddy's back and leaned against him. "I'm gonna miss you, Buddy."

A comfortable sound came from Buddy's nose. He brushed his head up against Max's and then lowered his furry chin down on top of his paws.

"Listen, Buddy." Max sat up and stared at his dog. "Don't get sad, because I'm coming back, okay? I'll come back just like Ramey said, and after that you and me will be together forever, okay? Okay, Buddy?"

The dog lifted his eyes and then let them fall back again. That's what Buddy always did when he was sad. Max leaned over and hugged the dog, held him close the way his mommy used to hold him when he had a hurt knee or a bad day at school. "That's okay, Buddy. I'm sad, too. But I have a sense. Everything's going to be okay, Buddy. You'll see."

One more time Max sat up, and this time he stood up. Warm ocean water ran down his legs, but he didn't think about it too much. He looked up at the sky one last time and smiled. Smiles could happen even if tears happened at the same time. Max had found that out ever since his mommy went away. He sucked in a breath and whispered one more thing to God.

"Thanks for the sense, God. I felt it." He wiggled his toes until his feet sank a little in the sand. "I'm sorry for getting mad. And could You tell my mom something, please? Tell her I'm not mad at her for making the part in the letter about going away for two weeks. I forgive her, okay? Could You tell her that, God?"

Max didn't need a sense this time. His mommy taught him a long time ago that God was good at passing on messages to people, and God 'specially liked it when people forgave each other.

"Know what love is, Max?" his mom used to ask him sometimes. "Love is what happens when people forgive."

Max was glad he thought of that. He loved his mommy very much and he couldn't stay mad at her.

He looked over his shoulder at Ramey. She looked old and tired and a little bit cold. He didn't want to stay mad at Ramey, either. The trip to Florida wasn't her fault. Max brushed the sand off his shorts and looked real quick at his dog. "Come on, Buddy. Let's go home."

Buddy followed him again, and as soon as he was close enough to Ramey, he said the things in his heart. "I thought about it, Ramey. I'll go to Florida."

Her forehead got bunchy lines on it and surprise showed in her eyes. "Really? You're not mad anymore?"

Max shrugged and felt the corners of his lips lift up. "I'm scared a little, but I'm not mad. God gave me a sense."

Ramey leaned closer. "A sense?"

"Yes. Sense is when God tells you some-thing. But you have to be very still to hear it."

"Oh." Ramey reached for his hand and wrapped her fingers around his. "What sense did you get?"

"That one day I'll know why."

Ramey's mouth stayed open and at first no words came out. Then she said, "Why what?"

"Why Mommy wanted me to go on the trip."

"Oh, right."

One more thing was in his heart to tell her. He took a step closer and looked at her eyes. "I'm sorry, Ramey. I didn't mean to be mad at you."

Then Ramey said the thing that his mother said meant love. In a happy sort of sad voice she said, "I forgive you, bucko."

And right then, as she said those words, Ramey got something happy in her eyes. Something happier than she'd had for a long, long time.

FIFTEEN

All week, conversation between Connor and Michele came in fits and starts, and the trip to the airport that Friday evening was no different.

Michele wanted to come, wanted to be there to see her husband's reaction when his only son walked off the Jetway. Other people might have to wait at the security staging area, but not Connor and Michele. Pilots had privileges, even with the changes in travel since September 11.

They rode in silence, and a Martina McBride song came on the radio. Michele wasn't really listening, but the point of the song seemed clear enough. "You'll get through this . . . you'll break new ground . . ."

She leaned over and changed the station. Martina had no idea what Michele Evans could survive or what type of ground she was capable of breaking.

Connor drove, his eyes locked on the road ahead. She didn't have to see his expression to know what he was feeling, that mix of fear and excitement over what lay ahead, the fact that he would finally get to see the boy whose existence had so thoroughly changed their lives in a matter of days.

He was driving sixty-five, seventy. Fifteen miles over the speed limit. She rolled her eyes and gazed at the traffic ahead of them. "Speeding won't get him here any sooner."

He shot her a confused look. "I'm not speeding."

"You are."

"No." He looked at the speedometer. "I always drive like this."

"Right." She hated the sarcasm in her voice, hated how it seemed part of her persona now. The bitter wife, still in the dark about why she hadn't been enough for her husband. The angry spouse, bent on punishing Connor for finding her less than perfect.

Connor exhaled and it sounded like steam releasing from the darkest places inside of him. "I'm not in a hurry, Michele. His plane doesn't come in for another hour."

She said nothing. These days if his statements didn't demand a response, she didn't give one. Twice he'd tried to sit her down and explain what had happened with the boy's mother. But always she stopped him before he got started.

"Spare me the details, will you, Connor? I'm not interested." She flashed angry eyes at him. "Besides, I can use my imagination. Long layover, planes grounded in a storm, some smart-looking flight attendant wants your attention and you think, *She looks a lot better than the one I have back home*." She uttered a poisonous laugh. "Believe me, Connor. I don't need the details."

Each time her response seemed to paralyze him. He'd stand there in front of her, his mouth open. As though he truly wanted to tell her more about what happened, wanted to explain his actions in some way. But then his mouth would close. He'd drop his shoulders and turn away. What could he say? That Michele had nothing to worry about because he'd never so much as called Kiahna after their time together? That he'd never loved the girl?

Michele turned away from Connor. She already knew that much.

Lust. That's what happened to Connor.

And now the product of his lust was about to walk into their lives. She hated that, too. The boy had nowhere to go, but still she felt nothing but spite for him. What had happened to the kinder, confident person she'd been two weeks earlier? How could she dream of holding anything against an orphaned little boy?

She had no answers for herself.

Connor took the next exit and the road veered in a semicircle. The sensation made Michele dizzy, not that it took much these days to do that. Her eating habits were completely out of whack. An entire pack of Oreos one day, nothing but water and herbal tea the next. She wanted to starve, never eat another bite of food again. But sometimes her feelings were so jumbled up she couldn't do anything but eat herself into a bloated state of oblivion.

She hadn't told Connor, of course. He didn't need to know about her binge eating. It wasn't something she did all the time. Only when her emotions were more than she could handle. He'd tell her the same thing Renee would tell her, the same thing her sister, Margie, would tell her. Get a grip. Get some help. Grab onto God and don't let go. Eating wasn't the answer; prayer and Scripture and counseling were.

But so far, she hadn't felt like doing anything but eating. Eating and crying and hiding in her craft room so the girls wouldn't see her tears. So Connor wouldn't see the cookie wrappers. She kept a role of paper towels in her bottom desk drawer. Any food trash was squished into a ball, wrapped inside a paper towel, and tossed in her trash can. That way no one would be the wiser.

Besides, what did it matter? Connor could say he was sorry, he could tell her that he still loved her, still found her beautiful. But he'd been saying that back in 1996, hadn't he? Why should she believe him now?

"What are you thinking?" Connor kept his eyes on the road ahead of them.

"Don't ask."

"Michele . . ."

The pain in his voice made her cringe. She was new at hating, and sometimes when his voice sounded the way it did now, she longed to lean over and hug him. Cry with him and scream at him and hold onto him for dear life. Instead she looked out the side window and said nothing.

"Michele, don't do this. What's Max going to think if this is how we are?"

She turned to him. "Max?" Her voice

rose a level. "Is *that* what's worrying you, Connor? What *Max* will think when he comes home to a family that's falling apart?" Another bitter laugh. "Well, don't be surprised when I tell you I don't exactly *care* what Max thinks." She clenched her fists and made a sound that was part moan, part yell.

"I'm just saying it'll be awkward." Connor's tone had lost all of its previous sureness. He sounded more like a nervous child dealing with an abusive parent than the conquer-anything pilot.

She lowered her voice. "You want awkward, Connor? Look at the faces of our girls when we get home. See the subtle knowing in Elizabeth's expression and the fear in Susan's. You think those girls don't know something's wrong?"

"Of *course* they do." For the first time that day, he raised his voice at her. She watched him make a straight line of his lips. "I'm sorry. I didn't mean to yell. What I'm saying is, nothing will be right as long as you stay mad at me."

He might as well have kicked her in the gut. Did he really think that's all this was? A case of her being mad at him? "You had an affair, Connor. You slept with some woman in Honolulu, and a few weeks later

227

you came home and acted like nothing ever happened. Every year since then you lived with the truth, but never, not once, did you come clean with me." She dug her fingernails into her thighs. "As long as I'm *mad* at you?"

"Okay, I get it, but at some point you need to listen to me, Michele. Let me explain what happened." He worked the muscles in his jaw, checked the traffic, and changed lanes. The West Palm Beach airport was two miles up the highway. "It was years ago." He clenched his teeth for a moment. "Yes, you just found out about it, but that doesn't change the fact that I've been faithful for almost eight years. It doesn't change the way I feel about you." He reached for her hand but she pulled away. He hesitated but only for a moment. "I love you, Michele."

Deep within her a voice echoed in her soul. *Don't say it . . . don't say it, Michele.*

"Yes." She closed her eyes and ignored the warning. "But right now you love that little boy more."

Connor said nothing after that. Michele stared out the window, but in the corner of her eye she could see her husband's expression harden. Again, she wanted to hug him, tell him she was sorry for being so mean. But the wall between them was cement block and razor wire.

She couldn't imagine a way over it, even if she wanted to.

They parked and headed into the airport, side by side. It struck Michele that they finally looked the way she'd seen other couples look in crowded places. Back before her world stopped turning, she and Connor would be walking together, holding hands and leaning in for an occasional whispered one-liner, when they'd pass a couple with dead eyes and three feet of space between them.

"Let's never be like that," she'd whispered to him more than once.

"Never."

But now here they were, just like that. Part of the community of walking dead, together but as cold and alone as if they were in separate parts of Alaska. They reached the gate as the boy's plane rounded the corner and pulled up. Michele crossed her arms and held herself tight as she watched the Jetway accordion out to meet the aircraft.

Fitting . . . that Connor's world would connect with the Hawaiian flight attendant here, in an airport. The same way they'd first connected that summer night in Honolulu.

Connor moved a step closer and focused on the tunnel leading from the plane. "He should be one of the first ones off."

Again she said nothing. What could she say? Good? Great, that they'd be seeing him sooner than later? She clenched her jaw and followed Connor's gaze. Two flight attendants came through first. They each took a waiting wheelchair and disappeared down the tunnel again.

Ten seconds passed. Fifteen. Twenty.

She was just about to turn away, to look across the concourse and wonder whether anyone else was waiting for a person who would forever alter their lives by merely getting off a plane. But before she could turn, she saw a blur of motion near the tunnel entrance. And suddenly a male flight attendant exited next to a brown-haired boy with green eyes and honey-colored skin. He was smaller than she'd pictured him, but he was only seven, after all. In the days leading up to his visit, the boy had taken on a larger-than-life image in her mind.

But the most striking thing about him was his face: There was no question he was Connor's son.

Michele wasn't sure where to look. At the boy and his uncanny resemblance to

Connor, the boy who was absolutely her husband's, or at Connor and the reaction he had to be feeling. In the end she tore her eyes from the child and watched her husband, watched the way he took a quick step forward, then stopped himself.

He wants to run to the boy. If I wasn't here he'd have the child in his arms in less than a minute. She turned back to the boy and saw the flight attendant notice them.

"Is he with you?"

"Yes," she heard Connor say. "We're here for him."

The words felt like daggers in Michele's soul.

The attendant walked the boy to them. Connor showed his pilot's identification and signed a release form. This time Michele looked at the boy, and a soft gasp filled her throat.

He didn't only look like Connor; he looked like Connor's father. She had expected that, when she saw the boy, she would find herself looking into the face of the woman who'd lured Connor into a one-night stand. Instead, the face was as familiar as it was beautiful. The same face she'd smiled at a million times, the one she woke up next to and looked at across the dining room table.

The only possible resemblance to his mother was his eyes. Piercing green eyes lit up his face and made a stark contrast against his tanned skin and dark hair. His mother must've been breathtaking.

The flight attendant finished his work and left them alone.

"Max?" Connor stooped down and held out his hand. "I'm Mr. Evans, your mom's friend."

The boy reached out and shook Connor's hand. "Nice to meet you, sir."

Something about hearing the boy's voice shot a crack through Michele's tough exterior. He sounded sweeter than an angel, and it took everything in her to remember that he wasn't just any other boy. He was her husband's illegitimate child. She stiffened and cleared her voice. "I'm Mrs. Evans." She nodded at the boy but stopped short of holding out her hand.

"Nice to meet you, ma'am."

Connor's voice was tight, pinched with a kind of glad emotion that only made Michele more angry. "Did you eat dinner yet?"

"Yes, sir. On the plane."

"Well" — Connor straightened — "we're happy you could come, Max."

Michele shifted her attention back to her

husband. His face was masked in nonchalance, but beneath that mask she saw a sort of awe, a light he couldn't hide. Hatred flooded her soul again. She had seen Connor look that way only three other times in her life. When they faced each other at the front of a church fourteen years earlier, when Elizabeth was born, and when Susan entered the world.

The fact that he felt that way now knocked the wind from her and nearly dropped her to the airport floor, even as passengers streamed by them. How *dare* he give a look like that to a boy he'd only just met? As if his arrival was packed with as much emotional meaning as any of those previous events? She leaned back on her heels to keep from falling.

As she did, Connor reached out his hand to the child and smiled at him. "Come on, Max. Let's get your suitcase."

Her body moved despite the fact that her heart had crashed to the ground somewhere back at the gate. The concourse was crowded, and though Michele tried to stay even with Connor and the boy, several times the foot traffic kept her a few feet behind, as though there wasn't room for all of them to walk the path together.

The irony slapped her in the face. Of

course there wasn't room for all three of them. Not on the concourse, and not in life. And sometime in the very near future Connor would have to decide who was going to stay.

Her or the boy.

They reached the luggage carousel and Connor leaned close to the boy again. "You remember what your bag looks like?"

"Yes, sir." The boy looked up at Connor and blinked. "Long and blue with a zipper on the middle. A ruffle bag, I think."

Michele watched Connor stifle a grin. "A duffel bag?"

"Right. That's it. That's the name Ramey called it."

Michele dropped her arms to her side and stared at them. Connor was in another world, as if he and the boy were the only two people on earth. Already he was bonding with the boy, becoming friends, finding humor in the things he said.

Connor looked at her and motioned her closer. "Help us find Max's bag, okay?"

The boy looked up, and for the first time his eyes held hers. It didn't matter that he looked like Connor; his eyes were his mother's. She had no doubt. Looking into them now made her feel like the woman was standing next to her, linking arms with

Connor and laughing at her for ever trusting him.

She blinked and managed the slightest smile in the boy's direction. "Yes, of course." Her eyes darted from the boy's face to the moving belt and the luggage that was just starting to spill onto it. "A blue duffel bag."

The boy looked, too, and after a few minutes he pointed. "There it is! I see it!" He took a step closer, but Connor took gentle hold of his shoulder and stopped him.

"I'll get it." He reached over and pulled the bag easily up and onto his shoulder.

As he did, Michele caught sight of the tag fastened to the black nylon handle. In big, black letters it said simply, *Kiahna Siefert, Western Island Air.*

The label was the last and greatest blow . . . the surefire explosion that ripped through her soul and told her the truth. Her husband had fathered a child with another woman.

Connor caught Max's hand in his once more, and Michele knew.

Whatever decision was yet to come, for the most part it had already been made. If the future held room for only two of them, then she would need to start thinking about where she was going to live. Because she knew Connor Evans better than she knew herself.

And the way he held that little boy's hand, he wasn't ever going to let go.

SIXTEEN

Connor's heart was killing him.

Wracked with a series of wildly varying emotions in a way he'd never experienced before, he was beyond exhausted long before the three of them pulled out of the airport and back onto the highway.

The scene that had just played out was destroying his wife; it had to be. And because of that, he was desperate with grief. But at the same time . . . at the same time a myriad of brilliant colors was going off in his mind. Colors he'd never even imagined before this day. The reason for them was simple.

He had a son.

All he could do as they headed home was replay the way he'd felt back at the airport, again and again and again.

From the moment he laid eyes on Max, he knew the boy was his. The child was strong and healthy and striking, just the way Marv Ogle had said he would be. And the resemblance to Connor was amazing. Same strong jaw, same dimpled chin, same forehead.

As Max came closer, Connor felt himself falling hard for the boy, allowing the child entrance into a very select place in his heart. A place from which there would be no return, whether Max stayed with them or not.

But it wasn't until he took his son's hand in his that he felt it. A connection different than anything he'd ever known. It was part remorse, part rejoicing. For here was a son he'd missed without knowing it. Missed Max's birth and his first smile, his first steps and early days of preschool. Connor hadn't been there to marvel over his son's first attempt at writing his name, nor had he been there to watch him take his first at-bat in baseball.

Those moments, all of them, were gone forever.

But the rejoicing came in knowing that, because of some twist of fate, they'd found each other. Now, if Connor had any influence on Michele, he would never let his son go.

Connor checked the rearview mirror and met Max's eyes. The boy gave him a shy smile. "Florida looks like Hawaii."

"Yes, I guess it does." Connor grinned back at him and cast a quick look at Michele. The comment hit its mark. She turned and looked out her window, refusing to take part in the conversation.

Five minutes passed, and the tension in the car felt thicker than glue. He turned on the radio and punched a series of buttons and zipped past one commercial after another until Lee Greenwood's "God Bless the USA" filled the car.

Max didn't say anything, but Connor watched him in the mirror, checking on him every few seconds. It occurred to Connor what a good job Kiahna had done with their son. He was painfully polite, and more than a little shy. Connor figured the shy thing had more to do with the situation than Max's real personality. If Max and Michele didn't want to talk, Connor would. He rambled on about the girls and their camping trip, trying to sound as normal as possible. Still, the tension remained.

They arrived home in thirty minutes, and Connor hesitated before getting out of the car. It was only seven o'clock. The girls would be up, anxious to meet the son of Daddy's friend. He'd sat them down earlier in the week and told them about Max, that he was coming for two weeks and that he'd join them on their vacation.

Neither of the girls seemed bothered by the idea, though they wondered if he'd have his own sleeping bag for the trip. Susan wanted to know if he liked climbing trees, and Elizabeth wondered if he was old enough to ride a bike in the street. He still hadn't seen the fear and doubt Michele was certain they were feeling.

Either way the moment at hand was a big one.

Michele climbed out in silence and went inside without saying a word. That left Connor and Max in the garage, making sure he had his blue duffel bag. Before they went inside, Max looked at him, his eyes wide. "Is this house all yours?"

Connor wasn't sure what the boy meant. "Well, not really. It belongs to my wife and daughters, too."

"Yes, but . . ." He looked over his shoulder at the garage and back at the entrance to the house. "It's so big. I thought maybe . . . maybe other families lived here, too."

"Nope." Connor kept his tone even. The boy had probably lived most of his life in near poverty, all because he hadn't had a father to help out. He smiled at Max and took his hand again. "Just us." They stepped inside and walked through the utility room toward the main living room. "Ready to meet the girls?"

Max nodded. "Ready."

They were waiting on the sofa together. Connor had hoped Michele would be with them, but she was nowhere around. When the girls spotted them, they stood and took a few steps forward.

Elizabeth dropped her eyes to the place where Connor held Max's hand, and instantly he let go. As he did, her expression changed and the sweet smile that was so typical of her personality flashed on her face. "Hi . . . you must be Max."

He nodded. "Hi."

Susan skipped the formalities. She took a few quick steps in his direction and then motioned toward the stairs. "Wanna see my new Lego set?"

Max's eyes grew wide. "You have Legos?"

"Sure. Not all girls play with dolls, you know." Her lighthearted laughter broke the tension, and the threesome started to move away.

Then, as though he'd only just remembered where he was, Max stopped and looked at Connor. "Is it okay? If I go up and play with them?"

Warmth beyond description filled the center of Connor's being. These were his three children. Playing together for the first time. He struggled to find his voice. "Yes, Max. Go play."

He listened to their silly chatter as they headed up the stairs.

"How was your plane ride?" The voice was Elizabeth's, less childlike, and more to the point. "I hate the turbulence."

"Yeah. Me, too. But this one was great. Not too bumpy."

"Hey, guess what?" Susan wasn't about to let Elizabeth have the upper hand in the conversation.

Connor felt a pang at his daughters' determination to make Max feel welcome. How would they feel if they knew the truth?

Susan was rambling. "And then I also have Lego sets that make a plane and a spaceship." Her voice faded as she must've run ahead of the others, intent on showing Max her entire Lego collection.

"Wow, could I play with it?"

Their voices grew too distant for him to make out. Only then did he remember to exhale. He needed to find Michele, needed to talk to her and see what she was feeling, why she left the family and went up to her room. Why couldn't she have made even a little effort that night?

But first he had something to do.

He crept into his office and opened the top drawer of his filing cabinet. Tucked behind a dozen manila files was a small stack of three picture frames he'd hidden years ago. He pulled them out, careful not to bump them on the cabinet. Then he looked at the one on top. It was a picture of him and his father, taken at his graduation from West Point. The photo was always one of his favorites because his father looked so proud of him.

He studied it now, studied the way his arm hung loosely around his father's shoulders. The way his other hand was linked to his dad's in a handshake to mark the moment. He pulled the frame closer, looked intently at his father's eyes. There had been no sign back then, no hint that one day the two of them would walk away from each other forever.

No sign except the obvious.

His father had often been proud of Connor's accomplishments, but he couldn't remember once when the man had been proud of him as a person. Proud just to call him his son. A memory began to take shape, one from the year before their falling out. Connor had been helping Elizabeth walk along a gravel path through his parents' backyard garden at the ranch in Cambria.

"What are you doing out there?" His father had barked the words from a distance, his hands on his hips.

Connor remembered smiling, wishing his father would smile back. When the man's mouth remained slack, Connor spoke up. "Helping my little girl take a walk, Dad. Wanna join us?"

"You'll spoil her, Connor. She's two years old; she can walk by herself." He walked away, shaking his head and muttering something about independence and knowing when to let go.

The thoughts that ran through Connor's head that afternoon were the same ones that ran through his head now. How could it be right to build independence in a relationship with a two-year-old? Didn't love factor into the formula anywhere? And wasn't that why he hadn't ever felt close to his father? Independent, yes. But close . . . definitely not.

Connor pushed the memory aside and set the picture back in his filing cabinet.

Next was a photo of his entire family, taken either his sophomore or junior year in high school. His mother was in the center, the way she'd been when she was alive. Her smile was vibrant and alive, reaching his heart even through the grainy finish of a yellowed photograph. On either side of her sat his three sisters, each of them younger than he and only a year or so apart. In the back, tall and proud, stood his father and him.

The photographer that day had suggested that Connor sit beside his oldest sister. Two children on one side of their mother, two on the other. But Connor's father wouldn't hear of it.

"Connor's a man, not a child," he snapped. "He'll be in the back with me."

The words seemed as strange now as they had back then. Connor's a man, not a child? How old could he have been, sixteen? Seventeen at the most? What was wrong with being a kid, anyway? And maybe that was another problem with him and his father. The man had never looked at Connor the way Connor had looked at Max an hour earlier.

That look of love and adoration and awe all mixed up and shining from his father's eyes was something Connor had never known, even in the best of times. Pride, yes, but love and adoration and awe, no.

He studied the eyes again, looked at the way his sisters seemed somewhat stiff and uptight. They were happy girls, all of them. And they'd grown up to have nice families, sweet children. But back then they had feared their father, no doubt. Yes, he could be the life of the party, whipping up a batch of ice cream, organizing a game of croquet. But he was the sergeant, the one in control at every gathering. For the picture, he had ordered everyone to do exactly as the photographer said, and in minutes he turned their normally cheerful dispositions into a front of fear and high expectation.

How different might the portrait have looked if he'd simply taken his place and let the natural light in the eyes of his children shine through?

Connor looked more closely. Of all the eyes in the photo, his own were the hardest to read. If he was remembering right, that day had been difficult for him. Right before the portrait sitting, Connor's best friend had moved across town with his family.

He might've been sixteen, but he remembered how his heart had broken in two when Mike Estes pulled away in his family's van. All he'd wanted was to find a quiet place in the woods, somewhere to sit and think for a few hours. Instead, they had to get ready for the picture.

His father pulled him aside before the family gathered outside on the lawn and warned him about his attitude. "I'll have none of this moping around stuff." He straightened his jacket and dusted a bit of white fuzz off Connor's sleeve. "You'll be happy for the picture, and afterwards we'll change out of our clothes and make some ice cream." He hesitated. "Friends come and go in life, Connor. Get over it."

Connor stared at the photo, searching his old man's eyes. *Is that how you feel now, Dad? People come and go in life, and get over it?*

Sadness flooded his heart, because the answer was obvious. Of course that's how his father felt. Otherwise he would've found a reason to call by now, whether he'd changed his mind about the money or not. His silence over the years was further proof that he had never really connected with Connor in the first place.

Connor set the photograph with the other one in the back of the drawer, and closed his eyes for a moment. He could never feel that way about his own children, not his daughters nor his son. Now that he'd met Max, if things didn't work out and the boy had to be sent back to Hawaii, he would hurt forever from the loss.

Get over it? Connor couldn't begin to imagine how.

He opened his eyes and looked at the third and final photograph. The moment his eyes connected with the image, he felt his heart skip a beat. This was the picture he'd been looking for, the reason he'd come into the office in the first place. It was a photo of his father as a boy, maybe eight or nine years old. What he saw in the frame told him what he had only suspected before.

Max was a mirror image of the man.

Yes, the boy looked like Connor, but the resemblance to his father was breathtaking. Connor stared at the image, at the young boy so fresh and untainted by the views he would later take on.

"If only you'd kept a little of what you were as a boy, Dad." Connor's words were barely audible, and he narrowed his eyes. "You should see him; his name is Max, and Dad . . . he looks just like you."

The longer he stared at the image, the more his heart filled with sorrow. Sorrow and anger and frustration over everything in his life that hadn't worked out. Not just the affair, or the way Michele had changed, or the idea that he'd fathered a child without ever knowing it. But the fact that his dad would never know he had a grandson.

And the pain that caused him as he stood there in his office, looking at pictures of his father, was one more thing Connor was sure he'd never get over. And it was then, standing there in a sea of realizations, that Connor made up his mind. He would call the pastor, after all. Not because he'd done anything wrong in the past eight years, but because he needed help figuring something out. Something that, between his pain and Michele's, he couldn't sort through on his own.

How in the world to move forward.

SEVENTEEN

Max wasn't afraid of the dark, at least not at home.

But this was his first night at his mother's friend's house, and nothing seemed right. Mr. Evans told all the kids to brush their teeth and go to bed, but he was pretty sure the girls were still up because he could hear girl voices down the hall.

Everyone had their own bedroom at the Evans's house. Even him. Mr. Evans showed it to him after he finished playing Legos. The bed was bigger than his whole room at home. If Buddy was here they both could've stretched out in it and still had room for Mommy to cuddle with him. Of course Mommy was gone now. She wasn't ever going to cuddle with him again.

He rolled over in the big bed and blinked. Light from the stars was bright in his window, and he squinted his eyes real small so he could see them. Was heaven out there somewhere? Just past the stars and the moon? It must be, because whenever people talked about heaven they looked up. And up had to be higher than the stars and moon.

But that meant there was another problem, because the stars and moon were very far away. His teacher told him so in class before he left for Florida. And if the stars and moon were very far away, that meant his mommy in heaven was even more far away. The thinking of it made his eyes get wet again. His eyes were always wet, because it wasn't fair, that's why.

He turned over again and thought about the Evans family.

They were nice to him. Susan's Legos were better than Kody's or Carl's or any of the guys in Mrs. Watson's second grade class. It was the best collection in the world probably.

But something wasn't okay with Mrs. Evans. She was more quiet than most mommies, and he wondered if she had a hurt tummy or a head pain. His mommy got head pains sometimes, and when that happened she didn't smile very much. Of course not anymore, though. Because

Ramey said in heaven you had no more pains or tears.

He smiled a little at that thought, because he was glad his mommy wouldn't have head pains ever again.

The voices down the hall got louder than before, and Max had an idea. Maybe he could walk sneaky quiet out of the room and listen to what they were saying. He liked to do that sometimes when his mommy was on the phone, or when Christmas was coming and she had a friend over to help her wrap stuff.

But this was different. This was someone else's house and maybe they wouldn't like seeing him in the hall sneaky quiet, listening to what they were saying. But he really wanted to hear. Because maybe they were talking about him, and how he was feeling, and maybe if he heard their words, he could pop his head into the room for a minute and tell them himself.

The more he thought about the idea, the better it seemed. Finally, he slipped his feet out of the giant bed and lifted them one at a time, as sneaky quiet as he could go. He opened the door with careful hands and pushed his head into the hallway. It was dark except for a light at the end.

Max was pretty sure that was Elizabeth's room down there.

He took more quiet steps until he was only a very little bit from Elizabeth's door. Then he stopped and leaned against the wall. His breathing was loud and so was his heartbeep. He waited for both of them to quiet down, then he started listening.

"I still don't understand."

Max did a big nod from his spot out in the hallway. Yep, that was Elizabeth. She had an older voice than Susan, plus also she was more serious. Serious meant you had a little trouble laughing about things.

Mrs. Evans made a sort of hurt sound. "Elizabeth, I've explained it the best way I know how. Daddy was friends with Max's mother. She was killed in a plane crash two weeks ago, and in her will she asked that Max be given a chance to spend a few weeks with us."

"In her will? Doesn't that seem a little strange to you, Mother?"

Max's heart started beeping louder. Were they fighting? About him? He looked down at his chest. *Okay, listen, heart . . . be quiet down there.* He said the words in his head, and he breathed out hard, the way he'd seen Ramey do when she was upset. It worked, too, because his heartbeep got a little more quiet.

"Yes, Elizabeth, it seems strange to me. But it's the truth. Max's mother wrote a letter and asked her attorney to find Daddy. She wanted Max to spend two weeks here before he goes on with his life in Hawaii."

Silent sounds came for a minute. "Did Daddy like Max's mother?"

"Of course he liked her, honey. They were friends."

"Not that kind of like, Mommy. You know . . . did he *like* her? Like a girl-friend?"

Outside in the hallway, Max held his breath. He had wondered the same thing. His mommy never seemed to have a boy-friend, but maybe Mr. Evans had been that for her. He made his breathing as quiet as he could.

"Look, Elizabeth, it's late. You need to go to bed."

"Okay, but I don't like it. What if Daddy did love Max's mother? What if he wishes he was with her?"

"The woman's dead, Elizabeth. There's no need to worry about Daddy wanting to be with her now."

"Not now, but before."

"Elizabeth, stop. Go to bed before I lose my patience."

The tears were back, and Max felt them hot against his cheek. He didn't want either Elizabeth or Mrs. Evans to see him crying, so he made fast, quiet steps down the hall and back to the big bed. Elizabeth and Mrs. Evans had been fighting about him. He knew it.

What he didn't understand was why? Why did they sound like they were mad at his mommy? If she and Mr. Evans were friends, then that should mean they would like her better, not worse.

The light from outside was still bright, so he reached under his pillow and pulled out his Bible. Ramey had tucked four things between the pages. A letter for Mrs. Evans, a letter for him, a picture of Buddy, and a picture of his mom. He set down the letter for Mrs. Evans on the edge of the pillow. Then he took the other letter and opened it. Ramey wrote it in big words so he could read it all by himself.

Dear Max,
Read this when you are sad and then you will feel glad. I love you and your mom loves you and Jesus loves you. Your mom used to tell you a little

song. You can sing it now if you like.
You are not alone, Max.

                                    Love, Ramey

Max dried his tears on his pajama sleeve
and gave a little nod at the letter. Ramey
was right. He should sing his special song
from his mommy. With quiet words, he did
a small throat clear and began to sing.

"I love you, Max, the most, I love to
make you toast . . ."

He wanted to finish, but a ball was in his
singing throat. Because he missed Mommy
so much, that's why. Not just his heart and
his hands and his feet missed her, but his
eyes missed her, too. Because every time
he wanted to see her, she was never there.
He missed her so much he could almost
feel her there beside him. That's when he
remembered the last part of the song.

When oceans we're apart, I'm right here in
your heart.

That's right! He sniffed some and dried
his tears again. She used to tell him that all
the time. And heaven was at least oceans
apart. He did four fast breaths and folded
Ramey's letter back into the envelope. As
long as his mommy was in his heart, he
could look at the next special thing.

He pulled out the picture of Buddy. The

dog's eyes seemed to say, "Hi, Max, I miss you."

"Hey, Buddy . . . I miss you, too. Hope you're being good for Ramey."

He counted in his mind for a minute. "Thirteen more days and I'll see you again, Buddy. I'll be there as soon as I can." He gave the picture a little pat and returned it to the right page in his Bible.

Finally, he took out the picture of his mother.

She was the most beautiful mommy in the whole world. She had hugging hands, and a happy face, and eyes that laughed when he did something silly. She had strong arms for throwing a ball with him, and good legs for running on the beach.

No one would ever be prettier than his mommy.

He studied the picture for a long time, then he remembered the last part of his song one more time. *When oceans we're apart, I'm right here in your heart.*

A little yawn slipped from his mouth, and he snuggled back down into the covers. He put the Bible with his other special things back up on the shelf, and accidentally knocked the letter for Mrs. Evans onto the floor. But that was okay. He could get it in the morning.

The only thing he kept out was the picture of his mother. Before he fell asleep, he kissed his mommy on the face, and smiled at her. "I love you. I hope God tells you I said hi."

Then he held the picture against his heart and tried to imagine her there, right inside him, telling him everything was going to be okay. *Be brave and strong, Max,* he could hear her saying. *Brave and strong. Everything's going to be okay.*

Max closed his eyes with the picture still up against him and his mother's face and words in his head. His mother's special song in his heart. By the time he fell asleep, he had almost forgotten about Mrs. Evans and her daughter, Elizabeth, and the fact that maybe they didn't like him or his mom. Instead he slept with just one thought in his head.

Mommy wasn't far away at all. Because the thing she'd always told him was true. Whenever he wanted her to be with him, she was. Right there in his heart where she would always be.

EIGHTEEN

The trying conversation with Elizabeth over, Michele tucked her into bed. But the moment her daughter lay down, the questions came again.

"So you think they were just good friends? Max's mother and Daddy?"

Michele dropped to the side of her bed. "It was a long time ago, honey. All I know is she and Daddy were friends."

The lie grated against her tongue and brought up a host of questions in Michele's own mind. What would the girls think if they ever find out? Would understanding how their father fell be more difficult knowing that they were lied to? That the boy sleeping in the room down the hall wasn't only the son of their daddy's friend, but their daddy's son, too?

And how was she supposed to go camping on Monday morning? An entire week at the lake, pretending her life wasn't falling apart? Michele couldn't think of a single reason why she should go. She reached out and massaged Elizabeth's shoulders. The girl felt stiff and tense, further proof of everything she'd guessed to be true about the boy's arrival. The girls were confused, of course. Elizabeth the most because she was older, old enough to wonder why, if the boy's mother and her father were such good friends, hadn't she been to the house once?

"Lie down with me, Mommy. Please." Elizabeth caught Michele's hand and cuddled it close to her face. "I can't sleep."

Of the many changing patterns that had come about since she'd had knowledge of the boy, this was one of them. Sleeping next to Elizabeth or Susan in their double beds, instead of spending a night awake and restless lying next to Connor.

"Okay." Michele squeezed her daughter's hand. "Move over."

Elizabeth slid to the other side of the bed, and Michele lay on the comforter beside her. When she was settled, she rubbed Elizabeth's back until the muscles along her spine began to relax. Michele turned off the bedside light and let her eyes adjust to the darkness.

"How come no one ever told us about

her?" Elizabeth lifted her head off the pillow high enough to make eye contact.

Michele's heart felt limp and drained, too weary to respond. She sucked in a quiet breath and tried to stall. "About who?"

"The woman." Impatience stirred in Elizabeth's voice. "Daddy's friend, the one who died. How come no one ever told us about her before?"

"Because." Michele gazed at the darkened ceiling. "They were friends when you were just a baby."

"But friends stay that way forever, right? How come they were friends back then and not now?"

Michele leaned up on one elbow. "Elizabeth." She couldn't answer another question if it involved the spelling of her own name. "I found out about your dad's friend the day before you did." She made an effort to keep her voice gentle. "Now, let's get some sleep. We can talk tomorrow."

"Okay." Elizabeth allowed her head to fall back to the pillow. She yawned and her voice was tired. "Sweet dreams."

"You, too, honey."

"I love you, Mom."

"Love you, Elizabeth."

With so many aspects of life suddenly foreign and uncomfortable, the familiar back-and-forth exchange with her oldest daughter was the only part of the night that felt right.

Connor was home, but last she'd seen him he was on the back porch. The place where he sat for hours lately, staring across their backyard, ignoring the way she was dying as she roamed around their house alone. Michele's heart skipped into an irregular beat, as though even her body couldn't remember how to act, in light of what had happened.

What was he thinking, sitting out there all that time? Was he asking himself if it had been worth it, passing the time in a stranger's bed when he had a family back home? Was he wondering how she was handling the news, whether their relationship would ever be the same again?

Maybe he was thinking about the boy, how strong the resemblance was between him and his father and himself. Or was it worse? Was he relishing the idea of finally having a son, masterminding a way to keep him longer than two weeks?

She could hardly be upset with Elizabeth. A dozen questions flashed in her own mind at least every few minutes. And the fact was, she and Connor weren't speaking enough for her to know the answers to any of them. A few times he'd pulled her aside and tried to talk to her. "Quit it, will you, Michele?" He took her hand and led her into the laundry room earlier that day, his face tight, etched with a kind of concern he'd never shown in all the years they'd been married. "You're treating me like a stranger."

She worked her hand free from his. "You are, Connor. Until a week ago, the man I've known and loved had been nothing but faithful and honest and true." She lowered her voice and gestured in his direction. "So give me time, okay? This . . . this man you really are is someone I don't know, not even a little."

"I haven't changed." His words held a quiet desperation. "It was one mistake, Michele. One mistake."

"Well, excuse me for not jumping right into my new reality and knowing how to swim in it." Her tone was callous and filled with hate. "I'm drowning, Connor. Give me a little space so I can figure out how to get to shore."

She'd walked out then, unable, unwilling, to look at him another moment. The rest of the day they'd avoided each other, and now that it was so late, she doubted they'd speak until tomorrow. And then what? Were they supposed to get up early and get ready for church, as though this Sunday wasn't entirely different from any other they'd faced as a family? Was she supposed to help the girls pick out nice clothes, and curl Elizabeth's hair? Get herself into something that didn't make her look too heavy, and then head off to the ten o'clock service pretending that the boy with them was nothing more than a cute little visitor, a family friend?

The idea made her tired, but not quite tired enough to fall asleep. She directed her attention to Elizabeth, and heard the tender rhythmic breathing sound the child had always made whenever she slept. Careful not to disturb her, Michele slid her feet onto the floor and tiptoed from the room.

Being tired was one thing; finding the sort of sleep she'd known before the news was another. She closed Elizabeth's door behind her and peeked in through an adjacent one at Susan. Her youngest girl was sprawled out across her bed, legs and arms widespread in varying directions. Susan had always been a restless sleeper, and having the boy in their home had done nothing to alter her normal routine.

The fact allowed a single ray of peace to shine a dim light across Michele's soul.

She took a few more steps and stopped at the door of the guest room. Without really wanting to, she went partway in, far enough to see the boy curled up and sleeping. He looked lost on the oversized bed, and for the first time since he'd arrived, Michele felt a twinge of pity for him. The thing she'd been telling herself since finding out about him was true, after all.

The mess they were in wasn't his fault.

She took a step closer. He was holding something to his chest, something Michele couldn't make out in the shadows. Probably a favorite toy, or stuffed bear. A special blanket even. Something to remind him of home. She let her eyes adjust to the light in the room and imagined how the boy must feel.

His mother had been taken from him without warning. In the days since, he'd been forced to live full-time with a babysitter, and then hop on a plane — the same kind of plane that had taken his mother's life — and travel across the ocean for a visit with a family he'd never known existed. Perfect strangers, really.

Yet if she was honest with herself, he was

handling the situation better than she was. She stared at him a moment longer. Something made her want to go to him, brush the lock of hair out of his eyes, and whisper to him that everything would be okay one day. That no one blamed him for the strange circumstances they were in.

But she stopped herself.

Nothing good could come from letting herself feel for the boy. Merely looking at him, connecting with those green eyes and that beautiful complexion, was enough to make her sick to her stomach. Not because of anything he'd done, obviously, but because his mother had managed to seduce the only man she'd ever loved.

Michele swallowed a lump in her throat. The woman she detested was the same one the boy cherished every waking moment.

She turned and left the room. What good could she ever do the boy when she felt that way about his mother? She padded down the hallway and into her bedroom. It was dark, but light from the hallway spilled halfway across the floor. Enough to see her way around, and with silent steps she went to the mirrored sliding doors that hid the closet she shared with Connor.

The mirrors were kind, the way only a few mirrors were.

When she needed to feel good about the way she looked she avoided the bathroom mirror and the one standing in an oak frame at the corner of their room. The mirrors in their foyer were no better. But the sliders . . . the sliders were far more friendly, making the too-curvy parts of her body look long and slender and almost beautiful.

She went there now and scrutinized her image in the semidarkness, first the side view, then the full front image her body made. Her pants stopped short above the ankle, Capri pants, they were called, a way to dress for the increasingly warmer weather without showing her legs. She angled her head and took in the way they made her legs look. The effect was supposed to be slimming, but was it? Really?

And what had happened to her plans to lose weight before the camping trip? Back in February she'd written out yet another eating plan, one she'd put together from the dozens of diet books she'd read over the years. Eggs in the morning, tuna salad and an apple at lunch, chicken and vegetables for dinner. She'd written it all out, calculated that if she followed that type of a plan and ate only a handful of raw almonds or a piece of string cheese when she was hungry between meals, she should lose at least two pounds a week. Maybe five pounds early on, since the first week always showed the most impressive loss.

Michele smoothed the material where it covered her hips. The fleshy feel of her body beneath her fingers actually turned her stomach. What had gone wrong? She hadn't only planned out the meals and written a list of the things she wouldn't go near — Oreo cookies in the afternoon and ice cream after dinner — she'd made a schedule about what to eat and when to pray for strength, and what she'd weigh week by week in the time leading up to the camping trip. If she'd stayed with it, if she'd eaten no sugar and no white flour, and kept her calories at roughly twelve hundred or less each day, then by now she'd be back to her wedding weight.

Thirty pounds lighter.

She thought back to the days after she'd made the plan. Days one and two were strong, doable, the way they often were. But by the third day she'd felt a strange sense of confidence, as if somehow handling the rest of the scheduled diet days would be a breeze now that she'd gone forty-eight hours without sugar.

The memory became clearer in her

mind. They'd been at an open house for Elizabeth's class. One of the parents had made oversized chocolate chip cookies, and the entire room pulsed with the smell.

"Be sure to try Mrs. Edwards's cookies," the teacher advised them. "Her recipe won first place at the Palm Beach County Fair last year."

And there it was. A reason to try the cookies — just a taste. She joined the others gathered around the tray of baked goods and slipped three cookies into her napkin. One for Susan, one for Elizabeth, and one for Connor. She took a piece off Connor's cookie just to say she'd tried it, then offered him the rest.

But he only shook his head and flashed her a smile. "Thanks, hon, but I'm okay. Too much dinner."

Michele gave a light shrug and turned to the girls. Only Susan accepted a cookie. The other two Michele folded into a napkin and set in her purse. But throughout the night she broke off and ate small pieces, and by the end of the evening, she'd eaten both cookies.

After that she noticed that the tray still held more, so when Connor was busy talking to one of the other parents, she worked her way back to the table, took two more cookies, and wrapped them in the napkin in her purse same as before. That way if Connor or the girls saw her, they'd think the cookies were the same ones they'd turned down. Not Michele's third and fourth cookie for the evening.

By the time she went home that night, she'd eaten six cookies, and was suffering from indigestion and a bad case of regret. So bad that she'd beaten herself into the wee morning hours, confirming everything that had ever been true about her and her struggle with weight. She was a wretch for not being strong enough, a weak-willed carbohydrate addict who would easily trade a thin future for a handful of chocolate chip cookies. She would never be thin, never lose the extra weight, never wear the clothes she wanted to wear.

The tape in her head played for hours, and the next day she simply hadn't had the strength to try again. Forget diets, she'd told herself in the morning. Eat healthy food, healthy amounts, and eventually the weight would come off. By that evening when she was eating ice cream with Connor and the girls, the critical voice in her head was little more than a distant memory.

Michele turned sideways and stared at

herself again. How many years had she wasted worrying about her weight? And why had she let a handful of cookies stop her from meeting her goal? Up a few pounds, down a few. The same rut she'd been caught in since being pregnant with Elizabeth.

Back then, Connor offered to help her, work out with her, or help make sure the house held only nutritious foods. But his offers only made her feel unattractive and self-conscious, as though he was watching every bite she ate. Finally one day after she'd gone shopping for clothes four sizes larger than before, Connor pulled her aside.

"What can I do, Michele?" The concern in his eyes had been genuine. "You're still beautiful to me, but I can see how miserable you feel. Tell me how to help and I'll do whatever you need."

Michele had leveled her gaze at him, hoping he would see that her anger wasn't directed at him, but at herself. "Stop talking about it."

His expression went blank. "Stop talking about it?"

"Yes." She reached out and took his hand. "I have to figure it out, okay? Every time you say something I think I'm . . . I don't know, ugly in your eyes."

He lowered his eyebrows and came to her, taking her in his arms and holding her for a long while. "I've never thought that a day in my life, Michele. You're the most beautiful woman I know." He kissed her. "So what if you've gained a little weight? No one would ever call you heavy or think you had a problem."

"Well, *I* do." Tears filled her eyes. "Obviously, I do. You know how I used to look." She sniffed hard and pulled back enough to look into his eyes. "I'm just saying it would be better if the changes came from me, without you talking about it."

"At all?"

"At all. It'll be my thing."

The memory broke into fragments and disappeared.

That had been nine years ago. Nine years and not once had she made good on her promise to Connor. Every plan she'd ever tried had ended in failure, while she survived by justifying her eating habits.

She would tell herself that she didn't need to diet because she'd stayed about the same weight since having the girls, or she'd remind herself that occasionally she'd still pass some man on the street and feel him smile appreciatively at her. She was still

272

nice looking, still knew how to dress to make the most of her strong points, her long legs and thick, dark hair. As long as she wasn't gaining ten pounds a year, why fret over it?

But nothing she told herself changed the overwhelming truth.

She hated being overweight, hated having a closet of clothes that didn't fit her. She frowned at her reflection again and felt her stomach turn. In nine years she hadn't once been successful in her battle to lose weight.

No wonder Connor had slept with another woman.

A thought flashed in her mind. Maybe it wasn't her weight; maybe it was something more, something deeper. Something she had done that might have pushed Connor away.

But the thought was gone before it could take root. She'd done nothing more than eat too much. And that was damage enough.

Michele slid the door open, flipped on the closet light, and walked to her section of summer clothes. Four pairs of Capri pants, three pairs of shorts, and a handful of short-sleeve blouses. Tomorrow she'd have to draw from that collection in order to pack for the camping trip.

She pictured how the scene would probably play out.

Connor would be glued to Max, teaching him how to bait a hook or ride a jet ski, all the while no doubt seeing the boy's mother every time their eyes met. Whoever she was, Michele was certain she'd been thin and striking. Otherwise her husband wouldn't have been tempted to sleep with her.

Michele stared at her reflection again. And what about her?

She was about to spend a week with Connor, knowing that every time he looked at her he was likely wondering why she was still wearing bigger sizes, not the petite sizes worn by the flight attendant. The thought of that left her trembling with fury.

The clothes hanging before her looked like prison issue outfits she'd be forced to wear as punishment for not taking matters into her own hands and doing what she'd said she would do. She backed away, stepped out, and turned the light off. In the time it took her to do that, she made up her mind.

They could go without her.

Elizabeth and Susan had been looking

forward to the trip for months, so they could still go. But certainly it didn't matter if she didn't come along this time. She could go to her sister's house, sort through the remains of what once was a wonderful life, and see if any sort of salvage was possible.

God would be okay with that, wouldn't He?

She would take time to herself at her sister's, read the Bible the way she'd been meaning to since hearing the news about Connor's affair. Maybe if she was away from Connor she'd be able to hear God's voice above the skirmishes in her heart.

She headed out of her room and down the hallway again. Yes, a little time away from each other would be good for all of them. After all, she wasn't the one who'd been unfaithful. Let Connor sweat a little, let him wonder whether she was leaving him for a week or forever. Connor could handle all three children by himself.

The girls were wonderful campers, fully capable of putting up the tent, rolling out their sleeping bags, and fishing on the edge of the lake. They'd been able to swim and jet ski since they were kindergartners, and they weren't adventurous enough to stray from Connor.

The boy? Well, he was Connor's problem. Single parents took kids camping by themselves all the time. With every passing second the idea looked better. Why walk around camp feeling self-conscious all week, worrying if Connor was dreaming of a woman he'd been with some long-ago August? She'd rather not go and avoid the comparison.

Once her mind was made up, she expected to feel better, expected the ache in her heart to ease some. Instead it felt worse, and that left Michele disoriented and nauseous, able to see something she hadn't seen until that instant.

There would be no shortcuts climbing free of the tangled web her life had become, because the idea of spending a week away from Connor hurt just as much as spending a week with him. All of which meant that even if she hated herself for it, even if it made her feel desperate and trapped and hopeless, at least for now one truth remained. It was a truth that surprised her.

She was still in love with her husband.

NINETEEN

In the end, Connor did everything he could to talk her into going on the trip.

Though they missed the service, he met with the pastor Sunday afternoon. He explained the situation and how his night with Kiahna had been a mistake. "The thing is" — Connor leaned forward in the chair opposite the pastor and took hold of the armrests — "it could've happened to anyone. It was a series of bad choices, and it's in the past."

"Not for Michele." The pastor was in his early seventies. He preached only once a month, handing over the pulpit most weeks to his younger associate. His voice was scratchy and unhurried. "For Michele it happened two weeks ago."

"I realize that, but I messed up just once. Now she's questioning everything, our entire marriage."

The pastor stared at him for a while.

"Why are you here, Mr. Evans?"

"I need help." Connor raked his fingers through his hair. "We leave for vacation tomorrow, and she doesn't want to go with us. All because of Max."

"I suspect she's troubled by more than Max."

"Look." Connor glanced at his watch. He'd come to the man for a quick fix, advice that might clear the fog of confusion and make everything right again. "I can't do anything about the past. And she doesn't want to talk about it, anyway." He exhaled in a short burst through his teeth. "Her attitude's bringing all of us down. I know she's hurt, but that woman meant nothing to me. It was an accident and it's long over. Everything's been fine for years. How can I make Michele forgive?"

"Only God can do that, but I can give you a hint . . ." He settled back in his chair, his gnarled hands folded across his lap the way he might look if he were praying. "It'll start with you."

With me? Anger filled Connor's senses. He clenched his jaw and then in sudden defeat he gave up and released a soft chuckle. The pastor obviously hadn't heard a word he'd said. "With me?"

The man gave a slow nod. "Yes. With you."

"Okay." Connor chuckled again. "Whatever."

They exchanged a few more words, but the conversation was over. Michele didn't understand him, and neither did the pastor. He'd have to figure a way out of the mess he was in without anyone's help.

As he left the church office, Connor shot a look at the scattered clouds above him. "God . . . looks like it's You and me on this one."

The statement was only half serious, and Connor heard no audible answer, no strong sense of knowing deep within him. If God had been listening to his prayers, he never would have run across Kiahna in the first place. Connor climbed in his car and strapped on his determination.

He would get home and do what he could to convince Michele to come with them.

When he found her in their bedroom half an hour later, he reminded her that their time with Max wouldn't be an actual trial run if she wasn't there; and he added that Elizabeth and Susan would certainly find it strange that their mother had taken a private vacation instead of joining the family at the lake.

By Sunday night, he resorted to begging.

"Please, Michele. Come with us." He found her standing at the rail on the balcony off their second-story bedroom, but still she kept her back to him. "I need you there."

She lifted her chin and stared at the dusky horizon, beyond the row of houses that made up their neighborhood. "I can't."

Anger splashed itself against the moment. "I've never asked much of you, Michele. But just this once —"

"*What?*" She spun around and faced him, her eyes wide. "*You've* never asked much of *me?*" She laughed in that new, acid way he'd come to expect. "You asked me to wait at home for weeks on end while you flew from Los Angeles to Honolulu . . . nine months of that, Connor. You asked me to care for our girls, keep up our home, and never stop praying that you'd get reassigned back in Florida. On top of all that you asked me to be faithful, and guess what? I was, Connor. Sure, it was lonely, but always I knew that someday you'd be coming home for good." She lowered her voice. "Let's talk about what I've asked of you."

He took a step backwards, knowing what was coming, knowing that listening to her spell it out was part of his punishment.

"Just be true to me, Connor. That's all I asked. Go to work and come home still in love with only me, forever and ever." She hesitated, seeming to gain some sort of control over her anger and hurt. When she spoke again, her voice was a quiet kind of steel. Gentle, but utterly unbendable. "Don't ask me to go, Connor. I can't." Her eyebrows relaxed some, and she turned once more toward the railing. "I won't."

She spent the night with one of the girls again, and made sure they were packed. He took care of himself and Max, and when it came time for bed, he tucked the boy in with a smile that took every ounce of his effort. "Excited about the trip?"

"Yes, sir." The boy pulled the covers up to his chin. Neither his tone nor his expression gave away any of what he might be feeling.

Connor sat on the edge of the boy's bed and pursed his lips. "Max . . ."

"Yes, sir?"

"You don't have to call me *sir* anymore."

A layer of formality faded from Max's eyes, but he said nothing.

"*Sir* is for strangers, and the two of us . . . well" — Connor cocked his head to the side and grinned at the boy — "we're more like good friends who never got to meet until this week. Okay?"

Max made a little gulping sound. He nodded his head a few times. "Okay."

In the moonlight, the boy's face, the angles and curves of it, were so like his own, so like his father's. He'd been too busy handling Michele to take time simply to study the child and marvel at the fact that the boy was his.

"Mr. Evans?"

"Yes, Max." He gave himself permission to run his fingertips along the boy's forehead, the side of his face, the way he had always done with Elizabeth and Susan.

"Could you give me my Bible? I forgot to look at it before bedtime."

His Bible? Hearing that sent a ray of guilt through Connor's heart. His son had a Bible? One he read every night? He blinked, for the moment unable to do anything but let that single fact work its way through him. What about his own Bible, lying dusty and unread upstairs in the bookcase near his bed? How long had it been since reading it was a priority? And how many hundreds of other little details did he not know about his own son?

"Mr. Evans?"

Connor jumped a little and scanned the bureau near Max's bed. There, on top, was a white book with the words *My First Bible* written in yellow, kidlike lettering across the top. Even before he picked it up, he could see that letters or photographs were stuck between the pages. He was careful as he moved it from the bureau to Max.

"Thanks."

"You're welcome."

Max held the Bible to his chest and gave Connor a look. Though he had only known the boy for a few days, Connor could sense that he was asking him to be a part of this nighttime routine. At least for tonight.

Connor twisted the button on the small bedside lamp so Max could see the words. "What part are you at?"

The corners of Max's mouth rose a bit. He sat up and leaned against the headboard, then he opened the book, took a handful of things from it, and set them on his lap. "I already read about John the Baptist." He kept his eyes on the book, studying the pages with an intensity that reminded Connor of himself.

After flipping through most of the Bible,

Max stopped and pointed to one of the pages. "I'm here." He looked up at Connor. "The Sermon on the Mount."

"Could you read it to me?"

"Sure." Max pulled himself up a little straighter and brought the book closer so he could see the words. " 'Jesus knew that the people needed Him. They needed His words so that their hearts would be right. One day He went to a place in the mountains and began to talk to the people . . .' "

Max kept reading, but Connor was no longer listening. His heart was stuck back on the first part, where Jesus knew that the people needed His words so that their hearts would be right. How simple was that? Simple and sound and true beyond anything Connor had told himself in the past ten years.

When was the last time he'd had those profound truths in the forefront of his mind? Back when he met Michele and the two of them began dating, definitely. But when had he stopped? When had he chosen to get through a week or even a day without God's words to guide him? And how come bells hadn't gone off, alarms to signal the fact that without the wisdom Jesus gave, he was bound to fall?

If his heart had been right that summer

eight years ago, he never would've been unfaithful, never. Tempted, maybe, but he would have seen the way out, the way promised by God Himself. But then, he wouldn't have this wonder child sitting before him to remind him of everything he'd forgotten.

Connor let the thought pass. It was a little late to be thinking about where he'd gone wrong with God. Even if he could figure it out, he wasn't sure where that would leave him now. He'd lied to Michele for nearly eight years. It was hardly time to pretend he could be counted among the godly.

Max was finishing up, talking about love and how it was the greatest command of all. Connor studied the boy, the way he read quickly and with voice inflection. Whatever Max had lacked growing up without a father, Kiahna had obviously done her best to make up for it.

" '. . . And this is what I want you to do.' " Max turned the page and looked up at Connor. "This isn't from the Sermon on the Mount, but it's my favorite part." His eyes fell to the book again. " 'I want you to love Me and love each other. This is the most important thing, that you love each other.' " He let his eyes fall to the bottom of the page, then he looked up at Connor. "Then there's a question time, but I'll read them in the morning."

"You read in the morning, too?" Connor shifted some. God might as well have shone a spotlight at him, searching his heart for a reaction to his son's faithfulness. Connor crossed his arms and bit the inside of his lip. The boy's example was more than Connor could absorb.

"Yes." Max closed the Bible. His expression was as open and earnest as an angel's. "Mommy says the days are better when you start them with Jesus." A shadow fell over his face and his eyes grew damp. "She used to say that, I mean."

The words caught Connor by surprise. His heart scraped along the ground for a few seconds and he reached for Max's hand. He needed to take things slow with the boy, build a friendship with care, especially since chances were he was going home in two weeks. Connor searched his face, the well of sorrow and fear there, and with everything in him he wanted to take the boy in his arms and rock away the pain.

But he forced himself to hold back. Neither of them would benefit by making that kind of connection, only to lose it.

Instead he nodded to the few things on Max's lap. "What do you have there?"

The sorrow faded and the boy's eyes held a sparkle Connor hadn't seen yet. "My special things."

"I see." Connor resisted the urge to stare at them, figure out what might be so special to his son. "Special things are good."

Max picked them up and held them with a care that went beyond his seven years. "Want to see?"

"Really?"

"Sure." Max shrugged. "Special things are okay to share." He picked up the first item, a dog-eared Polaroid photo, and held it out for Connor to see. "This is my bestest friend, Buddy."

Again the child's words were like a sucker punch to the center of his conscience. His friend, Buddy. The dog Connor had refused to allow to come. One more reason for the sorrow that came and went in Max's eyes. Connor exhaled through his teeth. "He looks like a great dog."

"He is." Max gave the photo a sad smile. "The best."

Connor's throat was too tight to speak. Seeing Max's special things was going to be more difficult than he'd thought. Because with each one, Max was giving him a glimpse of his heart, his little world. A part that would stay with Connor forever, even if the child sitting across from him had to go.

Max placed the photo of Buddy at the bottom of the small stack and picked up the next item. "This is from Ramey. It's a letter telling me to be good and remember the things my mommy told me. Especially our song."

Connor couldn't stop himself from asking. "Your song?"

"Yes." Max looked up again.

This time the protective layers he'd come with were gone, and Connor could see straight to the boy's soul. "Did your mom make it up?" Connor's voice fell some, respectful in a way that seemed appropriate given the level of importance Max's special song clearly held for him.

"Mm-hmm." Max looked back at the envelope from Ramey. For a moment he seemed to consider whether he might sing the song for Connor, but then he sifted the smudged white envelope to the bottom and took hold of the third and final item. "This is a picture of my mommy." He studied it before lifting it up to Connor. "You're her friend, so you already know what she looks like, but you can see it anyway."

Connor wanted to close his eyes, but it was too late. It hadn't occurred to him that one of the special things would be a picture of Kiahna. And now . . . now his eyes fell on her image and in a rush every memory of her came back. She looked the way he remembered her. But the picture brought into focus the tiny details he'd forgotten over time. The way her green eyes took up half her face, and her striking figure.

The picture showed her sitting on a log in some kind of forest setting, but as Connor looked at it he could see her at the airport restaurant, the way she'd looked when the two of them first met, the way she'd looked when they left together looking for a place to talk and —

He swallowed and directed his gaze back at Max. "She's very pretty."

"I know." Max looked at the photo again. "I think she'll be pretty in heaven, too." He lifted his eyes to Connor. "Don't you?"

Connor was grateful Michele was nowhere nearby. "Yes, Max." He patted the boy's hand. "I'm sure she'll be very pretty in heaven."

Max made a neat stack of his three special things and stuck them back in his Bible. Then he handed the book back to Connor. "Thanks for letting me look at it. I know it's late."

A Bible from his mother, two photos, and a letter reminding him what was important. The most precious things his son owned. Again Connor couldn't make his throat squeeze out the words. He took the book, set it back, and turned off the light.

Max yawned as he slid back beneath the covers. "When do we leave tomorrow?"

"Early." Connor took Max's hand and gave it a gentle squeeze. "I'll wake you and the girls in time to eat breakfast." He gave the boy another smile. "A good breakfast is the first part of taking a camping trip to the lake."

"Then what?"

"You mean, what happens after we get to camp?"

"Yeah, do we build a tent?"

Connor searched the boy's face. "You've never camped before, have you?"

"No." His eyes fell. "Mommy said we'd go, but we . . . we ran out of time." He looked up again. "What do we do when we get there?"

"First . . ." Connor coughed to clear the

emotions from his throat. "We'll set up camp. The tents are already made, but they need poles so they can stand up. Then we'll make up our beds, and put the food away, and probably do some fishing."

"Wow." Max's mouth hung open.

"I know, it's a lot." Connor smoothed out the wrinkles in the bedspread. "That's why we have to get up early."

Max was quiet for a beat. When he spoke, his voice was a mix of fear and concern. "What about Mrs. Evans? Isn't she getting up early, too?"

"Well . . ." Connor took in a sharp breath through his nose. "Mrs. Evans isn't going with us this year."

"That's what I thought." Max's eyebrows bunched together. "It's 'cause of me. She doesn't like me, right?"

Connor closed his eyes just long enough to gather his thoughts. When he opened them, he looked through the dark shadows of the room, straight to Max's soul. "No. It's not because of you, Max." Anger flashed inside him, but Connor ignored it. He could be mad at Michele later. "Mrs. Evans doesn't like to fish all that much, see. And this week her sister wanted her to come for a visit." Again Connor forced a smile for the boy. "So it worked out just fine. You and the girls and I will go camping, and Mrs. Evans can go see her sister."

Max's eyebrows stayed low and together. "Really?"

"Really."

"Okay." The frown eased some. "I wish she was coming with us."

"Me, too, Max." This time, Connor spoke despite the lump in his throat, but his voice was little more than a whisper. "Me, too."

TWENTY

The plans for Michele's trip to see her sister came together by Sunday night.

Once Elizabeth and Susan were packed and in bed, she worked from their home office. Connor was helping Max, no doubt. Earlier that day Connor finally gave up on changing her mind, and now he seemed content to keep his distance.

Convincing the girls hadn't been as easy.

"If you're not going, I'm not, either." Elizabeth had dug her fists into her waist, her eyes angry and narrowed. "You can't do this, Mom! We've been planning it for a year."

"I'll go next time." Michele kept her voice calm, hoping the girls would see her resolve and give up.

"But it won't be right without you." Susan sat on the edge of Elizabeth's bed for the discussion. "You're a better jet ski driver than Dad."

"Yeah, and plus he'll be busy with that

Max kid." Other than the first hour or so, Elizabeth still hadn't warmed up to the stranger in their house.

"He'll be with all three of you." Michele remembered to smile. She flipped the lid of the girls' suitcase open. "The important thing is that you have a good time. You don't need me for that."

"But you *never* do this." Elizabeth was bent almost in half, her cheeks red. She raised her hands and dropped them again. "It's just wrong, Mom. We're not a family without you."

"Okay." Michele set a pile of shorts into the suitcase, stood, and faced the girls. "You want the truth?"

"Yes!" Their voices came in stereo, equally hurt and frustrated.

"I want Daddy to have a chance to get to know Max." Michele didn't blink. She left out the part about not being able to stomach the idea of having to live up to the memory of an island affair, or not wanting to watch Connor fall in love with the woman's son.

Susan was on her feet. "He can get to know Max if you're there, Mommy."

"No." Michele crossed the room and set her hand on Susan's shoulder. "It'll go better without me. Besides, I haven't seen

294

Aunt Margie in almost a year. I need this time with her." She looked from Susan to Elizabeth and back again. "Okay?"

"Are we still going to Wisconsin this summer?" Resignation rang in Elizabeth's voice.

"Of course." She stretched out her arms, inviting the girls to come close for a group hug. "That vacation will just be our family, no friends along."

The girls exchanged a look, and Elizabeth took the lead. "Okay." She huffed a drawn-out, exaggerated sigh. "I still don't think it's right, but if that's what you want to do . . ."

"Besides, you know how Dad is . . ." Michele gave first Susan a kiss on her cheek, and then did the same for Elizabeth. "You'll be able to stay up later and eat twice as many s'mores as usual."

Susan allowed a grin. "Yeah."

"And we'll all be together again in a week."

A scowl still shadowed Elizabeth's face, but she lifted one shoulder. "We'll miss you."

"I'll miss you, too." Michele returned to the suitcase. "But think of all we'll have to talk about when we get back."

Michele slept very little that night, but

made up for it on the flight out west. She arrived in LA before three that afternoon, and two hours later she was northbound on the Ventura Freeway, the ocean on her left, mountains on her right, and Santa Barbara just five minutes away.

Margie Bailey and her husband, Sean, lived in Santa Barbara on a craggy plateau overlooking the Pacific Ocean on one side, and the hilly entrance to the Santa Ynez Valley on the other. The house was more of an estate, situated behind gated walls and giving Margie and Sean the privacy they wanted, despite the congestion that had come to mark most of the city.

Sean was a plastic surgeon. Margie met him at Westmont, a small, private Christian college on the south side of Santa Barbara. Sean's hours allowed him ample downtime to hike and bicycle and vacation with Margie. The two were content with having no children, and together they planned to spend the rest of their lives on California's central coast.

Despite their different lifestyles, Michele and Margie shared the faith they'd been raised with and a relationship stronger than time. They were also close to their brother, Paul, but the two sisters shared a bond so strong that they liked to say when

296

Margie was sick, Michele came down with a fever, or if Michele was having a hard day, Margie got a headache. Michele was eighteen months older, nicknamed *Mitch* when Margie was learning to speak. Michele hadn't told Margie about Connor's affair or the plane crash or the little boy staying at their house. The sum of the information seemed too big to condense into a single telephone conversation. So when Michele decided to forgo the camping trip, a visit with Margie was the perfect alternative.

Without talking about it, neither she nor Connor had made any attempt to get up for church on Sunday. Instead, she called Margie, explaining only that she needed to get away for a week, and that she wasn't going with her family on the camping trip.

"Something happened."

"Yes." Michele massaged the bridge of her nose to keep from giving in to the tears. "We'll talk about it when I get there."

Being the wife of a pilot meant that catching a flight wasn't a problem. She booked a standby reservation on a less popular 6:00 a.m. flight from West Palm Beach to Los Angeles International Airport. In LA she rented a car and drove to her sister's house.

Margie knew better than to ask questions right away.

They hugged, and Michele joined them for lasagna. Since Michele's encounter with the mirror the other night, she'd only picked at her food, and that evening was no exception. Four bites into her lasagna she crumpled her napkin and set it on her plate. She didn't want Margie to notice her lack of appetite, otherwise she'd get a lecture on how great she looked and how she didn't have a weight problem and definitely didn't need to starve to feel good about herself.

Not that Michele believed her. Margie hadn't gained three pounds since college, so topics involving food and excessive weight were ones they rarely discussed.

On this night, Margie didn't notice the uneaten lasagna, and Michele was relieved. They made small talk throughout the meal and afterwards during dishes. When they were finished eating, Sean muttered something about having work to do in their upstairs office. Margie kissed him and whispered a quiet thank-you, and she and Michele headed into the den to talk.

Michele took the spot at one end of their

leather sofa, and Margie took the other. They were barely seated when Margie met Michele's eyes and asked the question that had been coming all evening.

"Okay, big sister, what is it?"

"Connor's camping with three kids, not two."

Margie leaned back some. The subtle rise in her eyebrows made it clear she hadn't been expecting that answer. "Three?"

"Yes." Michele took hold of a nearby pillow and clutched it to her middle. Normally that was something she did to hide the fact that her stomach wasn't flat. But here with Margie it was the only way she knew to ward off the empty feeling in her gut. Her eyes met Margie's again. "He took the girls, and a seven-year-old boy named Max."

Margie wrinkled her nose. "Max?"

"Max is . . . he's Connor's son." Her voice cracked, and she hung her head. This wasn't the time to break down. She brought her back teeth together and sniffed. Then she found her sister's eyes once more. "Connor had an affair with the boy's mother back in 1996."

"No." Margie's face was three shades paler than before.

"Yes . . ." Nausea rose up and made further explanation impossible. "Yes, Margie."

"Connor's never loved anyone but you. The two of you are . . . you're the reason I believed in love enough to get married. Tell me you're making it up."

"I can't."

"Mitch . . . I can't believe it."

"It's true." Michele angled her head. She was still as confused as Margie about what had happened. "I wish it wasn't, but . . ." She gave a few quick shakes of her head and then all of it, every word of Connor's talk at the beach, every detail about his reaction to the boy and the way their lives had changed swept over her. And the flood of tears she'd held off threatened to drown her.

Margie said nothing. She slid over and put her arms around Michele's neck and held her until Michele could catch her breath and get enough of a grip to speak.

Then she explained everything she knew about what had happened. "There was a storm that weekend. All the planes were grounded. He met her at the airport in Honolulu; she was a flight attendant for Western Island Air." She sniffed and took a tissue from the box on the table. She wiped her nose. "I don't know how many days or hours they spent together, but they shared at least one night."

"That's all you know?" Margie sat facing her now, her eyes as wide with shock as they'd been when she first heard the news.

"I don't *want* to know more." Michele pulled her legs up and hugged her knees to her chest. "What good would that do?"

"Okay, so what happened? Why does she call now, why send her son off to your house after all these years?"

"She died." Michele felt herself sink an inch. "She was in the Western Island Air plane crash last week."

"Oh, Mitch." Margie's expression went slack, her voice dropped to a scratchy whisper. "No."

"Yes." Michele rocked a bit. The news was still so awful, she could hardly speak it. Even to Margie. "The woman left a will, asking that the attorney in charge of her estate contact Connor before putting the boy up for adoption." She paused. "He has no other family."

For a long while they said nothing. Then Margie took Michele's hand. "I'm so sorry, Mitch. You have no idea . . ."

"I have some idea." She uttered a sound that was more cry than laugh.

"But Connor isn't the cheating type . . ."

"I know."

"He wouldn't recognize a female who had something for him if she had the truth plastered on her forehead." Margie sat cross-legged. "He was the last one in the world who should've had an affair." She thought about that. "I mean, no one should have an affair, but Connor? Connor Evans?"

"Yeah." A sad sound escaped her. "I guess no one's safe."

"So . . ." Margie grew still, her normally bright eyes dark with the weight of the moment. "You're staying with him, right? I mean, you're going to work through it with him, aren't you?"

It was the first time anyone had asked her, and the first answer that came to mind frightened her. "I'm not sure."

"Mitch . . . what he did was wrong, but it was eight years ago, honey." Margie's eyes glistened. "You can't throw away what you have now over something that far back in the past. Unless . . ."

"No." Michele shook her head. "Connor says that was the only time." The words felt plastic, and for the hundredth time Michele let doubt have its way with her. "Of course, he's lied about the Hawaiian

302

flight attendant all these years. I guess he could be lying about other times."

"No, Mitch. You can't think that way."

"I don't know." Michele eased her hand away and folded her arms tight against herself. "Makes me wonder if my weight had something to do with it. I kept telling him I'd lose it on my own, but . . ." She patted her thighs. "It hasn't happened yet."

Margie gave her shoulder a small shove. "Don't be crazy. Connor's nowhere near that shallow. Whatever was going on with the two of you back then, your weight wasn't the issue."

Michele thought about that. "If not my weight, then what?"

"I'm not sure. Maybe it had nothing to do with you. Or maybe it's something God has to show you."

"Yeah, well . . ." Michele worked her fingers into fists. "Maybe Connor hasn't been attracted to me for a decade, Margie. Have you thought of that?"

"Mitch, Connor's in love with you. Maybe more since he moved back to Florida than ever before."

"Oh, yeah?" Michele allowed a sad smile. "How would you know?"

"Because . . ." Margie pulled herself up a bit straighter. "You send me pictures every Christmas. I can read the man's eyes like a book, Mitch; he's crazy about you." She reached out, caught Michele's closest hand, and squeezed it. "Don't let him go. You have the girls to think about . . . your future with Connor. Please . . ."

The conversation drifted, the two sisters alternately crying and laughing over memories from Connor and Michele's marriage. Like the wake after a funeral, Michele thought. Remembering the dead — both the good and bad times.

Margie recalled the irony when Michele told her that she'd met a pilot. "You were terrified of flying."

"I know." Michele rubbed her eyes. They were still swollen from the crying she'd done earlier. "I think that's why I fell in love with him. He was the only guy who ever made me face my fears."

"And you helped him with his."

"The delivery room, yes." Michele still had hold of the pillow. She laughed and let her head fall back a bit. "I thought for sure he'd faint the minute the doctor yelled, 'Push!' "

Every ten or fifteen minutes, the conversation would fall silent, and once Margie looked at Michele and said the thing neither of them had talked about in years.

"What about Connor's father?"

Michele's heart sank another notch. "He doesn't know." At least once a year, without Connor knowing it, Michele had called the old man, given him an update on the girls and the life the four of them were living. Always she would end the call with a plea. "Call him, Loren. Please."

The old man's answer was the same every time. "When he's ready, he'll call me. Let's leave it at that."

Michele had talked about the phone calls with Margie, so it was no surprise that she would bring him up now. "I've thought about seeing him this time, taking a drive up to Cambria and telling him what happened."

"You should." Margie rested her head against the back of the sofa. "Maybe it'll help."

"With him and Connor?"

Margie made two small lifts with her shoulders. "With all of it."

"I don't know." She was running on fumes, hungry after her half-eaten meal and working on East Coast time, three hours ahead of Margie. The idea of calling Loren Evans, telling him what had happened, seemed suddenly overwhelming. She raked her fingers along the legs of her jeans. "I'll see how I feel tomorrow."

The conversation went on for another hour and ended with the two of them holding hands and praying out loud, something Michele hadn't done since the last time she'd been with Margie.

"God, please give my big sister a miracle." Margie's voice grew tight and she hesitated a moment. "Her family needs so much healing."

When they were finished praying, they talked some more until finally there was nothing left to say. The fact that Michele was there had said it all. As she brushed her teeth and turned down the bed in the guest room, she pressed her fist against her stomach, the way she often did now to ease the knots there.

But the ache wasn't as bad as before.

Was that how powerful her memories of the past were? So strong that they could ease the pain of today? She lay in bed and wondered what Connor and the kids were doing. Still eating s'mores around the fire, no doubt. Connor would let them stay up as late as they wanted, and since he was a night owl, he'd enjoy every minute.

And what about the boy?

Was he liking his camping experience? Had the girls warmed up to him? Was

Connor falling for him? If she and Conner survived the affair, it would have to be without the boy. Michele couldn't begin to imagine a life with him in it, a reminder of Connor's unfaithfulness at every breakfast, every dinner, every family outing.

If only they could be sure the boy had a good home, a place where he'd be okay, then Connor would have an easier time letting him go. No doubt guilt was playing a role in Connor's thoughts and actions, guilt about what he'd done to Michele and the girls, yes. But guilt regarding the boy as well. After all, he'd done nothing to help the boy's mother, given no financial assistance, no emotional support.

Now that he was aware of the boy's existence, she was fairly sure Connor was struggling over not only his curiosity about having a son but also his obligation to the child. These thoughts played in Michele's mind for nearly an hour before she fell asleep.

When she woke the next morning, she had an idea. At first the idea felt sneaky and manipulative, the sort of thing she knew wouldn't be right. But by lunchtime, she'd made up her mind. Wrong or not, what she was about to do could give Connor the assurance he needed to let the boy go.

At one o'clock that afternoon she called information and found the number for Marv Ogle, the attorney in Honolulu. She was connected to the man after only a few minutes on hold.

"Marv Ogle." The voice was familiar, the one she'd heard on the answering machine before her current nightmare began. "How can I help you?"

"Mr. Ogle, this is Michele Evans, Connor's wife. Max is staying with us."

An instant warmth filled the man's voice. "Yes, how's it working out?"

"How is it?" Like sandpaper, guilt grated against her soul. She could hardly say she was giving it a try. She cleared her throat. "Things are fine, but . . . well, we were wondering what options Max has when he goes home."

"Options?"

"Yes." Michele closed her eyes and tried to believe she wasn't somehow manipulating the outcome of their two-week trial with the boy. "In other words, where would the boy live?"

"I see." Disappointment rang in the attorney's voice. "Like I told your husband, Max really has no one, Mrs. Evans. His baby-sitter loves him, but she's dying of heart disease, so that's not a permanent option." He paused. "My wife and I could take him until the state found a permanent home for him, but we're near retirement and we travel quite a bit. Our lifestyle isn't conducive to raising a young boy, you understand."

Mine isn't either, mister. Michele bit her tongue. "So what about adoption? Are you aware of anyone, any situation where a family might want him?"

"Not at this time." The attorney sighed. "I suppose I could put feelers out, let the private adoption attorneys know about him." Silence filled the phone line. "Are you saying that it isn't working, Mrs. Evans?"

Michele tightened her grip on the receiver. "Max is a lovely child." She covered her eyes with her free hand. "But taking him into our family, Mr. Evans . . . it's more than we can do." She clenched her teeth. "You understand?"

The attorney's hesitation lasted only a few seconds. "Of course. If this is something you and Mr. Evans agreed on, then I'll get to work on it right away."

"Yes." She opened her eyes and stared straight ahead, her resolve intact. "Both of us feel he'd be better off with an adoptive family." The lie tasted bitter, but she pressed on. "We'd like to know as soon as you receive any interest in him."

"Mrs. Evans." The attorney seemed at a loss for words. "Max is an older child. Interest in an older child can take some time. A year or more. Sometimes older children never get adopted. I hardly imagine we'll have interest in the next week or so."

"I realize that." She bit her lip and begged God that someone would come along, someone interested in a boy Max's age. "But please, if you hear anything, contact us right away."

Michele clicked the off button and sat unmoving, the receiver in her hand. What she'd told the attorney was true — the boy needed a different home. One in Honolulu, with a family who wanted him. Connor couldn't possibly expect her to agree to keeping the child, so if God was going to work a miracle the way she and Margie had prayed, then the call to Mr. Ogle was her way of helping make it happen.

That's what the miracle would be. Sometime in the next week the attorney would hear of a family simply desperate for a boy like Max. Connor would get word of the family's interest, and feel practically obligated to let the boy return home. It would be the perfect solution, the only way she could move ahead and rebuild the life she and Connor and the girls had always shared.

Michele stared out the window at the palm trees that lined her sister's courtyard. *Okay, God? Will You do that? Will You let that be the miracle, please?*

In response, something her sister said ran through her mind again. Whatever was going on with Connor and her back then, her weight wasn't the issue. But if it wasn't her weight, then what? What had she done to make Connor vulnerable to a woman like Kiahna Siefert?

Or maybe she hadn't done anything wrong at all. She closed her eyes and tried to picture the scene at the campground that afternoon. Connor, Elizabeth, Susan, and Max. Fishing and playing on the shore together. Riding jet skis and eating around the campfire, laughing at Connor's silly stories and having a great time.

The images made Michele sad in a deeper sort of way than anything else that evening. Not because of the bonding they were probably doing, the girls and Connor and the boy. But because if God didn't find a family for Max, if for some reason Connor chose to keep him, then a separate family vacation was hardly a temporary solution.

It could very easily become a way of life.

TWENTY-ONE

The girls and Mr. Evans were fishing from some chairs near the water, but Max wanted to find pretty rocks. Ramey liked pretty rocks, because whenever he found one walking home from the bus stop, he'd give it to her and she'd set it on the shelf by the TV.

He wanted to bring a whole bagful of pretty rocks home from his Florida trip.

"Mr. Evans?" He took careful steps between the folding chairs because 'Lizabeth said fish don't come if you bump someone's fishing pole. When he reached his mommy's friend, he put his hand on the man's knee. "Can I walk along the water and look for rocks?"

"Sure, Max." Mr. Evans patted his hand very nice. "Just stay close so we can see you."

"I will." Max smiled, then he took more careful steps through the chairs and walked just along the edge of the water.

Being at the lake made him remember the ocean, and the times when he and Mommy walked near the water. Sometimes they found pretty shells or sand dollars. But whenever he found a pretty rock, he gave it to Ramey. Mommy never got jealous about that. She liked the pretty shells, and Ramey liked the rocks.

Max stopped and took his tennis shoes off. Next he pulled off his socks and squished them into his shoes so they wouldn't get lost. He set them a few steps away from the water in case the tide came in. Did lakes have tides? His toes liked being free, and he pushed them into the sand. It was different than the beach sand back home, more bumpy and rough. But it felt good.

He headed back to the water.

Their camping trip was going pretty good. He wasn't afraid to sleep in a tent anymore. The first night he made a plan to sit up in case a bear or an alligator or a snake tried to climb inside. But Mr. Evans saw him and asked what the problem was.

When Max told him, Mr. Evans's eyes got soft. "Move your sleeping bag over here for tonight, by me."

The tent was big inside, with two rooms and a zipper wall in the middle, but Mr.

Evans said they would leave the wall open for the trip. 'Lizabeth and Susan were sleeping together in the front part, Mr. Evans in the back, and Max in the middle. A warm feeling came into his heart when Mr. Evans asked him that thing, so he moved his sleeping bag right up next to where his mommy's friend was sleeping.

"Nothing's coming into our tent, Max, okay?" Mr. Evans rubbed his back for a minute. He used a whisper voice because the girls were already asleep. "You're safe with me."

"Okay." Max liked the sound of that. And after he lay down, it was true. He felt safe next to Mr. Evans, and that night he fell asleep holding hands with that man. Mommy's friend was tall and strong and smart. Bears and alligators and snakes wouldn't think of hurting him with Mr. Evans nearby.

Something caught Max's attention and he stopped. In front of him was the bestest rock he'd ever seen, just laying there on the ground. It was shiny black like a marble with four snowy white little stripes on it. He picked it up and turned it over in his hand. Dirt covered up the back, so he quick put it in the lake water and rolled it around in his fingers. When the dirt was off, he looked hard at it and saw a wonderful thing. The stripes went all the way around! Like white rings on a black marble. Only it wasn't a marble, it was a rock, and that was even better because God made rocks.

Wow! Ramey was going to love this one!

He took one more close look, and then stuffed the rock in the front pocket of his jeans. Pockets were a perfect place to save rocks. Max walked a little bit more and he saw a big rock, the kind good for sitting on. He wasn't tired, but he stopped anyway. Big rocks were also good for thinking. He grabbed onto the top of it and pulled himself up. Then he sat so he could see the lake water. Mr. Evans and the girls were back some, but even if he looked straight out he could see them in the side part of his eyes.

Max did his best thinking near the water, and even though this wasn't an ocean, it was still water. And Max had a lot of thinking in his head.

The first thing he wanted to think about was Buddy. Max was pretty sure the old dog would love camping, especially the fishing part. Buddy got pretty excited whenever he smelled fish. But also the tent part, because Mommy used to say Buddy liked being a watchdog for him. He could probably even keep Mr. Evans safe.

Sunshine was out that day and it was hard to see over the water. Max made a shield with his hand and put it over the top of his eyes. Right away seeing was better, so Max kept his hand there.

The other thing in his head was something his mommy had told him in that letter, the one Mr. Ogle read him. Not the part about being brave and strong and remembering that she loved him. The part about having a daddy somewhere out there. At first he didn't want to think about that thing. He wanted his mommy back, not a daddy he didn't even know.

But now, after being with Mr. Evans, the idea of a daddy was in his head a lot. Sometimes he woke up thinking how it would feel to have a dad like Mr. Evans, someone strong and nice who would love him for always. 'Lizabeth and Susan were lucky to have Mr. Evans for a dad, but Max wasn't sure they knew they were lucky.

He remembered how he used to think that way before his mom died. But back then the thinking lasted only a minute because he didn't need a daddy, not really. His mommy was all he needed.

But now she was gone . . .

Plus she must have wanted him to find his daddy someday. Or else she wouldn't have put that part in the letter, right?

Max's hand was tired, so he let it fall back to his lap. He lifted his face to the sun and closed his eyes. How was he supposed to find his daddy when the world had so many dads all spread out everywhere? Or maybe his daddy was looking for him and one day he'd walk up to Ramey's door and knock and there he'd be. The daddy his mom had told him about. He squinted his eyes and looked up at the sky where God lived.

God . . . Hi, it's me. Max. He kept the words in his head. *I was thinking about my daddy somewhere out there. The one my mom told me about. Do You think maybe You could ask my mom where I should look for him? Because there's a lot of dads and what if I don't know what he looks like or what his voice is?* He thought for a minute. *And tell my mom I miss her. The missing doesn't make my stomach hurt as much, but well, my heart still hurts. I think it always will. A'course if I find my daddy that would help.*

Max kept his eyes closed and decided

this was a good time to sing his mommy's special song. That way she would feel close again. He opened his mouth and let the words come quiet and small. "I love you, Max, the most . . . I love to make you —"

"Max?"

He opened his eyes speedy quick and turned around. It was Mr. Evans, and he had worry in his eyes. Max hopped off the big rock and looked at his mommy's friend. "Hi."

"I saw you sitting up there." Mr. Evans put his hands in his pockets. "I don't know. I thought maybe you might want to talk."

Max made a line in the sand with his big toe and then made his eyes find Mr. Evans again. "My brain had some thinking in it."

Mr. Evans nodded. "That happens to me a lot." He looked out at the water. "Especially lately."

"Me, too."

"So . . ." Mr. Evans looked at him again. "What thinking was your brain doing today?"

Max leaned back against the big rock. He didn't like talking about the thinking in his head unless it was with his mommy. But Mr. Evans was her friend, so it was probably okay this time. He put his hand over the top of his eyes again so he could see better. "About my daddy."

Surprise went across Mr. Evans's face. He turned around and rested against the rock, too. Max liked how their arms were side by side, the way he was sometimes side by side with his mommy when they had their talks. Mr. Evans made a long breathy sound. "What do you know about him?"

"Well" — Max felt his pocket to make sure the rock for Ramey was there — "Mommy said he's out there somewhere, and that one day maybe I'll find him."

Mr. Evans waited. "That's all? That's all you know?"

"Mm-hmm. Mommy just told me about him in her letter, the one Mr. Ogle read to me after . . . after she didn't come home."

"I see." Mr. Evans squinted at the sun a little. "So that's what you were doing? Thinking about your daddy?"

"Not just thinking." Max made his bottom lip wet with his tongue. It gave him a little nervous feeling talking about this, but Mr. Evans was a good listener. "I asked God about it, too."

"You did?"

"Yep. Because so many dads live out there, I don't think I'll ever know who he is

319

unless God shows him to me. So I asked God."

For a minute it seemed like Mr. Evans might hold him close with both arms, the way he'd seen the man do with 'Lizabeth and Susan. But then instead he felt the man pat his head and watched him move away from the rock. "Max, I think God's going to answer your prayer."

"Really?" A happy feeling filled Max inside. If a smart man like Mr. Evans thought God would answer about helping him find his daddy, then maybe that's exactly what God was going to do.

Mr. Evans turned and looked at him. "Really."

Max moved his head up and down, and then he remembered the rock. "Look what I found." He used tight fingers to pull it from his pocket, because he didn't want to drop it into the lake. Then he held it up for Mr. Evans to see.

"Hey, that's a beauty." Mommy's friend leaned close and looked at it. Sometimes grown-ups looked real fast when a kid had something to show. But Mr. Evans really liked the rock because he looked at the top and bottom and even at the sides. "Who's it for?"

"For Ramey." Max put the rock back in

his pocket. "I always give her special rocks."

"I see." Mr. Evans looked at him for a long time. "Ready to try some fishing?"

Max still had more thinking in his head, but he liked Mr. Evans a lot. "Would you show me how again? I messed up last time."

"Sure." Mr. Evans held out his hand. "Come on, we'll walk together."

Max reached out and took hold of Mr. Evans's fingers. On the walk back they talked about rocks and tides and what kind of worms fish like best. But Max wasn't thinking very hard about that stuff, because he kept thinking about how his hand felt in Mr. Evans's, and how he hoped one day when he found his daddy that the two of them could hold hands, too.

In fact, he hoped his daddy would be just exactly like Mr. Evans.

TWENTY-TWO

Connor knew the score from the moment they set out on the camping trip. A week with Max — teaching him to fish, taking walks along the shore, watching him play with the girls — would make it impossible not to bond with him.

But he hadn't expected it to happen so fast.

The girls had set their poles down and taken their water noodles down to the lake. He could see them floating in the roped-off swimming hole, so he directed his attention to showing Max how to bait a hook.

"You can't kill the worm, because the fish need to see it moving."

"That's how you trick 'em, right?"

Connor stifled a grin. "Right."

When Max's hook was out in the water a ways, Connor baited his own rod and cast out a few yards away. They fell into a comfortable silence, fishing side by side with the girls splashing and playing a ways off. Connor took his eyes off his bobber and let them settle on Max.

The feelings he had for Max went beyond anything he'd imagined. Marv Ogle had been right, his son was easy to love. Not just for him, but for the girls, too. Before the trip, Michele had pulled him aside one last time and warned him to be careful of the girls' feelings.

"Elizabeth is suspicious of him." She kept her voice low so the children wouldn't hear her. "You need to respect that, Connor. Don't force them to be friends."

He'd done nothing of the sort. Instead, the children had found their way all by themselves. The first night Max was struggling with his sleeping bag, an older bag Connor and Michele had kept in the storage closet. Connor was still unloading things from the car, but when he peeked in the tent, what he saw made his heart sing.

Elizabeth had stationed herself next to Max, and she was showing him how to guide the zipper.

"The cloth gets in the way sometimes," she told him. "So push it away with one hand and then it'll zip up just fine."

Max did as she said, and when it got

stuck two more times, Elizabeth helped him get it back on track. When the bag was zipped up and smoothed out in the middle of the tent, Elizabeth patted Max's back. "Good job, Max. You'll be a camper before you know it."

They were midway through the trip, and that type of scene had played out dozens of times each day. The night before, Max announced he was making s'mores for each of them. Susan and Elizabeth exchanged a giggly smile, but they nodded their approval. "Okay, Max. Thanks."

Each marshmallow caught fire before Max had a chance to back it out of the heat. But he went ahead undaunted, and for each girl he placed the gooey black-and-white mess on top of a piece of chocolate, sandwiched between two graham crackers. "Here!" He handed a s'more first to Elizabeth, then to Susan.

Connor half expected them to give the boy a stiff thank-you and then dump his creation in the nearest trash can. Instead they each hugged him and remarked that his was the best s'more they'd ever seen. And they ate the entire thing. Both girls.

If only Michele could see them. If only she'd let her guard down enough to give Max a chance. Connor was convinced she'd fall in love with him, the same way he and the girls already had.

He studied Max, the intensity in his young face as he made slight movements with his fishing pole.

Max shifted his eyes to his and smiled. "Like this?"

"Perfect." Connor had told him to keep the bobber moving, because that meant the worm would move. And moving worms were the kind that attracted fish. "I'll bet every fish in the area is thinking about that worm right now."

The boy turned back to the lake and once again studied his bobber. Connor understood the reason Michele didn't want to be around the child. It was one thing for her to know he'd had an affair, but to see living proof of his betrayal . . .

So far she hadn't been able to look past that part to Max himself. In the past few days, that had become Connor's prayer. That Michele would see what she was doing, and by the time they came home, she might understand how well Max could fit in their family.

He cocked his head and watched his son's mannerisms, the look in his eyes. No wonder Michele struggled. As much as he could see the Evans family resemblance there, he was definitely Kiahna's son.

He remembered the photograph Max kept tucked in his Bible. Yes, Kiahna had been as likable as Max. Their time together had been wrong, wracked with the kind of life-strangling sin that still sucked the life from his relationship with God. Nothing about his time with her had been right. But he'd gotten a glimpse of the woman's heart that weekend. A look he remembered even after years of trying to forget.

Except on rare unguarded moments, Connor didn't go back. But here, now, he felt time slip away, felt his heart going down the old forbidden roads, following a trail to that stormy evening in Honolulu. Back to a time when he broke the most important promise he'd ever made.

The meal had been the icebreaker.

Once Connor and Kiahna combined tables to eat together, conversation moved quickly from surface talk about their similar tastes, to formal introductions, to Kiahna and the reason for the sadness in her eyes.

Most flight attendants stayed together in groups, moving across the concourse, visiting the rest room, or grabbing a bite to eat. They were easy to spot, slim and fit, sharply dressed in their pressed airline uniforms, hair pulled back, makeup just so. Each pulling a smart-looking bag behind them.

They'd laugh and talk while they walked, waving animated hands, catching up on the latest passenger story or the way one of them had stumbled over the preflight preparation talk or some irresistible tale from back home. Where pilots might never make emotional connections with each other, flight attendants quickly moved beyond the surface details of their job. They shared about family and children, broken romances and budding relationships.

Rarely did they keep to themselves the way Kiahna was, and the picture she made — sitting alone at the table — intrigued Connor.

"Where's the rest of the group?" He caught his straw between his thumb and forefinger and took a long swig of iced tea. The conversation refreshed something in his soul, something that had been gasping for air in light of the troubles in his life.

"The other attendants?" Kiahna set her fork down and smiled. "We go our own ways."

"Oh." Connor cocked his head. "How come?"

"They're too fast for me."

"Too fast?"

Kiahna gave him a sad smile. "Surely you know Western Island Air's reputation?"

Connor thought for a minute. "Maybe not."

"My crew flies nights, Captain Evans."

"Connor." His response was quick. For some reason it mattered that the girl sitting across from him drop the formalities. "Call me Connor."

"Okay." Her smile was utterly guileless. "My crew flies nights, Connor. It takes more than Diet Coke for most of them to stay awake."

The truth of what she was saying sank in. "Drugs?"

"Cocaine." She shrugged one shoulder. "Cocaine before the flight, and men after. I do better to stay by myself."

Connor sat back and studied her. "Strong convictions, huh?"

"I guess."

"Why?" He figured maybe she was married, living a quiet, conservative life in which there would never be room for the racy lifestyle her peers were living.

"Faith, I guess." She tugged on a slender chain she wore around her neck and pulled a simple cross from beneath her uniform. "I'm a Christian." She let the cross fall back in place. "My parents used to say faith wasn't something you could pretend about. It wasn't real unless it looked like faith and acted like faith." She folded her hands on the table in front of her. "I buried my mother three days ago, six months after we buried Dad."

A hundred questions fought for position, and he asked her the one that jumped out in front. "How did they die?"

"Dad died of a heart attack. He was Irish; heart attacks ran in his family." Her eyes fell and she stirred her straw in slow circles through her soda. "Woke up one morning and never made it to the breakfast table."

Connor wished he could take away the raw pain in her eyes. "I'm sorry."

"It's okay." She shrugged and gave a quiet sniff. "They're in heaven, right?"

"Right." Connor didn't want to think about heaven. "Your mom?"

Kiahna's eyes fell to her drink again. "She was Hawaiian, a strong woman who would've lived to be a hundred." She looked up. "But the cancer got her first."

She hesitated. "I think her body gave up after Dad died. Her immune system shut down and cancer took over."

Connor had the strangest desire to walk around to her side of the table and hug her. He tried to guess her age, and figured she couldn't have been more than twenty-three, twenty-four at the most.

He took another sip of tea. "Are you . . . are you married?" She wore no ring, but that wasn't proof. His own wedding ring was in his bag somewhere. He'd taken it off that morning before his workout and forgotten to put it on again.

"No. I live with a roommate, a flight attendant for another airline."

"No siblings?"

"I was an only child." Her smile warmed some. "My parents used to tell me they had just one baby because they couldn't imagine ever loving another child as much as they loved me." She lifted her eyebrows. "We were very close."

Connor was still stuck on the thing she'd said a moment earlier. She had no family? Only a roommate? A fiercely protective feeling welled up within him. How fair was it that a girl with such faith, such desire to live for God, had lost her parents and didn't have anyone more than a roommate to come home to?

She seemed to read his thoughts. "It's okay. I'm in school full-time. My roommate's a good friend."

"What are you studying?"

"Medicine. I'm going to be a doctor." She gave a sideways nod of her head. "Maybe God will use me to cure cancer. So that people like my mother would have a chance to live."

Connor stared at her, speechless. She was amazing. Faithful, true, and with a determination that was all but extinct in the self-centered society they shared. He forced himself to focus. "How far along are you?"

"A year away from my bachelor's."

Connor tried to do the math. "So you're what, twenty-two?"

"Twenty-one." She lowered her mouth and took a sip from her drink, keeping her eyes on his the whole time. "I know . . . most people think I look older."

"Definitely." Connor was thirty-three that year, and the girl's age reminded him he had no business asking about the details of her life. Bad enough that he was married and having lunch with a young, single flight attendant. But a twenty-one-year-old? She was barely out of her teens.

"I'm alone by choice, Connor." She sat back. "I was in love once, a young professor at the college. But he didn't understand. He wanted to marry me and take care of me, have me drop out of school so I could be there for him." Her eyes didn't waver. "But I don't want that, not yet. I'm going to be a doctor; nothing's going to stop me. Love and marriage, raising kids, all that can come later." She softened some. "For now it's me and God and my studies. The flight attendant thing is the best way to pay the bills."

Their conversation shifted to the task of piloting a commercial aircraft, and Connor was impressed with how well she listened. He added intelligent to her list of attributes. Intelligent and driven.

When they were finished eating, she insisted on paying for her own part of the bill. Together, they moved into the concourse, intent on finding out information about the approaching storm. They each had their pull-behinds, but their pace was unhurried.

She gave him a smile that held no pretense, nothing flirtatious. "I like you, Connor. Most pilots are arrogant. But you're . . . you're easy to talk to."

He felt the compliment make its way

through his body. It was time to mention Michele. "That's what my w—"

"Attention, please." The voice was loud and made it impossible for Connor to finish his sentence. "Because of a storm system, the airport is closing down until further notice. Repeat, there will be no landings or takeoffs until we've been given the clear from the weather service."

Connor stopped and let his weight fall back on his heels. "Great."

"Maybe it'll be gone in an hour or so." Kiahna moved ahead toward the counter. "Let's ask."

Trailing a few feet behind her, Connor thought about how long it had been since he'd seen Michele, and how he would've visited her this weekend if it weren't for the storm. But maybe Kiahna was right, maybe it would pass in an hour or so. One thing about that moment stood out even now.

How badly he had hoped she was right.

TWENTY-THREE

Connor drew himself from the memory and focused on his girls. But he couldn't shake off his thoughts.

The affair hadn't been his idea any more than it had been Kiahna's. He'd forgotten how determined he'd been to leave Honolulu, to get home and make contact with Michele. As intriguing as he found Kiahna, as much as she reminded him of a younger Michele, he had no interest in spending another hour with her, let alone a night.

No, what happened next, even at the time, had felt like some sort of orchestrated drama over which he had no control. He blinked and let the images from that hot August evening continue.

A line of passengers swelled around the counter. Connor stayed close behind Kiahna as she approached the gate agent from the side. "What are they saying about the delay?"

The agent checked her computer. "Looks like nothing leaves until tomorrow morning at the soonest."

"Excuse me." Connor stepped forward. "I need to get back to Los Angeles to-night." He glanced at his watch. "Are any of the flights cleared for takeoff? Mine's supposed to leave in an hour."

The woman gave him a blank look. "We made an announcement."

"Yes." He gave a quiet huff. "But please . . . I need to get back."

"Captain, the airport is shut down." She pointed at the window. "Those are hurri-cane-force winds. Phones are out along the coast." She turned back to the growing crowd of passengers around her counter. "You'll have to wait with everyone else."

They found a bench not far away and sat down. Kiahna caught his eye and twisted her mouth up some. "I think it could be a few nights, actually."

She barely had the words out of her mouth when another announcement came on. "Attention, please: The Honolulu Air-port is now closed for the night. Officials will review the situation with the weather at noon tomorrow. The weather service has advised us that flights might be grounded for two to three days."

The traffic in the concourse froze during the message, but the moment it was over, passengers scattered toward the doors and a bank of phones along both walls. Connor watched them, running and fighting for position. He wasn't sure whether to join the rush or sit back and wait for the crowd to pass. "Everyone needs a room."

Kiahna made a little frown. "It'll be too late for most of them."

"You think so?"

"The weather warning's been around all day. Tourists planning to leave will have changed their mind and kept their rooms. Twice as many tourists for the existing rooms? At the peak of summer?" She stared at the throng of people moving past them. "Most of them will be sleeping in an airport chair."

He looked back at the gate counter. "I'll call my supervisor and see what they want me to do."

Five minutes later he was back with the news. "I'm in the same boat as the rest of them. The pilots' club is full, no rooms anywhere, and no flights until tomorrow at the earliest." He leaned back and stretched out his legs. "I better get comfortable."

Kiahna watched him, saying nothing. Now — years later — he could guess what she might've been thinking. Probably that the two of them had known each other for less than an hour, so maybe she shouldn't make the offer. Or possibly that if she invited him, he would get the wrong idea.

Whatever had gone through her mind, she made her decision and broke the quiet between them. "You could stay at my place, Connor. My roommate would be there; you could have the couch."

Instantly, two thoughts flashed in his head. First, he hadn't yet told her he was married. Without his ring, she may have assumed he had no one waiting at home for him. Second, if the phones were out, he'd have no way to call Michele and tell her what he was doing, where he was going.

After that, a series of thoughts bombarded him, one after another. Thoughts that screamed for him to get up and run the other direction, ones that reminded him he was a married man and spending the night on this single woman's sofa couldn't possibly be a good idea. But she had a roommate. Besides, he wasn't attracted to her; he merely needed a place to sleep. He sat up a bit and met her eyes. "Really?"

"Sure." She slid to the edge of the bench. "It'd be safer than any place near the water."

Safer . . . The word played in his mind for a moment. He was quiet. What would Michele think? Maybe he should stay at the airport, wait for an opening at the pilots' lounge, even find a few seats where he could stretch out at one of the gates.

"It's okay, Connor." She gave a light laugh at his obvious struggle. "You're a pilot for one of the largest airlines in the industry; I wouldn't have asked you if I didn't have a roommate. We won't be alone." She lifted her chin, and her tone held not a trace of teasing or flirtation. "A good night's sleep is important."

He made a deal with himself. He would stay, so long as he told her about Michele. Between that truth and Kiahna's roommate, there would be no room for danger.

"Okay." He stood, and she did the same. "I should probably call home and —"

Before he could finish his sentence, a teenage boy walking past and slurping something from an oversized cup, tripped, and fell flat out onto the concourse floor. As he did, his drink lid popped off and what felt like a quart of root beer shot from the cup and doused the front of Connor's uniform.

"Hey!" Connor stepped back, arms out, shocked by the sudden cold against his chest.

Kiahna helped the boy to his feet and in a flurry of red-faced apologies, the teenager was gone. Kiahna turned to him and covered her mouth with the tips of her fingers. "You're a mess."

"Thank you." Connor made a slow exhale. With a polite smile, he nodded at Kiahna and pointed toward the rest room. "Watch my bag, will you? I'll be back."

By the time he returned, Kiahna was laughing out loud. "Come on." She set off toward the airport's front door. "Let's get you to my place so you can clean up."

They were just out of the airport parking lot in her beat-up Honda Civic when Connor remembered about Michele. "Listen, I'll need to use your phone. My w—"

Kiahna's scream stopped him short.

In a heartbeat, a trash can blew into the road and an oncoming car swerved into her lane to miss it. Almost as quickly the other driver yanked his car back onto the right side of the road. Kiahna straightened out the car, breathless from the near disaster.

"Nice work." Connor's voice shook, the adrenaline rush as swift for him as it must have been for her.

"I thought we were dead." Kiahna drew a slow breath and pulled back onto the road. "Let's see if we can do this."

When they arrived at her apartment, they hurried inside as soon as Kiahna had the door unlocked. "Whew!" She fell back into an oversized chair and used her fingers to brush her hair from her face. "The wind hasn't been like this since I was a little girl."

He stood, awkward, beside his suitcase and gave her an uncertain smile. "Where's your roommate?"

"I don't know." Kiahna glanced at the kitchen and toward the hallway. "Lara?" Her voice hung in the air, but no one responded. Kiahna took a few steps into the apartment. "Lara, I'm home."

"Maybe she's sleeping." Connor hoped so. He couldn't ask Kiahna to go back out in this weather. But he'd call a cab before he'd stay the night with just the two of them.

"She should've been home hours ago." Kiahna went to a narrow table that lined the hallway a few steps away. Her answering machine was blinking, and she pushed a button. A voice came through the speaker.

"Hey, this is Lara, I'm stuck at work." Fear colored the caller's voice. "The road's blocked by trees. It could be a few days before they clear it away, so a bunch of us are staying at the house of one of the clerks here."

Kiahna clicked a button and turned off the machine. Then she lifted her shoulders twice and looked at him. "Now what?"

Connor fell against the door. "Look, Kiahna, if she's gone for the night I should call a cab."

She dropped in the nearest chair and frowned. "Sorry about this. I had no idea . . ."

"I know." Connor opened a phone book beside the phone and flipped to the taxi section. "I'll have them take me back to the airport. The floor of the pilots' lounge will work."

He lifted the receiver and hit the on button. But instead of a dial tone, it was dead. "Hmmm." He tapped on the button four times and tried again. Still dead. "Are the phones out?"

"They were out near the coast." She

stood, made her way toward him, and held the receiver to her ear. She repeated the same moves Connor had made, tapping the button several times. But each time she held the receiver up she only shook her head. "Not a spark of life."

Connor took a step backwards and considered his options. He was stuck there, like it or not, about to spend the night alone with a flight attendant he'd only just met. Suddenly he couldn't draw another breath without telling her the truth. "Listen, Kiahna, I tried to tell you before. I'm married."

There. He'd said it.

Her smile was quick and uncomplicated. "That's fine. You're safe; I told you that. Besides, I figured you must be married; most pilots are." She gave him a curious look. "I could go stay with my neighbor if it'd make you more comfortable."

Suddenly he felt foolish for worrying. "No, that's okay." Neither of them had ulterior motives. She was still grieving the loss of her mother, alone in the worst storm to hit the islands in decades. Of course he could stay. He'd take the couch and make sure she was safe for the night. Then in the morning the phones would be back up, and he'd call for a cab.

The ominous clouds outside brought an early nightfall, and Kiahna put together a chicken salad and warm bread for dinner. They talked about their faith and the dreams they'd had as kids. Halfway through the meal, she narrowed her eyes and said something that made his heart skip a beat.

"How long have you and your wife lived in LA?"

"Actually . . ." He let his eyes fall to his plate. "She lives in Orlando. It works out better that way. At least for now."

"Oh . . ." Her expression changed, but not enough for Connor to comment on it. Again her mannerisms, the shine in her eyes reminded him of Michele. But the realization only made him miss his wife, the way she'd been before her depression. Either way, he felt nothing but kindness for the stranger across from him. And the certainty of that convinced him that Michele would understand his predicament. What else could he do?

They finished dinner and moved into her tiny living room for a movie. Connor took the seat farthest from her and outside the storm intensified. Halfway through the show, the electricity went out.

"Okay." Kiahna didn't sound frightened.

"Now if I can remember where I put the flashlight."

"We should have thought of that earlier." He wondered if she could hear his pounding heart from across the room. "Want help?"

"No, stay there. I think it's in the cupboard by the refrigerator."

He heard her grope her way from the living room into the kitchen, and after a few seconds of shuffling sounds, there was a click, and light sprayed from the place where she was. "Found it."

He gripped the arms of his chair. "What time is it?"

She appeared in the doorway and returned to the spot where she'd been sitting. As she did, she shone the light at her wrist. "Nine-fifteen."

"No wonder I'm not tired." His words felt awkward on his tongue. Why not turn in early? Send Kiahna off to her room and crash on the couch? Before he had time to process that, she interrupted his thoughts.

"I know." She shone the light toward a cabinet at the other end of the room. "Want to play poker?"

"Poker?" He couldn't contain a chuckle. "What would your God-fearing parents say about that?"

"Dad loved a good game of poker." She headed toward a small lamp stand with a set of drawers at the base. "He used to say cards were good for the mind. But no gambling, never that." She cast him a shadowy smile over her shoulder. "He taught me to play when I was six."

"All right, then." Connor chuckled again. "Where should we play?"

She grabbed a deck of cards and a box of poker chips from the cabinet, and tossed them on the small coffee table in front of her sofa. "This works for me." She dropped to the floor cross-legged. "You can have the sofa."

After a while, she owned all the chips, and he tossed his cards on the table. "Okay, you got me. Your daddy taught you good." He grinned at her, struck by the picture she made sitting across from him, her hair still windblown, innocence shining in her eyes.

What he wouldn't give to have Michele there, looking at him like that right now.

Her smile faded. "Yes. He was a good teacher and . . . and a good friend." She met his eyes and the sadness in her face lifted. "Tired yet?"

"Not really."

She bit her lip and looked around the

room. A gust of wind howled outside and they heard a crash of something blowing across the road. "Wicked storm."

"I know." Connor stared at the window. Mature trees lined the apartment perimeter; he hoped the winds didn't get strong enough to topple them.

"Hey. Wanna see my scrapbook? I put it together after my parents died . . . sort of a walk through my childhood."

"Think that'll put me to sleep, huh?" It was fun to tease her.

"Well" — she grinned at him — "if it does, then I guess that's a good thing. Should I get it?"

Don't do it, Evans . . . tell her good night. Flee . . . flee as fast as you can.

Connor immediately recognized the voice echoing on the inside of his heart. *I hear you, God . . . I've got it under control. Besides, I'm not interested in her.*

She was waiting for an answer. "Sure. I'd love to see it."

They sat side by side looking at the book. Toward the end, she turned to him and tapped the open page. "That's it."

He glanced down and saw that a few pages remained. "What's on those last ones?"

She hesitated, and for the first time since

he'd run into her at the restaurant, a vulnerable look flashed in her eyes. "A few poems I wrote."

He held her eyes and felt something begin to stir in his gut. "Show me."

Her eyes fell to the book, and after a few seconds she looked at him again. "Okay." She slid the book from her lap to his, and her hand grazed his leg with the slightest sensation. "No one else has ever seen them."

The poems were beautiful, deep and heartfelt, and Connor felt privileged that she was trusting him with a glimpse of her soul. As he read them, he ached for how much she still missed these two people who had been her parents. When he finished, he looked up and saw tears in her eyes.

Slowly, he shut the book and placed it on the coffee table. "Kiahna, you're a gifted writer. Those poems . . . they're beautiful." He yawned then. "Well, I think we both need some sleep."

"You're right."

They said good night, and she left for her bedroom. He was almost asleep on the couch a half hour later when he heard her scream. Even in the darkness, he was at her side in an instant. Glass glinted in the moonlight, covering the floor on the window side of the bed. He walked around it, grabbed the flashlight from her nightstand, and clicked it on.

"Something hit me." Kiahna was huddled on her bed in a nightshirt, her hand pressed to her head.

"Let me see." Connor held the light near her forehead and caught his breath. A gash ran from the end of her eyebrow toward her temple. Already a knot was swelling near the wound. "Do you have a first-aid kit?"

"Yes." She made a soft moaning sound. "I feel sick, Connor."

He shone the flashlight on the floor and saw what had happened. A tree branch had crashed through the window near her bed and hit her head. If she was nauseous she might have a concussion, and there was nothing he could do about it. "Let's get out of here."

She struggled to her feet, and he helped her into the living room and onto the couch. Once she was seated, he put a pillow beside her and covered her bare legs with a blanket. "Don't lie down yet. Where's the kit?"

"In the bathroom." Her words were slow and deliberate. "Under the sink."

Once more he aimed the light at her head. Blood was running down the side of her face. "Keep your hand against your head until I come back."

"Mmm-hmm." She swayed some.

"Let's see if the phones are back up." He grabbed a phone from a nearby nightstand and checked for a dial tone. None. He whisked his cell phone from his pocket, but the message in the window still read *No service.*

A sense of urgency filled him. He had to work fast. If she was in trouble, he'd take her in the Honda and they'd drive until he found help. He found his way to the bathroom, grabbed the kit, and soaked a washcloth. "Don't fall asleep, Kiahna," he called to her as he headed back to her side.

"Mmmm."

He cleaned the blood, dried the area around the gash, and used seven small bandages to pull the edges together. One larger bandage went over the smaller ones, and in fifteen minutes the bleeding had stopped.

"How're you feeling?" He stepped back and used the flashlight to study her look. Her face was pale, even in the dark of the room. "Still sick to your stomach?"

"A little."

"You didn't black out, did you?"

Kiahna leaned her head back against the sofa. "I don't think so. I'm not as dizzy as before."

Connor recalled a few things about first aid from his time at West Point. A blow to the temple was the worst kind, and even if she hadn't lost consciousness, she should be watched, woken every hour at least. He aimed the flashlight at her eyes, and both pupils responded to the light. He lowered it a few inches below her chin and tried to study her expression in the glow. "You feel well enough to stay here? I can take you for help if you need it."

"No . . ." She shook her head. "I can stay here. Really. I'm too tired to go anywhere."

"You can sleep here on the couch. I'll stay beside you on the floor and wake you every hour just in case."

"All right." She fell sideways and stretched out, asleep before her head hit the pillow.

As a pilot, Connor had pulled all-nighters before. He was trained to stay awake in difficult situations. But after waking Kiahna twice over the next two hours, he was overcome with exhaustion. The floor was hard, the wood damp against his pants.

He clicked on the flashlight and sized up the sofa situation. It was wider than most, easily wide enough for both of them. He shone the light on his watch and set it to wake him up in an hour. Then he stretched out alongside her and turned his back to her. He rested his head on the armrest and closed his eyes. Just an hour. He'd sleep some, and when the alarm sounded he'd wake her again and make sure she was okay.

But within minutes he was sound asleep.

To this day he could remember the dream he'd had that night. It had been of Michele and him, back when they first fell in love. Back when Michele believed in Connor the way Kiahna had said she believed in him. That he was a doer, a man of competence and confidence.

When the alarm went off, Connor heard it, but only at some deep, half-asleep place in his brain. He groped around the floor beside the sofa and pushed the button to stop the beeping. Then he turned and felt a body beside him.

Michele. He smiled and put his arm around her, pulling her to him, running his fingers along the side of her body.

She stirred, and before he knew what was happening, before he remembered that he wasn't home, and that the woman beside him wasn't Michele, but a flight attendant he'd met only that afternoon, his lips found hers. The kiss was slow and easy, but with an aching need that doubled with each second.

A minute passed before they pulled back, and in a moment he would remember forever, their eyes met. Only then did Connor realize where he was and what he was doing. That the woman in his arms was Kiahna, not Michele.

And in that moment he knew something else.

He'd been lying to himself about his attraction to her. She was young and passionate and riddled with a terrible loneliness. She needed someone . . . almost as much as he did.

"Kiahna . . ." His ragged voice gave clear evidence of his desire.

That's when he'd heard it. A warning as clear and distinct as if God was standing beside him shouting at him: *Get up and apologize, move away from her . . . Flee, Son. Flee . . .*

Connor made a subtle press of his body against hers. *Everything's okay. I'll flee later.* "I'm sorry . . ."

She swallowed, her eyes wide. "It's okay."

Flee, Son . . . move away . . .

His lips drew closer to hers, guided by a force stronger than anything he'd known before or since. And as they began to kiss he knew it was too late. He couldn't break free of the wave of longing suffocating him, moving him closer to her with every heartbeat.

Flee, Son . . .

He pulled back and studied her once more. "Kiahna, come here."

She came to him.

The warning voice grew dim. *Flee . . .*

He kissed her again. *Just a little more . . . I'll move across the room in a minute.*

It was the last lie Connor told himself that night.

After that he didn't give another thought about her concussion or the wind or the rain or whether the entire roof might come off in the storm. He was completely and utterly consumed by her, by being with her.

When he woke the next morning he wanted to throw up.

What had he done? How had he allowed things to go so bad? The storm had cleared overnight, enough for her to take him to the airport. They were silent, awkward as they made their separate ways around the apartment. Her dizziness was gone, and he was no longer worried about her head.

He was worried about his own.

What had he been thinking to kiss her like that? And how come they'd lost control so easily? At the time he had no answers. Only later would he be able to piece the nightmare together. Michele's depression, the distance that caused between them, his troubles with the FAA, his tiring commute from LA to Orlando, the troubles with his father.

All of that, combined with the way Kiahna had looked at him, the way she'd talked to him . . . the same way Michele spoke to him in their early days.

It all added up now, but back then on that awful morning after, he was too shocked to make sense of anything but the obvious. He had to get home.

The ride to the airport was even more strained, neither of them saying a word until she parked the car at the departure area, climbed out, and met him on the curb.

"I'm sorry, Connor. I've never done anything like that in my life." She could barely look at him. When she did, her eyes brimmed with tears. "I feel awful."

"Me, too." He took a step back and held

the handle of his suitcase. "I'm sorry, I . . . I don't know what to say."

"You were lonely. I should've gone to the neighbor's."

Lonely? He let her word play in his mind. "Not that lonely. It's no excuse."

"But your wife?" Then she asked a question that haunted him still. "How long have you been separated?"

"Separated?" He searched her eyes, confused. "I told you, Kiahna. I'm married. Everything about last night was . . ." His eyes fell to the ground for a few seconds. "It was wrong. It never should have happened."

"But . . . you said you lived alone in Los Angeles. I thought . . ."

And in a rush, the realization hit him.

She thought he and Michele lived in separate states because they were on the verge of divorce. "No, it's . . . it's nothing like that. I live in Los Angeles because I'm stationed there. My wife and the girls, our life is in Florida. I commute back and forth." His eyes shifted to the ground again. He wanted to disappear, close his eyes, and never again have to see the island girl standing before him. He exhaled hard through pursed lips. "Los Angeles is temporary, until I get assigned back to Orlando."

"Oh. I . . . I misunderstood." Her cheeks grew red, and she took small, jerky steps back to the driver's door of her car. Then she stopped and met his eyes one last time. "Good-bye, Connor. I'm sorry . . ."

"Me, too."

That was the end of it. He never heard from her again, never heard anything about her.

Until Marv Ogle's call a week ago.

A noise caught his attention, and Connor released the memory.

"Hey! Mr. Evans, I think I got a fish!"

"Good." Connor blinked, still trying to clear his head. He turned to Max. "Hold onto him!"

"Okay." The boy was on his feet struggling with his fishing pole, eyes dancing, a grin plastered across his face. "I always dreamed I'd catch a big fish like that one."

He moved in a single fluid motion from the chair to a position behind Max, where his arms came around the boy and surrounded his smaller hands on the rod. "You're right. Feels like a big one." Connor used his wrists to jerk the pole. And a flash of silver jumped from the water twenty-five feet out. "Oooh, I think it's a trout!"

Elizabeth and Susan were still swimming, talking to a few girls and unaware of the commotion. Together, Connor and Max reeled in the fish and fought to hold it while Connor removed the hook from its mouth.

"Looks like you caught us dinner, Max." Connor gave the child a quick squeeze, then fastened the catch chain through the fish's mouth and tossed it into shallow water where it would stay fresh until later.

"Yeah." Max moved to the shoreline and stared at the fish, flopping only once in a while now. "I bet it's the biggest fish in the whole lake."

Connor helped the boy bait his hook and then returned to his chair. But all the while he couldn't stop thinking about Max's statement, how he'd always dreamed of catching a fish that big.

His eyes narrowed, and he looked out beyond the horizon. Kiahna had dreamed of something, too. Becoming a doctor and curing cancer. It hadn't occurred to him until just now, but there could only be one reason why she didn't make it to med school. She'd gotten pregnant.

From what Mr. Ogle had said about Kiahna, her son came first from the moment she found out she was carrying him. She must've made the decision to go it alone, knowing that he had a family of his own in Florida. And the decision cost her every dream she'd ever had. Kiahna raised Max in a small apartment, probably the same one where he'd stayed during that stormy August night. Mr. Ogle said they lived paycheck to paycheck from the day Max was born.

Connor let the truth settle into the barren, sandy bottom of his heart.

Then another thought hit him, the worst one of all.

Kiahna should've been a doctor by now, practicing in some medical building, making rounds at the local hospital, and finding a cure for cancer. The only reason she was on the doomed Western Flight 45 in the first place was because he'd gotten her pregnant, forcing her to keep her flight attendant job and focus entirely on raising Max.

The truth hit him like a city bus, square in the chest. And in that moment he made a decision.

Through his own selfish behavior and ignorance, he'd done enough harm to the precious boy sitting a few feet from him. It was time to step into his life, not out of it. Time to do whatever he could to make Max's life happy and warm and safe, time to shower him with the kind of love Connor was dying to give him. One day he would make up for all he'd cost Max.

Even if he spent his whole life trying.

TWENTY-FOUR

Michele was trying her best to concentrate.

Margie and Sean had invited a few friends over, two couples and Bobby Garrison, an old high school friend of Michele's whom Margie ran into at an art show a few weeks earlier.

From the beginning, the group seemed to be trying too hard to tell funny stories and keep up a light banter. Almost as though Margie had warned them Michele's marriage was on the rocks, so don't let the mood get too somber.

One of the men was talking about a trip he and his wife had taken to Sanibel Island, Florida, a few weeks ago.

"You know Sanibel Island, right, Michele?" The man gave her a quick look, his eyebrows raised, ready to tell whatever story was going to come next.

"Yes." Michele allowed a polite smile. She and Connor spent an anniversary on the Gulf Coast once and stayed a night on Captiva Island, just north of Sanibel. "I know the area."

"Anyway" — the man turned to the others — "we're flying home and we have this layover in New Jersey." He raised one eyebrow. "I know, not exactly a straight route."

His wife laughed and patted the man's knee. "So we have an hour, and John goes to the men's room with the old gray back-pack, the one with the broken zipper that we've been meaning to throw away." She paused only long enough to grab a quick breath. "You know, we used it for our wallets and a bag of snacks, a few books, that kind of thing."

"How was I supposed to know Melinda had her makeup bag inside?"

"So he goes in, with all these tough New Jersey guys and New York businessmen coming and going, and the bag comes open." Melinda was already laughing.

"Makeup spills all over the floor, I mean all over. Foundation and mascara and pencil-type things." He spread his hands out in front of him and made a whooshing sound. "All over the men's room floor."

Other people joined in and were chuckling now. Melinda was gasping for air between bouts of laughter, dabbing at tears in her eyes. "So every one of the guys turns and looks, and there's John." Another burst of laughter. "Scrambling around the floor stuffing makeup into his backpack."

John rolled his eyes. He was laughing so hard his whole upper body shook. He sucked in a breath. "I look up and tell them, uh, it's not like it looks. The makeup belongs to my wife."

"And then . . ." Melinda hooted a few times. "A construction worker heads out the door, rolls his eyes, and says, 'Sure, pal, and I'm the Easter Bunny.' "

The stories continued for the next half hour.

Michele chuckled at the appropriate times, but only because she didn't want to attract attention, didn't want people feeling sorry for her. Every now and then she made eye contact with Bobby across the room, and finally he motioned for her to follow him out onto the back deck.

She waited until he closed the sliding glass door behind them before turning to him. "Thanks."

"Don't worry about it." He leaned against the railing and studied her. "You looked like you needed rescuing."

Michele took up the adjacent rail, a few

feet from her old friend. A cool ocean breeze blew across the deck, and high clouds blocked out the stars. This was the first time she'd been alone with him all evening. "I wasn't in the mood."

They were quiet for a few minutes.

"So . . ." Bobby's eyes held hers. "It's been a long time."

"Twenty years at least." She took in the length of him. "You look good."

"And you."

Michele dismissed the compliment. She was thirty pounds heavier than she'd been the last time she saw him. "Margie says you're an artist."

He shrugged, his grin setting off familiar dimples in both cheeks. "I paint some."

"She says you're good." Michele still held his gaze. "I'd like to see your work."

"Okay." He stretched his legs out some and crossed them at the ankles. "Someday."

She shifted so she could see him better. "Did you and Tammy ever marry?"

"We did." He drew a slow breath. "She left me two years ago for her nursing instructor."

Michele felt her heart sink. Was no one safe? "Tammy?" She looked up and let her gaze settle on the silhouette of mountains in the distance. "You were perfect for each other."

"I thought so, too."

More comfortable silence settled over the moment, and Michele was glad for the chance to see him. She and Bobby had never dated, but they ran in the same circles through junior high and high school. She couldn't remember the number of times the two of them stayed up late talking about one teenage drama or another.

"Margie tells me you're having trouble at home." Bobby hooked his thumbs on the front pockets of his navy Dockers.

"Some." Michele met his eyes again. "Connor had an affair eight years ago. I just found out last week."

Bobby winced.

"Apparently he got the girl pregnant and didn't know it." Michele crossed her arms and willed away the pit in her stomach, the same one that came each time she thought about the situation. "She died in that plane crash in Hawaii; her attorney called Connor because he was listed in the girl's will. The boy has no one, apparently."

A knowing look filled Bobby's expression. "That's why you're here."

"Yes." Michele looked at the animated

discussion still going on inside, and then back at Bobby. "Trying to figure out my life."

His smile was comfortable and easy. He held out his arms. "C'mere, friend. I think you need a hug."

Their hug stirred warm memories — but nothing more. "Thanks, Bobby. I'm glad you're here."

"Me, too." He pulled back. "What is it you want, Michele? Have you thought about it?"

"Yes." She searched his eyes, grateful for the chance to consider the question. "I want to call Connor and tell him I love him."

He did a slow nod. His expression held no disappointment. "Then go. I'll be out here if you need to talk."

For the first time in days, Michele's smile felt genuine. "You're still a great listener, Bobby."

"My pleasure." He gave her a mock bow. "Anything for an old friend."

Michele crept inside unnoticed, slipped into the guest room, and used her sister's phone to place the call. Connor had his cell phone, but she hadn't called once since the trip began. Now it was Thursday night.

She hadn't realized until now just how much she missed Connor. Funny, too, because Connor often was gone longer than three days in the course of flying. But she always knew they'd be together again soon.

This time . . . she wasn't sure.

The number came easily, and after three rings Michele heard a click. "Hello?"

It was Elizabeth. An ache spread across Michele's chest, and she closed her eyes, imagining her oldest daughter sitting with the others around a campfire. "Hi, honey. It's Mommy."

"Mommy!" Elizabeth's voice faded some. "Hey, guys, it's Mom!" She paused. "We miss you so much . . . and we're having such a good time. You should be here, Mommy, can you come? Can you?"

The rush of words left Michele speechless for a moment. She allowed a gentle laugh. "I'm a long ways away, sweetheart. But I miss you, too." Michele bit her lip, not sure she wanted to ask. "How's it going with Max?"

"Great!" Elizabeth's tone held an unreserved happiness. Nothing like the doubt that had plagued her before the trip.

"That's good." Michele hated the way her heart sank at the report. "Tell me about it."

"Well, the first day we helped him with his sleeping bag because he didn't know about the zipper and he had the middle spot and we had the room near the front door, so we helped him. And the next morning we made blueberry pancakes and you won't believe it, Mom. That's Max's favorite kind!" She barely took a breath. "And that day we showed him how to fish, only he didn't catch a big one until yesterday, and he and Daddy reeled it in together and we ate it for dinner, and everyone told him it was the best fish of the trip so far. Oh, and I forgot about yesterday when we went swimming and Max is the best swimmer, Mom. Even better than me and Susan because . . ."

Michele tuned out the rest of the report. Connor and Max caught the best fish of the trip? The image turned her stomach. Why had she called in the first place? After another minute of Elizabeth's report, Michele cut in.

"Honey, is Daddy there?"

"Oh." She made a quick giggling sound. "Sure, Mom. Here he is."

As the phone was passed, Michele heard voices in the background. Susan was singing, and a boy's voice — obviously Max's — was joining her at full volume.

Connor came on. "Hey, just a minute. I'm going to move over by the tent so I can hear." A few moments passed. "Okay. There." He breathed in. "How are you?"

"Fine." She could hear the bitterness in her tone, but she was helpless to do anything about it. "Just thought I'd see how the trip was going."

"It's good." His voice was light and cheery. Didn't he feel any of the emotional turmoil that haunted her every waking moment? "I wish you were here."

She closed her eyes and rested her forehead in her free hand. The small talk was killing her. "Sounds like you're having a good time."

"We are." He hesitated. "Max is getting along great with the girls."

"That's what Elizabeth said."

"He's a great kid, Michele. If you were here, you might think so yourself."

"Connor." She wanted to scream at him. "I didn't call for a glowing report about the boy."

"His name is Max."

Something in her husband's tone — something almost steely — caught her short and made her heart skip a beat. What had happened in the past three days? Was the connection between father and son already so strong that Connor felt the need to defend the boy to her? She held her breath and waited until her heartbeat resumed. Then she gritted her teeth and found her voice. "I know his name, Connor."

"You're always calling him 'the boy,' that's all." His words were gentle again. "Maybe it would help if you called him Max."

"Help what?" Anger stirred. This wasn't at all how she'd expected the call to go.

"Help you accept him." A long silence followed. "Michele, I think we should consider keeping him. He's . . . he's a great kid, and he needs a home." He paused. "How can we turn him away?"

Her eyes flew open and she was on her feet, pacing the length of the room. "Do you *hear* yourself, Connor?" Her voice rose a level. "I thought I made myself clear before I left. I can't bring the son of some floozy flight attendant into my home. I'll think of your . . . your backstreet affair every time I see him!"

"First of all" — Connor was angry now, his words a study in controlled fury — "she wasn't a floozy. And second, it wasn't a backstreet affair. It was wrong, but until you let me explain myself you won't understand how it happened."

Michele's head was spinning, and she thought she might faint. "Connor . . ." She sat on the edge of the bed. It took all her energy to finish her sentence. "You're defending her to me?"

"Michele, you don't understand." The anger was gone, and in its place, Connor sounded defeated.

"No, I don't." She massaged her fingertips into her brow. "I need to go."

"We just started talking."

"I can't think of anything else to say."

"Michele . . . don't do this."

"Good-bye, Connor. I'll call you some other time."

"You're coming home Saturday, right?" He sounded resigned to the fact that they weren't going to get any further tonight. "Same as us?"

"Actually —" Her voice cracked. Her throat was thick, and she waited a moment to find her voice. "I think I'll stay a few more days. I don't know. I'll be in touch."

"Time away isn't going to make any of this any —"

"Connor." She was exhausted, unable to take any more of his pleading. "I'll call you later."

She hung up without saying any of the

things she'd planned to say. Without asking him to tell the girls she was thinking about them, without telling him how badly she missed them, and without doing the one thing she'd set out to do.

Tell him she still loved him.

The receiver was still in her hand. She lay back on the bed and brought her arm up over her eyes. Okay, so he had feelings for the boy. Couldn't he have waited until they were together again to let her know? Did he have to take over the conversation right from the beginning, going on about how great the child was, how well he was getting along with the girls?

She sat up and looked around the room until her eyes fell on her purse, hanging from the back of the door handle. An idea hit her, and though she felt a decade older than she had an hour ago, she struggled to her feet, took the purse, and found the address book in the side pocket.

Connor would've hated the idea of her calling him. But in that moment, nothing could have made the possibility more intriguing. She thumbed through the tiny pages until she reached the *E* section, and there it was.

Loren Evans.

She sniffed and dabbed at her tears once

more. Then she dialed the number. He picked up on the second ring.

"Hello?"

"Loren?" Her tone held none of the sorrow she was feeling. "Hi, it's Michele."

"Why, Michele . . ." His voice filled the phone line, rich and full. She could almost see his smile. "How are you, little girl?"

It'd been six months since she'd called the man, but years since they'd seen each other. *Don't let him guess why I'm here, God . . . please.* "Hey, I'm in Santa Barbara visiting Margie."

Her father-in-law was quiet for a moment. "Brought the whole family?"

"No." She knew her response would come as a relief. Loren would've wanted to see the girls, but certainly not Connor. "I'm by myself." She clicked her fingernails together. "I was thinking about coming by tomorrow, if you're not busy."

"No, ma'am." His chuckle stirred memories of the past. "Not too busy for my favorite daughter-in-law. What time you want to come?"

"After lunch. Say, two o'clock?"

"Great." He stopped. "Everything okay, Michele? You sound upset."

She wasn't sure whether to laugh or cry. That was the exact response she had hoped to get from Connor a few minutes ago. "I'm okay, Loren." She tightened her grip on the receiver and managed to sound believable. "We can catch up tomorrow."

"Okay then. Two o'clock it is."

They hung up, and Michele replaced the receiver on its base.

As she slipped her address book back in her purse, she shook her head. What was she doing? What good could come from spending an hour with Connor's father? It wasn't as if the man had any influence on his son, not anymore. She lay back on the bed again and analyzed her motives for several minutes.

The reason wasn't all that complicated really. Loren Evans represented a part of her past, the part that was honest and real and before her husband's affair. Maybe by spending time with the old man, she could figure out what to do next.

She thought about her sister's party a few rooms away, and Bobby, who was probably waiting for her. But she couldn't face any of them. She changed into her sweats and a T-shirt, brushed her teeth, and climbed into bed. Before she fell asleep, she thought about her faith, the faith she and Connor had always shared.

It had grown dusty in recent years, no

doubt. People wanted their hair cut on Saturdays, and that left only Sundays to run errands and prepare for the coming week. Their combined schedules made church attendance a hit-and-miss event at best. Elizabeth and Susan barely knew their Sunday school teachers, and it had been years since Michele and Connor had offered to help out with one of their classes.

How much softer would the blow of Connor's affair have been if she'd been more connected with the Lord? Would forgiveness have come easier, sooner? She let her thoughts drift, and they landed on a memory from last summer. One of the secretaries at church had called and asked if they still wanted their names on the church registry.

"Of course." She'd given the woman a nervous laugh. "We've been members forever."

"Good." The woman's voice was tender. "We haven't seen you around and we thought we'd ask. I'm glad nothing's changed."

But something had changed, hadn't it?

Connor had cheated on her, and buried the truth for all those years. No wonder he chose yard work instead of church so many Sundays. The guilt probably made being in church just about unbearable.

But what about her? Had she known in the center of her being somehow that Connor had cheated on her, that what they shared wasn't as wonderful as it felt or appeared? She thought about that, and the answer came easily.

No, she hadn't known at all. Not on the surface, and not in the deepest places of her heart. She trusted Connor without reservation, holding nothing back in the way she loved and believed in him. But maybe if she'd been closer to God she would've seen the truth for what it was. Maybe she would've asked more questions about his time in LA or the stormy night when he couldn't call home because he was stuck in Honolulu.

A sigh lifted from the basement of her soul and made its way through her teeth. "Why, God . . . why did we drift?" Her voice was a whisper even she had trouble hearing. "And how are we supposed to find our way back from here?"

She waited for some type of response, but the only sound was the distant party banter.

"God . . . only one thing will save our marriage now." She spoke the words aloud again. They seemed more real that way, more heartfelt. "Please, God . . . find a home for the boy. He needs to be out of our lives, the sooner the better. Please, God."

It would take years to ease the pain of what Connor had done to her. A hundred years to forget it. And if the boy lived with them? The healing would never come, never. It wasn't just the affair, of course. It was the fact that the woman had given Connor the son he'd always wanted. And worst of all, that Connor had lied to her. His deceit had robbed her of even the sweetest memories, because everything about the past looked tainted in light of the lie Connor had carried with him.

As Michele fell asleep she thought about the extent of the damage, the sum of the disaster he'd wreaked on their lives.

Every I love you, every kind word, every happy moment.

All of it was suspect now.

Despite her talk with God, Michele was restless that night. Several times she woke up in tears, and thought about her family and the camping trip they were enjoying with the boy. No question that with him in the picture, their marriage would never work. But unless someone stepped forward to adopt him, Connor wasn't about to let him go. And that was the saddest thing of all. Because of the boy, Connor hadn't only robbed her of her past.

He'd stolen her future as well.

TWENTY-FIVE

It was Friday morning, time for Ramey to pray once more for a miracle.

She was sitting in her recliner with Buddy on the floor beside her. Dogs still weren't allowed at the apartment, but due to the circumstances with Max, she'd gotten an exception from the manager.

In her lap was Kiahna's journal.

Ramey had read all of it in the past week, desperate to better understand the relationship between Kiahna and Max's father. What she'd learned both touched and grieved her. After Connor Evans, Kiahna had never loved another man. Her entire life was devoted to Max and making a good life for him.

If Kiahna had cared about this Connor man so much, then maybe that was really where Max belonged. Maybe it was the very thing that would cause Kiahna to smile from heaven and know that things had worked out after all.

But there was a problem.

Marv Ogle called a few days earlier and told her about the Evans woman's request. Apparently things weren't working out with Max, which meant that he'd come home and be put up for adoption.

"I'm in touch with several private adoption attorneys," Mr. Ogle had told her. "Older children are usually harder to place, but I think we can find a home for him."

She was supposed to be happy with that bit of news, but she couldn't be. She'd read the rest of Kiahna's journal in the days since Max left and she knew the entire story now. The way Kiahna and Connor Evans had met at the airport and how she'd invited him home only as a way of being kind. Island hospitality, really. Or maybe it was the hospitality she drew from her faith.

In the short time that she'd known Connor, Kiahna had come to love him. One journal entry stayed with Ramey and came to mind several times each day since she'd read it.

After Max was born, Kiahna realized something was standing in the way of her and God. Unforgiveness. How dare

Connor sleep with her, make her pregnant, and leave without ever looking back? Didn't she deserve more than that? His callous ability to walk out of her life after what happened was something she couldn't come back from.

Until Max was born.

At that point she realized that love had power beyond anything she'd ever known. And it occurred to her that with bitterness and hate in her heart, she never would be able to love Max the way she wanted to love him. After Max was born, she wrote in her journal that she'd finally figured out what love was.

Ramey found the entry and read it again.

Love is what happens when people forgive. I forgive Connor Evans. A part of me will always love him, but from this day on I won't hate him. Not for one minute. I forgive him because he gave me Max.

If only the Evans woman could understand that simple truth. Love happens when people forgive.

Ramey flipped a page just as the phone rang. She picked up the receiver from the table near her chair and clicked the on button. "Hello?"

"Ramey, it's Marv Ogle. How are you?"

She'd been to the doctor the day before. Heart disease was making an uncontested run at her body, but that didn't matter. Her focus was on seeing that Max had a family. "Fine. What's the news?"

"Good, I think. I got a call this morning from an attorney on the big island. He says he has a family who owns a B&B near the beach. They've decided to adopt a young boy, someone to help them keep the place up, and take over the business one day."

Ramey scrunched up her face. "Where's the good part?"

"I know." The attorney was trying to sound positive. "That's what I thought. But I called the couple and talked to the woman. They lost their boy in a drowning three years ago. She's interested in Max, Ramey."

"Sounds like she needs a hired hand." Beside her, Buddy lifted his furry head and gave a sad-sounding yawn. Ramey reached down and patted him. "Max is a little boy, Mr. Ogle."

"I know. We talked about that. She said she'd homeschool him and teach him how to make pottery and build wicker furniture and put together an authentic Hawaiian luau. It doesn't sound too bad, really. They live in a pretty remote area; sounds like they want a child to keep them company. Someone to leave their life's work to."

"What about Buddy?" Ramey heard the suspicion in her voice, but she didn't care. Kiahna had loved Max with all her heart. Placing him in a situation where he wouldn't receive that type of love would be the greatest tragedy in Ramey's life.

"Yes, well, that's a problem."

"How come?" Ramey rubbed the soft fur under Buddy's ear.

"The woman's allergic to dogs, apparently."

Ramey smacked her lips. "That would never do for Max. He needs a lot of love and he needs Buddy."

The attorney exhaled in a way that rattled Ramey's nerves. "You need to understand something, Ramey. Older children don't get adopted easily." He paused. "Mrs. Evans said she and her husband were praying for the boy to find a family in Hawaii. They aren't interested in keeping him."

"Then *you* keep him." Her voice was louder than before. Buddy sat up and rubbed his wet nose against the back of her hand.

"We've already discussed that. My wife

and I are too old to be the boy's parents. We love him, of course, but we're on the road half the year traveling and neither of us are home during the day when we're on the island. Max needs a family."

Angry tears filled Ramey's eyes, and she rubbed her back teeth together to keep from crying. When she could speak, she made her voice more calm than before. "Wanna know what I think?"

"What?" The attorney sounded tired.

"I think Mr. Evans wants to keep Max. It's just a hunch, but every time I pray about it that's the picture I get." She tapped her finger on the cover of Kiahna's journal. "It's that wife of his we need to pray for."

"I'll tell you what, Ramey. You pray for the wife, and I'll pursue the couple on the big island. One way or another we'll find Max a home. Deal?"

"Deal." Ramey didn't like the sound of that, but she had no choice, really. She said good-bye and hung up the phone.

Buddy cocked his head and made a whining sound. "You miss him, huh, boy?"

The dog gave a sharp bark.

"I know, me too." She scratched Buddy beneath the chin and turned her attention back to God.

The praying had to get stronger, twice as often, twice as long as before. Because either God worked the forgiveness miracle for Max, or the boy would lose everything he had left in life. With that thought, Ramey bowed her head and began to pray for that forgiveness miracle she'd asked God about before Max left.

Only this time she prayed as if her next breath depended on the outcome.

TWENTY-SIX

Loren Evans had moved twelve paper towers from the living room into various other parts of his ranch house. It was one o'clock on Friday afternoon, and Michele was coming in an hour. He wanted the place to look respectable.

Now that he'd finished tidying up, he found his Bible, the one he'd purchased for himself a year ago Christmas, and sat with it at the dining room table. With gentle fingers he flipped to the back of the book, to a place where he'd made a list of the things he was asking God for.

The things he was begging Him for.

First on the list was that somehow, someday, he and his son might find a way to bridge the ocean that lay between them. And now, after years of not seeing Connor or his wife, Michele had called and wanted to visit. Loren studied his handwriting, the way he'd carefully written out the request:

Span the bridge, God. Bring me and my boy back together.

Yes, this visit from Michele had to be part of the answer, he had no doubt. The thing he wasn't sure about was exactly what part her visit would play. After all, seeing her couldn't possibly remove the thing that stood largest in the way of bringing the two of them together.

Because that thing was pride. A pilot's pride. After twenty-five years in the skies, Loren Evans knew a thing or two about pilot's pride. A pilot couldn't afford to be wrong, not ever. Not that pilots didn't make mistakes; that wasn't it. But when a pilot erred, he didn't view his actions as a mistake. He viewed it as a change in plans, something to be battled and dealt with.

Wrong was almost never admitted, at least not among the more talented pilots.

It had been that way for Loren, and he was certain it was that way for his son. That type of pride didn't always fall away when a pilot stepped out of his uniform at the end of a day.

The very thing that made Connor and him strong as pilots was the reason the two of them hadn't spoken in nearly eight years.

For most of that time, Loren had been

content to wait. His decision not to give Connor the money for the airport was the right one. He stood by it even now. The boy had no idea what it took to run an airport. His only reason for wanting to buy the property was so he could run from the FAA investigation.

Loren understood. No pilot liked being scrutinized by the FAA. But Loren had followed the case from a distance, talking to pilots in the know and getting the rest of the details when Michele called each Christmas. Connor's case had been dropped, just the way Loren knew it would be. Connor was most certainly a stronger pilot for the trials he'd gone through that year.

So through the first six years, Loren waited for Connor's call.

Once, halfway through that period, Michele asked him the obvious. "Don't wait for him to call you, Loren. Call him. That would solve everything."

Ah, but that's where she was wrong. It was where she was still wrong.

A year ago Christmas, Michele called and conversation turned to Connor. "Does he forgive me yet?"

She made a tired sound. "Honestly?"

"Honestly."

"No, Loren. He's holding onto it like his life depends on it." Her voice had filled with tears. "I'm sorry. It's Christmastime, and I wish . . . I wish more than anything that he'd call you."

The brokenness of her voice that year stayed with him for days. Later that week, his doctor expressed concern about his blood pressure.

"People don't live forever, Mr. Evans," the doctor had said. "You're on as much medication as we can give you. If the pressure keeps going up, it'll only be a matter of time."

Combined with Michele's sorrow, the events of that December caused him to do something he hadn't done since his beloved Laurel was alive. He went to church and prayed for his son. But he realized a truth that stood to this day. A hundred phone calls from him wouldn't help bridge the distance between them.

Not as long as Connor thought he was right.

No, it would take a change on Connor's part. A realization that he no longer had a need to stay angry about the money Loren hadn't lent him. An understanding that he was wrong to walk out that day, wrong to make a declaration that their relationship was over. And until he could admit that much, Loren was helpless to make a move.

Still, he prayed about it.

And since that Christmas, he hadn't missed a week at church. The new awareness of God and His workings in Loren's life had caused some changes in him, made him a little less rough around the edges, a bit more quick to recognize his faults.

He saw less of Connor's sisters these days; the girls were busy with their children, caught up in their own lives. The extra time allowed him more golf games with his friends from church, more time to play croquet with a few of the guys from the local school board he'd been appointed to.

But most important, it gave him more time to pray for Connor.

And for the next thirty minutes, until he heard Michele's car pull up in the driveway, he did just that.

Michele's palms were sweaty as she headed up the walkway and knocked on Loren Evans's door. She wore a pair of beige slacks and a navy blazer, and she pressed the wrinkles out of it as she waited. Maybe he wouldn't notice the weight she'd gained.

The moment he opened the door she chided herself for worrying about her looks. Loren lit into a smile that filled his entire face. He was out on the porch hugging her before she had time even to say hello. "Michele, my girl, you look gorgeous!"

Connor's father had always been like this. Gregarious and outgoing, friendly in a way that made people want to come back soon for another visit. He'd only been reserved around one person — his son. Connor explained it was because his father expected more from him than from other people. Either way, Michele always found it sad that she could hug Loren more easily than his own son could.

Loren still had his arms around her as she leaned back and took in the sight of him. His hair was whiter than before, thinning some. But otherwise he looked the same. Tall and robust, the same way Connor would no doubt look when he was in his sixties. There was something different about his eyes, but Michele couldn't quite place it. Maybe it was just old age. She kissed his cheek. "How are you, Loren?"

"I'm good, but I've missed you." He removed one arm and pointed the way into the house. "And how about those grandbabies of mine?"

"They're not babies anymore." Michele followed him into the house and onto a sofa in the front room. Loren sat in an adjacent recliner. "Elizabeth's ten and Susan's eight. They're getting taller every day."

"I bet they're beautiful. Just like their mother."

There it was again, and this time Michele was certain. It wasn't old age or her imagination. Connor's father had a softness in his eyes that couldn't be explained by something as simple as the passing of time.

She searched his face, looking for clues. "What's new with you, Loren? You look different somehow."

He cocked his head and winked at her. "Evans men age well, that's all."

"You've been keeping busy, then?"

"Actually . . . I've been hanging out with the church crowd." He gave her a smile that warmed the room. "Going to service each week, reading the Bible, walking with the Lord." The smile faded. "Praying for Connor."

Michele was glad she was sitting down. She had always liked Connor's father. But even when his wife was alive, he'd only gone to church once in a while to please her. Before their fallout, Loren's lack of faith was one of Connor's gravest concerns.

And now — despite the season of pain and separation between father and son — God had brought Loren into a place of believing. The reality of what had happened shot a thrill through her, one she had hardly expected from their visit.

"So how is he, Michele?" Lauren settled back into his recliner and lifted the footrest. "Any closer to breaking?"

Michele folded her hands and looked to the deeper places of Loren's heart. "I think he might be further than ever." She bit her lip, warding off the tears that already threatened her voice. "Things aren't so good, Loren."

He pursed his lips and gave a single nod. "I didn't think so. Something in your voice yesterday."

"He and the kids are camping this week. Our annual trip to the lake."

"And you're here with your sister?" A shadow fell across his expression. "Then it's worse than I thought."

"Yes."

Loren returned the footrest to its normal

position and slid to the edge of his chair. "Tell me about it, Michele. I want to know."

She hated telling the story, hated the way it drained her and confirmed her new reality all at the same time. Her eyes held his until she found the courage to speak. "Connor had an affair."

Loren's reaction played across his eyes like one of those animated billboard signs. Shock, then hurt, then anger. Proof that Loren still had a tough attitude reserved for Connor. "Whatever was the boy thinking?"

"It was eight years ago, right after the two of you, well, after the two of you stopped talking."

Connor's father closed his eyes for a moment. When he opened them he looked as if he'd aged two years in as many seconds. "Has it happened since?"

"No. Connor says it hasn't, and I believe him, crazy as that sounds."

Loren made a fist with one hand and covered it with the other. He exhaled hard. "So, he kept it from you all these years?"

"Yes." Michele blinked so she could see through the wetness that had gathered in her eyes. "He wouldn't have told me at all, but we got a phone call a few weeks ago from an attorney in Hawaii."

"Hawaii?"

"That's where he had the affair." Michele rattled off the details as she knew them, up to and including Kiahna's death in the plane crash. After a few minutes she came to the point. "Connor has a son, Loren. A boy named Max Riley. He's seven years old, and he's with Connor and the girls right now."

Loren's face grew several shades paler. "He got the girl pregnant?"

"Yes." Michele used the sleeve of her blazer to dab at her tears. "He didn't know until now."

"Connor always wanted a son." The man's words sounded like he was in a trance, the facts not even close to settling in yet. "And now . . . is he . . . is he going to live with you?"

"Connor wants that, I know he does." Michele felt her chin quiver. "But I don't think I can do it, Loren. Every time I see the boy I think of his mother."

"He looks like her?" Connor's father was spellbound, as shocked by the news as Margie had been.

"No." She sniffed. "He looks like Connor." Her eyes held his. "Actually he looks a lot like you, Loren. But his eyes are

394

green like hers, and . . . I don't know what to do."

"Does Connor know how you feel?"

"Of course." She lifted her hands and let them fall again. "Honestly . . . I don't know if we're going to make it."

"Hmm." He stood, crossed the room, and sat down beside her. "I'm sorry, Michele. So sorry. For all of Connor's stubborn pilot personality, I never thought he'd be unfaithful. He was never that kind of man."

"I didn't think so, either."

He patted her knee. "I guess I have something else to pray about, don't I?"

"Yes." She peered up at him through fresh tears. "Pray for Connor to change his mind about the boy. And pray for me. That I'll hear what God's trying to tell me, okay, Loren?"

For a long time he looked at her. Then he stroked his chin and his eyes grew thoughtful. "Sometimes the thing He's telling us is not what we expect."

The man's words settled like rocks in Michele's heart. If he meant that maybe God wanted her to keep the boy, she wanted to tell him he was wrong. But before she could answer back, Loren smiled and patted her knee again. "I didn't even offer you something to eat."

The moment Michele pulled out of the driveway, Loren knew.

Eighteen months of praying about his relationship with Connor convinced him that what had happened in the past few weeks, the revelation of his son's affair, the reality of the little boy, were not mere random events. Rather they were part of an intricate plan God was working in Connor's life.

Perhaps in all their lives.

His first instinct was to work on Michele, wear down her bitterness, convince her that perhaps the little boy should be part of their lives after all. But after sharing a cup of coffee with her, he recognized something about that option. It was self-serving. Because deep in his heart he loved the picture of one day — before his own death — reconciling with Connor and meeting his grandson. The only boy to carry on the Evans name.

Toward the end of his visit with his daughter-in-law, he silently asked God about it. *Tell me, Lord, what do I say to make her change her mind?*

Son . . . be still and know that I am God. My ways are not your ways.

Often since that amazing Christmas, Loren had sensed God putting a knowing in his spirit, his soul. Not audible words or even a direct voice, really, but an understanding that the thought currently on the stage of his mind had been sent straight from heaven.

But this time . . . this time the words were so clear, Loren couldn't resist glancing over his shoulder. At almost the same time he realized what had happened. No one behind him had spoken, but rather God was determined to make His point.

Be still and know that I am God . . . My ways are not your ways . . .

Both Bible verses had come up in his reading over the past two months, but now, put together, they formed a message that stopped Loren in his tracks. No question what God wanted him to glean from the words. Though with all his being he wanted to be in control here, help Michele accept Connor's son and find a way to make everyone come together, God wanted him to let that idea go and instead to consider what was best.

For heaven's sake, not his own.

And so for the rest of Michele's visit, up to and including the moment when she pulled out of the driveway, Loren thought

397

through the scenario. Michele wasn't being selfish, not really. On a practical note, she and Connor had decided long ago that two children were enough. She ran her own business and would hardly have time for one more set of homework papers, one more load of laundry.

And this wasn't any other child. It was — as Michele had said — a boy with his mother's eyes, one who would be a constant reminder of Connor's unfaithfulness. Maybe it was Connor who was being selfish in wanting to keep the child. Maybe the greatest way he could show his love for Michele and the girls would be to give the boy up.

Then there was the boy.

At first Loren thought that having him stay with Connor and Michele was the best situation for him. But was it?

The child had spent all his life in Hawaii. He had friends there, and — in the attorney and his wife, and the older babysitter — the boy had adults who cared a great deal for him. The sum of it made up his home, the place where he would best remember his mother and feel connected to his past.

These thoughts, all of them, came as Loren allowed God to bring them. Not as some sort of wishful thinking or attempt to manipulate the outcome, but quiet and slow and true. The way God often brought His ways into focus.

As Michele left that afternoon, Loren's understanding of what God wanted from them was not only clear, it was urgent. Urgent enough that as he caught his reflection in the entryway mirror, he felt a sureness well up inside him, a prodding of what he had to do next.

It was something drastic, something he wouldn't have considered doing earlier that day or any other time in the past eight years. He would have to wait until Monday, of course, until the camping trip was over and his son was back home with his three children. But then he would do it, because if God wanted him to, then even a pilot's pride couldn't stop him.

Come Monday afternoon he would do the one thing that — in light of the recent events — truly could change all their lives forever.

He would call his son.

TWENTY-SEVEN

Max liked fishing, but he liked sitting beside Mr. Evans even better.

It was the last day of their camping trip, and he and Mommy's friend had an idea that they wouldn't fish in their chairs. 'Lizabeth and Susan found some friends and so they were swimming. Susan said it was 'cause sometimes even tomboy girls got tired of putting worms on a hook.

But Max wasn't tired at all. His mommy always said she would teach him to fish. She said it when he was five and when he was six and later when it turned to summer. But she didn't. Mr. Evans said because she ran out of time, that's why. And now that the camping trip was almost up, Max and Mr. Evans were running out of time, too.

So that morning Mr. Evans smiled at him and roughed up his hair. "What about something different today, Max?"

Max wasn't sure what that meant, but he shrugged his shoulders very big and said, "Sure." Because he trusted Mommy's friend about everything.

The different thing was that today he and Mr. Evans took their fishing stuff down the beach to the big rock, the one he'd found a few days ago when he wanted to talk to God about his mommy. The rock was tall and warm and just enough bumpy so that they could sit on it side by side and do their fishing.

Catching fish was really cool, cooler than he ever thought it would be. But sitting beside Mr. Evans was better because they could talk about lots of things. Things like Ramey and Buddy and the stuff he would miss most about his mommy. Mr. Evans didn't treat him like a kid, because guess what? He really listened! His eyes and face told Max that he wanted to know the things Max was saying.

And that felt better than catching fish.

Another thing was that his arm was up against Mr. Evans's arm ever since they climbed up and sat on the rock. Mommy's friend had big arms with strong muscles in them. Next to him, Max felt safe.

Sometimes he even pretended Mr. Evans was his daddy.

That's the thing he was thinking about right now. Because maybe he would never find his own daddy, but if Mr. Evans would let him get Buddy and come back to Florida, maybe he could stay there and pretend forever that Mr. Evans was his daddy. 'Lizabeth and Susan liked him better now, and maybe Mrs. Evans wouldn't be mad at him when they got back from the trip. So maybe it could work out.

At breakfast that morning he made a secret plan about that idea. A secret plan was when you had a thing in your head but didn't tell anyone else, not even grownups.

His secret plan was to talk to Mr. Evans that day and ask him if he was really good and if Buddy didn't bark very much, could they come and live there forever.

Now, sitting on the rock with their arms touching, Max swallowed hard. It was time. The secret plan had to happen now, because there might not be another chance.

"Mr. Evans?" Max had on one of the man's baseball caps so he didn't have to use his hand as a shield. He squinted up at his mommy's friend. "I have a question."

"Okay, Max." Mr. Evans moved his

fishing rod to his other hand, and then Max felt the man's strong arm come around his shoulders. He hoped his question wouldn't make Mr. Evans mad because he didn't want him to take his arm away. Not for a long time. Relaxed was in the man's eyes, plus also a smile. "What's your question?"

"Well . . ." He was about to do the secret plan, but all of a sudden a butterfly landed on his fishing pole, just a little space up from his hands. He made his voice into a hushing sound. "Look!"

"Hey, how about that." Mr. Evans leaned in and looked close at the butterfly. "It's a monarch."

"That's the same kind we have!" Max still used his best whisper voice. Only now his throat felt funny, because this was sort of like a special butterfly day, but his mommy wasn't here to see it.

Before he could say anything, a couple of tears slipped from his eyes and landed on his dirty jeans.

"Max?" Mr. Evans looked at him. "What is it, pal? Why the tears?"

Max did a quiet sniff because the butterfly was still there, but it was moving its wings very slow. Butterflies did that when they were thinking about flying away. He wiped his cheek on the shoulder part of his T-shirt and told the tears to go away. When they left a little, he looked at Mr. Evans. "Butterflies were special for me and my mommy."

"Oh." Mr. Evans's face made a sad, thinking sort of look. "I didn't know that."

Max felt his mommy's friend scratch his arm a little, the way grown-ups did when they felt sorry for you. "Yeah." He stared at the butterfly again. "We used to have special butterfly days, where we'd see tons of 'em." He looked at Mr. Evans again. "A whole butterfly village."

Mr. Evans bit his lip and studied the wings of the butterfly. "I'd like to see that, a whole village of butterflies. They're very pretty."

"God's bestest artwork."

"Yes."

The butterfly took a few tiny bug steps toward Max's hand, and he remembered some of the things Mommy always said on their special butterfly days. "Know what Mommy says about butterflies?" He felt his smile fall. "What she used to say?"

The sad in Mr. Evans's face got worse. "What, Max?"

"She said they prove that God gives second chances."

"Butterflies prove that?" Mommy's friend tilted his head.

"Yeah, because a butterfly spends all those days as a callipillar, scooting on the ground. Did you know that?"

"I did." Mr. Evans eyes were serious. Max figured it was because he liked this story.

"Then one day" — Max stared at the butterfly — "one day he gets tired of scooting around, so he builds a little room and takes a nap there." Max made his voice quiet again because sometimes it would get loud when he told a good story. And the story of his special butterfly days was a very good one. "But know what the bestest part is, Mr. Evans?"

"What?" His face was closer now, because they both had shushed their words so the butterfly wouldn't leave.

"One day the callipillar wakes up and God has done an amazing thing. The callipillar shakes his shoulders a little, and what do you know? There's something on his back!" Max shook his back a very little to show Mr. Evans what he meant. The butterfly gave a big flap of his wings, but still he stayed on the fishing pole. "That thing is wings, Mr. Evans. And now the callipillar doesn't have to scoot around on the ground because —"

"Because he can fly." A smile came on Mr. Evans face. "And that's his second chance, right?"

"Right! And Mommy always said one day me and her aren't going to scoot anymore, either, because God loves us more than He loves the butterflies."

The butterfly started taking small steps again, only this time Max felt him walk his scratchy little feet right up onto his fingers. "Wow." Max made the word as hushed as he could. "I never felt a butterfly walk on me before."

Mr. Evans set his fishing pole down and did a closer look. "How does it feel?"

In that second Max had tears in his heart because of something he remembered. Something from his mommy's letter. The tears spilled out again, quiet and slow, and even when he tried he couldn't make them stop.

"Max? You okay?" Mr. Evans got worry in his lips where the smile used to be.

"I remembered something my mommy said in the letter. The one Mr. Ogle read after she was gone."

Little bumps came in Mr. Evans's chin. Maybe he didn't want to know what his mommy's letter said. Plus also his eyes had some new wet in them. But then he said, "Would you like to tell me what she wrote in the letter?"

"Yes." Max nodded very slow because the butterfly was still moving its little feet on his hand. "I would like that very much." Max tried to remember his mommy's words from the letter. "She told me that she was in heaven now and that . . . finally she was getting her second chance."

"Like the butterfly?" A teardrop rolled down the side of Mr. Evans's face, but his words were clear. Not stuck in his throat like Max's sometimes got.

"Yes." He blinked so he could see the butterfly better. "She said that one day soon we'd be together again and we'd never scoot around on the ground. Instead we would fly. Forever and ever we would fly."

The butterfly did a tickly dance step on his hand, first one way, then the other. Then he flapped his soft wings faster than before. So fast it was hard to see the lines of brown and orange and black because they mixed all together.

In a quick rush, the butterfly lifted up and stayed above the big rock, bouncing and lifting and falling until finally it moved up over the beach and toward a faraway tree.

Max watched him go and the whole time he wished he could have real wings, so he could chase the butterfly and catch him again, keep him so he would never forget about special butterfly days. When the butterfly was gone, the hole in his heart felt the same big as it did when he first found out about his mommy being dead.

"Max . . ." Mr. Evans hugged him close. Then he looked at him so their eyes were hooked together. "Thanks for telling me that story. I know how special it is for you."

"Yes." He sniffed again, but not as soft as before. He wanted to cover up his face and cry, but he wanted to talk to Mr. Evans even more. And you couldn't talk very much when you were crying. Plus, his mommy told him whenever he was sad or afraid to be extra brave. "Mommy had something else special for me, too."

"You can tell me if you want, Max." Mr. Evans voice was soft like the wind from the lake. He began to turn the little handle on his fishing pole.

"She had a special song for me." He tugged the hat on his head to make sure it was still there. It belonged to Mr. Evans and it was too big, so he was extra careful not to lose it. "Me and her sang it all the time."

Mr. Evans said nothing at first. He kept turning the little handle, and now the bobber and hook came out of the water and right back to Mr. Evans. The worm was gone, so he reached into a little box of dirt and took out a long squiggly one. Then he bunched it up, put it on the hook, and stood up. Next he jerked his pole real hard to the side and the hook and worm and bobber went flying out over the lake. Then he sat down and said, "Do you remember it?"

"O' course." Max smiled at Mr. Evans, but inside his heart felt sad at that thing. He looked at his bobber and decided it was time to check his worm, too. He began to turn the handle and he watched the bobber come bouncing closer on the water.

Mr. Evans brought his legs up high and rested his fishing pole on his knee. "Could you sing it for me, Max?"

Max kept turning the handle on his fishing pole, but inside his head he was thinking very hard. Because this was a big thing. He never sang his special song with anyone but his mommy. After she died he sang it to Buddy, because Buddy was his best friend. But no one else in the world ever heard it. Still . . . He looked at Mr. Evans and tried to tell if he just asked

409

about the song to be nice or if he really wanted to hear it.

And right then he knew. Because Mr. Evans's eyes had a serious look that grown-ups got when they really meant something. He took a break from the handle on his fishing pole and set it on the big rock, the way Mr. Evans had done before. Then he folded his arms tight and looked at Mr. Evans again. "It has hand motions."

"Okay."

Max nodded. Then he put his hands over his heart and started to sing. "I love you, Max, the most . . ." He brushed one hand against the other. "I love to make you toast . . ." Wide open arms. "When oceans we're apart . . ." Hands back over his chest. "You're always in my heart."

"That's beautiful." Mr. Evans eyes were shiny.

"My mommy had to stay in Japan some nights because of her plane didn't come home at night. It came home in the morning time." The peanut-butter feeling in his throat was back, but he pushed the words out anyway. "She made up that song so I would know she was always with me. Even if the ocean stood in the way."

This time he was sure Mr. Evans looked sad, and he put his hand over his eyes and pinched his nose. The same way Mommy used to do when she was feeling extra much like a callipillar. After a minute he made a hard breathing sound and wiped his hands across his cheeks. "Could you sing it one more time, Max?"

So he did. This time he looked out across the lake and sang it with no hand motions. Just his hands on his heart so he would remember that she was there still.

"I love you, Max, the most . . . I love to make you toast. When oceans we're apart, you're always in my heart."

After that, they didn't talk for a long time. Max's head was busy thinking about his mommy and whether he had a worm on his hook still or not. He turned the handle until the bobber and hook came flying out of the water. Only they didn't come in nice and slow like when Mr. Evans did it. So Mommy's friend leaned close again, caught his pole, and helped him catch the hook.

"Can I pick the worm?" Picking the worm was the best part of fishing. Unless you caught a fish, o' course.

Mr. Evans made a little laugh. "Go ahead." He held the worm box over, and Max picked the biggest, fattest one he could find.

"The fish will love you, Mr. Worm."

It was extra strong, though, so Mr. Evans helped him put it on the hook and shoot it back out across the water. They sat like that for another long time, and then Mr. Evans turned to him. A little sad still stayed in his eyes.

"Okay, Max. Now what were you going to ask me, remember?" Mr. Evans took his arm away and picked up his fishing pole again. "Before the butterfly came?"

Max sat a little straighter. He almost forgot about the secret plan. He did a little cough so his voice would be extra strong. "Well, this week has been a lot of fun for me."

"Yes." A smile came into Mr. Evans's face and moved all the way up to his eyes. "It's been fun for me, too."

"Okay, so remember I told you about my prayer, that I would find my daddy out there somewhere?"

"Yes." More sad colored Mr. Evans's smile. "I remember."

Max tugged on the front of his cap and squinted up at Mr. Evans. "I did some thinking in my head about that, and what if I never find that daddy?" Max leaned back a little so he could see Mr. Evans better. "And so the thinking in my head told me what if I could pretend *you* were my daddy, Mr. Evans. I could go home and get Buddy and the two of us could live here with you and Mrs. Evans and 'Lizabeth and Susan forever."

Little muscles came out on the sides of Mr. Evans's mouth and he looked out at the lake. After a minute he made a sound in his throat and said, "That would be wonderful, Max."

"Do you think maybe I could do that? Because Ramey said she's too old to keep me and Mr. Ogle and his wife are never home and the manager is giving my apartment to another family, so I'm not even sure where my home is right now." Max told himself to stop talking. His mommy told him he talked too fast when he was excited, and he wanted Mr. Evans to understand every word he said.

"You want to stay with us, is that what you're saying?"

"Yes, sir. Mr. Evans, I mean. If that would be okay with you then I could get Buddy and pretend you were my daddy. If you don't mind too much."

"Max . . ." One more time Mr. Evans put his fishing pole down against the big rock, and this time he hugged him with both hands, the way he always did with

'Lizabeth and Susan. "I want that, too. I do." He pulled himself back some so they could see each other. "We both need to pray that God will help us work that out."

Something inside him said that maybe there was a problem with his plan. "Because Mrs. Evans might not want me to stay, is that why we should pray?"

"Mrs. Evans likes you, Max."

Max felt Mr. Evans move his fingers along his forehead. Then the man looked straight into his heart. Max did a little gulp. "Really?"

"Really. But still I think we should pray about it."

And so all that afternoon, even when they each caught the two biggest fishes in the lake, Max prayed. He prayed during dinner and while they built the campfire, and he prayed that night when he fell asleep in the tent next to Mr. Evans.

He prayed that maybe he wouldn't have to wait until heaven for his wings. Because if he could live with Mr. Evans and Mrs. Evans and 'Lizabeth and Susan, then they could be his own family forever. Then he would be sure his mommy was right, that God really did give people second chances. And so he prayed that if it was okay with God, Mr. Evans could be his pretend daddy. That way he wouldn't have to scoot around on the ground anymore, and he wouldn't have to wait till heaven for his wings.

Instead, he would fly right here in Florida.

TWENTY-EIGHT

Connor and the kids were home less than an hour when the call came in.

They'd been busy since pulling into the garage, unloading the camping gear, and cleaning it for next time. Max and the girls were so at ease with each other it was hard to tell they hadn't known each other forever.

Something in the genes, Connor told himself. *They're related, after all, even if they don't know it.*

The only sobering part of the afternoon was the obvious. Michele wasn't home. He hadn't heard from her since her cell phone call midway through the week. Her silence angered him. How was he supposed to help her understand the situation when she kept her distance in every way?

He planned to call her after everything was put away and the kids were busy in the backyard, but not until then. It would take that much time to let his anger cool, to re-member that even if she was making things more difficult, the mess they were in wasn't her fault.

At just after four, he was helping Max put away the fishing gear when the phone rang. "Be right back." He set down the tackle box and jogged into the house. He clicked the on button just before the an-swering machine picked up. "Hello?"

"Mr. Evans?"

"Yes." The voice was familiar in a vague sort of way. Connor leaned against the kitchen island and forced himself to con-centrate. "Can I help you?"

"This is Mr. Ogle, the attorney in Hono-lulu."

"Mr. Ogle, hello." Connor glanced at the calendar. It was Monday. They still had five days before the two weeks were up. "Things are going very well with Max."

"Oh." Surprise filled the man's tone. "I'm glad. A good two weeks together has to be better than the alternative." He paused. "Anyway, I went ahead and did as you asked. I put out feelers with the attor-neys I know, and late last week I found a couple that's very interested."

Connor's chest felt suddenly tight, and he couldn't take a deep breath. What was the attorney talking about? "Mr. Ogle, I never asked you to . . . I've been camping all week with the children."

"But your wife said . . ."

Heat filled Connor's cheeks. A picture was taking shape, one he couldn't fathom. Because the Michele he knew and loved would never have done such a thing. He gave a shake of his head, as if maybe that could clear up the situation and make sense of it. "My wife said what?"

"So you don't know?"

"Mr. Ogle" — Connor massaged his brow with his thumb and forefinger — "I have no idea what you're talking about."

"I see." The weight of the predicament sounded heavy in the attorney's voice. "I should explain, then." He gave a tired-out breath. "Your wife contacted me last week and said you'd made a decision. Max needed to come home at the end of the two weeks. She asked me to start looking for an adoptive family for the boy, the sooner the better."

Connor could feel the blood draining from his face. She couldn't have done that, not without talking to him. When he remained silent, Mr. Ogle continued.

"I explained that finding adoptive parents for an older child could take months, years even, but she told me she was praying it would happen sooner. She told me the two of you wanted a phone call if I found anyone."

Connor's heart was pounding so close to the surface, he could feel the beat in his neck and temple. "And now . . . now you've found a family?"

"Yes." He hesitated. "They've already started the process."

"But they've never even *met* Max." How had he lost control so quickly? His son was all but gone from his life, and they'd never had a chance to see that things turned out different.

"They run a bed-and-breakfast on the big island, Mr. Evans. Apparently they lost their son in a drowning accident a few years back. They want a boy about Max's age, someone to keep them company and learn the family business so he can take it over when they're too old to run it."

Connor couldn't believe any of it. He groped his way along the counter and dropped to the nearest kitchen stool. Not only had the attorney found adoptive parents for Max, but he had the boy's entire life planned out. All because of Michele's phone call. He wanted to scream that none of this was fair, that Max didn't want to live at a bed-and-breakfast or keep some older couple company all his life.

God . . . help me, here. This can't be happening.

"Mr. Evans?" The attorney sounded tentative, as though he understood the dilemma even before it was spelled out to him. "I'm sorry all of this comes as a surprise to you."

"Yes." Connor squeezed his eyes and tried to think of what to do next.

"Daddy . . . can we go out and play?" The girls ran into the house, with Max on their heels. "Please, can we? The car's cleaned out."

"Sure." He forced himself to smile. "I'll be out there in a bit."

When the blur of noise and motion was out in the backyard, Connor felt a lump choking his throat, cutting off every important thing he wanted to say. He massaged his neck for a moment, then did two short coughs. "Mr. Ogle, my wife and I never discussed this."

"So there's a chance you might want to adopt the boy after the two weeks are up?"

"Yes, there's a big chance." Connor didn't need even a moment to think about his answer. "The girls and I, we've connected very . . . very strongly to Max."

"And Mrs. Evans?"

"She didn't go with us on the camping trip." He gritted his teeth. "I'm expecting her home anytime, though. After that, I'm sure she'll feel the same way."

The attorney paused. "And if she doesn't?"

If she doesn't?

If Michele didn't fall in love with Max the way he had, was that what the man meant? For the past week he'd convinced himself that such a possibility didn't exist, that of course his wife would go along with the most obvious, most loving solution for Max. But now the attorney's question caused his heart to beat faster and harder than he could ever remember.

If Michele didn't love Max, if she didn't want him to stay, then he would have to choose, wouldn't he? The very idea made his head spin, and dropped his heart to his knees. God wouldn't let that happen, would He? Michele would come to her senses, surely she would.

But what if she didn't . . .

"Mr. Evans, I need to know what to do. The couple is very interested in Max. They want me to give them pictures and move ahead with the process." Kindness filled his tone, but clearly he needed an answer.

"What should I tell them?"

Connor drew in a long, slow breath and straightened himself. "Could you hold off for a few days, Mr. Ogle?" He moved to the patio door and stared at the children — his children — playing together on the backyard swing set. "You told us we had two weeks before we had to make a decision. Give us that at least. Please."

The attorney considered that for a beat. "Okay. I can put off moving ahead with their application until Thursday afternoon. I'll need to know by then."

Relief like a drug flooded Connor's veins and made his knees weak. He hadn't lost the boy yet. "Thank you, Mr. Ogle. I'll be in touch."

He was just hanging up the phone when he heard the patio door behind him. A quick look over his shoulder and he saw Max, a tired grin stretched across his face. The resemblance to himself, to his father, was striking. "I think I'm tuckered out."

Connor set the receiver down and tried to ignore the heaviness in his heart. He turned and gave Max his full attention. "Are the girls tuckered, too?"

"No, they're playing house."

"And they let you get away?" He raised his eyebrows.

"They wanted me to be the little brother, but I told them little brothers sometimes take rests."

"I see." Connor grinned but contained a chuckle. He motioned for Max to come closer. "Good call."

"Yeah." Max stretched his arms over his head and yawned.

"You really are tired." Connor put his hand on Max's shoulder and gave it a soft squeeze. "Wanna rest with me for a minute?"

"Okay." Max looked straight up and smiled with his eyes.

They walked side by side into the family room. Connor sat in the oversized leather recliner and patted his knee. As if he'd done so all his life, Connor watched Max crawl up into his lap and snuggle against his chest. "Is it okay if I fall sleep?"

Connor pictured Michele coming home to the scene of Max and him in the chair. He looked down at his son and the thought vanished. "Of course." He wrapped his arm around Max and stroked his back. "Fishing can tire out a man real good."

"Mmm-hmm."

It was all Max got out before his breathing changed and became slower, more even. His body went limp against

Connor's, and the feeling was exhilarating. All week he'd fought against this very feeling, the sense that he and his son had bonded beyond anything time or distance could tear apart.

Gentle snoring sounds came from Max's nose, and Connor tightened his hold on him. The poor kid must've been more tired than he thought. Not only the fishing and camping and unloading the car, but the mental exhaustion of wondering about his future.

How could Michele send him away? How could she have made the phone call to the attorney without even talking to him? It was completely unlike her. Michele — of the two of them — had always had the bigger heart, the kinder spirit. She was the fun parent, the one always suggesting a picnic at the beach or a walk through the park.

Couldn't she set aside the past long enough to imagine what Max might be going through this week? Couldn't she have asked, before making the call?

He hesitated. She did ask; she asked Elizabeth when the two of them were on the phone early in her midweek call. He hadn't heard Michele's part of the conversation, but he heard Elizabeth's. The child was effusive, going on about what a good time they were having and how he'd taught the boy how to fish, and how well Max was fitting in.

So she knew, after all.

She knew how he felt, how Max felt, and she'd called the attorney anyway. He looked down and gave the boy a light kiss on the top of his head. Then something caught his eye and he looked up.

It was their wedding portrait, a canvas oil painting of Michele and him on the day they married. He narrowed his eyes, studying the look on her face, the openhearted love that shone for anyone to see. Her beauty had been breathtaking back then, and not only because of her dark looks. There was that certain intangible quality of her heart, her ability to soar within him, even when he was in the air and she was on the ground.

Had his affair caused her such grief that she'd lost that look, lost her ability to love, in so short a time?

He breathed in the fragrance that was Max, warm and dirty from the camping trip, and let the question simmer in his heart. The answer, of course, was obvious. Michele couldn't possibly have lost her ability to love. No, she was only anxious and afraid and paralyzed with anger.

And in that instant something the old pastor had said to him a week earlier, the day he'd gone in for some quick advice, came back. He had asked the man how he could get Michele to forgive. The pastor had given him a hint.

It'll start with you.

Suddenly, for the first time, he understood what that meant.

The affair hadn't simply happened. It hadn't been a mistake or an accident or the result of a terribly tempting set of circumstances. He couldn't blame the FAA or his father or the distance he'd felt with Michele. No, fault couldn't be placed there or on Kiahna. She was only a girl, an idealistic faith-driven girl, who had trusted him one stormy night.

The affair didn't happen because of any of them.

It happened because he made a choice to break the most important promise he'd ever given Michele and his family. The promise of faithfulness. Because of that, this mess — the one that involved Kiahna and Max and Michele and Elizabeth and Susan, the one that even involved some Hawaiian couple with a bed-and-breakfast and a hole in their hearts where a little boy used to live — all of it was his fault.

His fault alone.

The truth came at him like a battering ram and planted a mountain of sorrow squarely on his chest. How come he hadn't seen that before, hadn't owned the fact that he didn't merely play a role in what had happened? *He* caused it. Pure and simple. It was his fault Kiahna had gotten pregnant, his fault she'd been forced to give up her dream of becoming a doctor, his fault she was on Western Flight 45 that fateful morning.

The truth grew heavier still.

It was his fault that, after leaving Kiahna, he hadn't found the courage to tell Michele, the courage to go home, look her in the eye, and tell her the truth so they could start rebuilding their lives. It was his fault the boy was without a father, and his fault Michele was on the other side of the country, sinking in the quicksand of anger and unforgiveness.

The sorrow — thick and oppressive — came then, and he let his head rest against Max. At the same instant another thought made its way into his conscience.

He hadn't even apologized.

Not to Kiahna, or to Mr. Ogle, and especially not to Michele.

Every time he talked about the affair, all he did was try to excuse it, rationalize it, explain it somehow. But he'd never looked Michele in the eyes and told her he was sorry.

This was the truth he couldn't stomach, couldn't figure out no matter how long he sat there. Why hadn't he taken the blame?

Max stirred and made a slight shift of his position. Again, Connor soothed his hand along the boy's back. His voice came in the gentlest whisper. "Max . . . what have I done?"

He closed his eyes and thought of where his choices had left him. *God, what sort of hypocrite am I? I've been running from all of it . . . from Michele, from the truth. Most of all from You.*

Connor tried to imagine God Almighty — how would such a holy God view him, Connor Evans, after all the mistakes he'd made? *I wouldn't blame You if You walked away from me for good, God.*

Son, I will never leave you nor forsake you . . . Return to Me.

Return to Me? The call blew across his soul like a whispery summer breeze. The response to his misery hadn't been his imagination. After all this time, after all he'd done wrong, God still cared. He was still just a prayer away, waiting to make peace with Connor the moment Connor asked. A flashlight of joy shone into the moment's dark despair. He blinked his eyes open and looked at Max. *God, he's my own son; I love him. But if I lose him, it's my fault.*

He had a choice to make now, one that would mean keeping Max or keeping Michele. And even that choice could be blamed on no one but him. The quiet sobs simmering deep in his soul tried to get the better of him, but he pushed them back.

On the surface, the choice wasn't difficult. He opened his eyes and looked at their wedding portrait once more. No, he'd made his choice a long time ago in a central California church before a hundred of their friends and families.

He would do whatever Michele wanted him to do, because he owed her that much. Without meaning to, he held Max a little tighter. He owed something to the son on his lap. But he owed Michele first. First and always.

He and Michele shared something rare and wonderful, something few couples ever know. It had been that way most of their lives together, even after his affair. It was the reason he never considered telling her the truth. Because after he was stationed in

Florida again, after he came home from Los Angeles for good, things between Michele and him became better than they'd ever been.

He couldn't imagine jeopardizing that by telling her what had happened. Besides, back then it had been easy to justify his actions, easy to tell himself he'd had no control over the situation, no other way to handle his frustrations than to give in to the temptation that stormy night.

Now he knew he'd been wrong. The bond between them would've been stronger if he'd told the truth. Of course, they still would've faced the dilemma with Max, and his sudden arrival in their lives.

He kissed the boy's head again, felt the soft dark hair against his cheek. No question he could keep the boy, love him and raise him, and revel the rest of his days in the fact that he had not only two wonderful daughters but a son. A boy to carry on his name.

But if losing Michele was the price he would pay, then he'd been right when he first sat down with Max. The decision was already made. He loved Michele with all his heart, all his being. His life was with her, and when she came home he would tell her how sorry he was, tell her he'd been wrong about everything involving that awful summer.

Then he would wait until Thursday, in case she had a change of mind. If not . . . he would call the attorney and tell him to contact the Hawaiian couple. Max would spend his days working in a bed-and-breakfast, keeping company with a couple he knew nothing about. And one day he'd be the operator of a bed-and-breakfast on the big island.

Pain sliced through Connor's chest at the thought, and he knew why. The idea of Max growing up that way, of his son never knowing of his love, ripped Connor's heart in half. Taking Max away from Connor now would be like cutting off his right arm. No, it would be worse.

But it would be nothing to losing Michele.

He thought about Max's future again. By then, by the time he was grown and running the bed-and-breakfast, the memory of his mother's friend in Florida, and the camping trip on the lake, and the fish, and the butterfly, would be but a distant fleeting thought.

And his desire to be part of the Evans family, his desire to call Connor his daddy, would have long since disappeared.

TWENTY-NINE

Michele flew home the next day, more because she missed the girls than because she'd figured out a solution for her life. Throughout two plane trips and the cab ride back home from the airport, she sorted out the details every way she knew how. By the time she walked through the front door, she was beyond drained.

The weather was more humid than when she'd left, and though she'd lost a few pounds at her sister's house, she felt hot and frumpy and more than a little grouchy. She should have stayed at Margie's until the boy was gone. That way she could come home with at least a good attitude, a sliver of hope that somehow she and Connor could find common ground again.

But of course she had to come home before the boy left. Because she had to see what had happened between him and Connor since she'd been gone. Not that it mattered; her decision was made, and if Connor wanted to make an attempt at their marriage, the boy would have to go home. But even after the child was gone, Connor would carry him in his heart. At least to the extent he carried him now.

And Michele had to see for herself just to what extent that was.

She set her bags down in the hallway and straightened out the wrinkles in her Capri pants. A quick glance in the mirror told her she'd picked the wrong shirt. This one showed the hint of a bulge on either side of her waist. She huffed and lifted the shirt enough to create a few bunches. Bunches hid bulges, any woman battling her weight knew that.

"Hello?" She called out and waited, but there was no response. Then as her ears adjusted to the quiet of the house, she heard the sound of distant voices coming from the backyard.

Dreading whatever she might see, she made her way to the glass door and stared outside. Connor was giving Susan a piggy-back ride around the yard, while Elizabeth and the boy stood not far off, giggling and talking together. When Susan's ride was finished, she jumped off and Elizabeth climbed on. Susan gave Max a quick hug and held his hands as they jumped up and down.

"Go, Daddy!" she yelled as she turned back to her father and sister. "Go faster!"

Michele watched, hidden in the shadows of the china cabinet, as Connor picked up speed and went twice more around the yard. Then he dropped her off where the other two were standing and collapsed in a heap of laughter and weary legs. The kids piled onto him, poking him and tickling him, but after a few minutes, Elizabeth and Susan headed off toward the swings and seemed to forget about the piggyback rides.

Back with Connor, Max laid his head on the left side of Connor's heart. Then just as fast, he lifted it and made a rhythmic motion with his head, all the while grinning the same grin she'd seen a thousand times on Connor's face.

Michele felt her blood run cold. What was the boy doing? Listening to Connor's heartbeat? And what had happened to the formalities, the distance the boy had kept even from Connor before she left?

Suddenly she realized the truth. She should've gone on the camping trip. She could've kept Connor busy, and Max would've had no choice but to spend his time with the girls. Instead, the girls must've spent much of their time playing together, and whenever that was the case, Max must've spent his time with Connor.

Of course they'd gotten close.

She kept her eyes trained on her husband and his son. Connor struggled to his feet, his motions exaggerated as though he was too weary to go another round. Max flung his arms around Connor's waist, looked up at him, and said something Michele couldn't make out.

Then Connor lifted the boy into the air and spun him around. When he set him back down, his arms came around Max's shoulders and held the boy in an embrace that was no different from one Connor would've given to Elizabeth or Susan. Or maybe it was different. Maybe Connor held on a little bit longer to Max, aware of the fact that their time together was short.

Connor stooped down and kissed the boy on the top of his head, and just at that moment he caught Michele watching them. He said something to Max, and the boy nodded and ran off to join the girls. Connor stood and faced her with a hopeful smile. His mouth opened and she could read the word "Hi" as he came closer.

She stepped back. Could she run away?

The last thing she wanted was to talk to Connor now that she'd seen firsthand the love he felt for his son, the way the two of them — the way *all* of them — had connected. Anything she said was bound to sound cold and bitter and thoughtless.

But she had nowhere to run.

Connor slid the door open, stepped inside, and closed it again. "Hey, when did you get home?"

"Just now." She took another small step backward, tried a smile, and let it die on her lips. "I missed the girls."

"Oh." The excitement in Connor's eyes dimmed. He didn't try to close the gap between them. "What about me?"

She let her gaze fall to her feet for a moment before finding his eyes again. "Of course. I missed you, too."

He brought his lips together and exhaled in a sharp burst. "Michele . . ." His eyes stared at something on the ceiling, and he ran his fingers through his short hair. When he looked at her, his eyes were deeper, more honest, than she'd ever seen them. "We need to talk."

"Okay." She crossed her arms, her heart tense and unmoved within her. No matter how he looked, she knew what he was doing. This was his attempt to change her mind, to convince her they could take the boy, after all. That she would grow to love him. But nothing he could say would make her see the boy as anything other than what he was.

The son of a woman who had slept with her husband.

Connor walked past her, and she followed him into the living room. He sat on one side of the sofa and motioned for her to sit beside him.

Every ounce of her wanted to refuse him, to take a chair on the other side of the room, but she wanted to be near him, wanted to hear what outlandish argument he was going to make about the boy. Because of that she sat down next to him and turned to face him.

He watched her, and the look in his eyes told her that she seemed more a stranger than the wife he'd married. The look fell away, and he knit his brow together. He looked even more handsome than she remembered.

"Michele, there's something I have to tell you. Something I should've said a long time ago."

A war was taking place in her heart, half of her wanting to throw her arms around his neck and tell him whatever it was, they'd work through it, they'd find a way to survive and come out stronger on the other end.

But the other half was winning, the part that hated him for what he'd done to her and the girls.

"All right." She kept her face free of expression. "What is it?"

The lack of love in her voice took even her by surprise. Why was she talking to him like this? Hadn't she missed him, hadn't that been at least part of the reason why she had to get home? And couldn't she simply have hugged him when he walked in from the yard, his face lit up at the sight of her?

The answer to every question was a resounding no, because Connor didn't even understand what he'd done. Couldn't see past his desire for the boy long enough to realize what his unfaithfulness had cost her.

"You're not making this easy."

"You haven't made it easy, either."

He looked down for a moment, and she watched him work the muscles in his jaw. When he lifted his head again, the remorse was back. "Michele, what happened in Honolulu that August was my fault." He rushed ahead as if she might stop him. "It was my fault that I wasn't seeing you as often as I should, and my fault that I was in trouble with the FAA, my fault that I agreed to spend a stormy summer night at the house of a flight attendant I didn't even know, and my fault the situation resulted in an affair."

Michele stared at her husband and felt her mouth fall open a bit. She couldn't remember Connor ever saying those words, "It's my fault." She bit the inside of her cheek and waited.

"It's all my fault, and I want to ask your forgiveness." He ran his tongue along his lower lip and searched her face, desperate for some kind of response. "I should've told you the truth when I came home from Los Angeles, but I told myself it was one of those things, something I couldn't have helped. I thought it would be easier on both of us if you never knew."

"Yeah, well, you thought wrong." The acid reply was out before Michele could stop it.

Connor jerked back the slightest bit and stared at her. "I know." His face was a study in control, his tone less desperate than before. "That's why I'm telling you this." He sat back. "What I'm trying to say is, everything that happened is because of me. But since I found out about Max, all I've done is think about myself and how much I owe that child, how much I owe —"

"*What?*" The word was a shriek, a cry that came from the most wounded part of her heart. She pointed toward the backyard. "How much you owe *him?*"

An exasperated huff slid through Connor's clenched teeth. "Not just him, you didn't let me finish." He shielded his eyes with his right hand for a moment, and then snapped it back to his side. "Michele, you're not hearing me."

"I hear you loud and clear. I knew what this was as soon as you told me you wanted to talk. It's some sort of build-up . . . tell the wife you're sorry so you can convince her to keep the boy." She stood up and glared at him. "Can't you just say you're sorry, Connor? For once can't you just leave it at that?"

Without waiting for a response, she rushed out of the room. She grabbed her bags and made her way up the stairs before she heard him get up, stride across the kitchen floor, and return outside to the backyard where the kids were waiting for him.

The hurt came the moment she

slammed the bedroom door behind her. Up until the point where he talked about what he owed the boy, she was tracking with him, believing that this time maybe he understood the gravity of what he'd done.

She wanted to forgive him, really she did.

But not when he was only using it to convince her of his ultimate goal — his desire to keep Max, and never send him home again.

She yanked shirts and shorts and pants and underwear from her suitcase, tossing them either in the dirty clothes hamper, or putting them away where they belonged. When she was finished, she stared out their bedroom window, then took slow steps toward it.

The window overlooked the backyard, and from her position she could see all of them. Connor and Max and the girls were playing Frisbee now, jumping into the air to snag the disc, and high-fiveing each other after a particularly difficult catch. Angry sorrow choked her throat and her heart and her ability to see straight.

So much for his apology.

Their argument hadn't meant a thing to Connor, hadn't made him lose a step. She'd been right all the time, his reason for talking to her had been clear-cut from the beginning. He wanted the boy. And the longer she stood there watching the two of them laughing and playing together, the more she felt inclined to let him have what he wanted. To put her things back in the suitcase and head back out the door.

Not just a few things to get her through a week or two, but every single thing she owned.

Connor was more confused than ever.

He'd worked on his plan ever since Max fell asleep on his chest in the hours after the camping trip. As soon as he saw Michele, he would smile at her, welcome her home, and then ask her if they could talk. Once he had her alone, he would take responsibility for every awful thing he'd done by having the affair. He would take the blame for all of it, and do his best to explain his feelings about Max.

Michele was wrong about his intentions.

Not for a minute had he planned to use that talk to convince her to keep Max. Oh, he wanted that, sure. Wanted it more than he wanted his next breath. But he'd already made a deal with God that if she was going to change her mind about the boy, she'd have to do it on her own. If he convinced her, she'd be tempted to hold the decision against him for the rest of their days.

And neither of them could live with that.

But right from the beginning, his plan went terribly awry. Like a perfectly sound flight plan that somehow falls apart in the air and ends up with an emergency landing. Only this time they didn't even get that. The conversation crashed and burned long before Connor had time to say even half of what he'd wanted to tell her.

Now here it was, ten o'clock Tuesday night, and Connor sat alone in the family room, staring into the darkness and wondering what was going to happen next, how either of them could salvage their relationship.

Maybe he'd been wrong about Michele. Maybe it was too late to save their marriage. If he was going to lose her anyway, then he might as well keep Max. That way when he and Michele had to share the girls, at least he'd always have his son. The boy would never have to grow up with a couple he didn't know, his future as predictable as the seasons.

He thought back over the night, and the tension that filled the house like a poisonous fog. Michele finally came down from her room, stood at the patio door, and called out a hello to the kids. Elizabeth and Susan came running, of course, but Max hung back. Poor guy, of course he didn't come running. Even in those first welcoming moments, she made her feelings for him clear. Her eyes never even looked for him in the yard, and once she hugged the girls, she put an arm around each of them and headed back into the house.

Connor went outside then, found the boy, and played catch with him. But Max wasn't fooled.

"Mrs. Evans is still mad, isn't she?"

"Not at you, Max. At me . . . at something I did."

"You?" He flipped the ball across the yard, and Connor couldn't help but notice that he had a great throwing arm. "I don't think so . . . I think it's me."

After a quiet dinner, they spent the rest of the evening apart, he and Max watching a movie together; Michele with the girls upstairs, getting them ready for bed, reading to them, and brushing their hair. She was asleep in one of their rooms now. At least that's what he guessed. She hadn't been down since dinnertime.

Meanwhile, Max fell asleep against his side, and when the movie was over, he carried his son upstairs to the guest room. As he tucked him into bed, he hovered over him a few minutes longer than necessary. Max had carried his Bible with him on the camping trip, looking over it, reading small passages, and checking the special things he kept inside.

The Bible was back on the nightstand next to his bed now. A reminder of all he held dear. But after the past week, it wasn't all he held dear, was it? That night as Max read him a book and prayed with him, he hadn't even reached for the special things in his small white book. The reason was as clear as the stars outside his window.

Max was growing to love Connor as much as Connor already loved him.

Connor leaned down and kissed Max's cheek, just as the phone rang. He crept out of the room with quiet steps and headed for his bedroom. There he grabbed the phone on the third ring and clicked the on button.

"Hello?"

The silence on the other end was long enough that Connor almost hung up. But just as he moved the receiver from his ear he heard a familiar voice. "Connor . . ."

He brought the phone back. "Yes?"

"Connor, this is your father."

A hundred other times in that instant he would have been first shocked, and then angry. He'd told his father not to call, that the relationship they'd once shared was over. But now, with his own son's sweet smell still fresh on his sweatshirt, his knees grew weak and he could do nothing but drop to the bed.

The word that came from his mouth was small and filled with sadness, a sadness Connor hadn't fully understood until just now. "Dad?"

His father's voice was thick. "How . . . how are you, Son?"

Connor had never cried over losing his father, but now his heart was strangled by sorrow. He pictured Max, then pictured the way his own father must've felt about him, regardless of how he'd chosen to show it. And out of the ashes of eight years of silence, a sprig of hope began to grow.

Connor's words were shaky. "I'm . . . not too good, Dad. Not too good."

"I heard." He paused. "Michele came by a few days ago."

He wanted to be angry with her, but he couldn't be. Couldn't do anything but grip the phone and realize how good it felt to have his dad on the other end. "I messed up."

"Yes. We all mess up once or twice."

What was his father saying? That he himself had made a mistake by turning his only son away all those years ago? Connor fell back on the bed, and tears blurred his view of the ceiling. "I never thought the affair was my fault." He pulled his arm across his wet eyes. "Until the other day."

"You know why, right?" The man's words were gentler than they'd been before. Gentle and kind and wise.

"Not really."

"Pilot's pride, Son. You and I both have it."

"Pilot's pride?" Connor twisted his face and gave a shake of his head. "What's my job have to do with it?"

"Everything." His father took a long breath. "Pilots — good pilots — carry with them a certain kind of pride, an ability to see everything that goes wrong as a problem he can fix and move away from. If a pilot thought himself capable of error, he wouldn't be much good with a plane full of passengers. See, it's a confidence thing that works wonderfully in the cockpit." His voice fell a notch. "But not so well on the ground."

Pilot's pride? Was that his problem? If so, he'd been crazy to let it go this far, to let it get in the way of every person he'd ever loved. "What made you call?"

"I have a few things to say." A smile sounded in his tone. "And God gave me the go-ahead."

"God?" Maybe this wasn't his father after all. The man had never owned the faith they'd been raised with. That had been his mother's area.

"Yes. My pilot's pride has faded since our last meeting. God wanted me to wait until the time was right, and after Michele came by I knew. This was my time." The humor was gone. "Our time."

"Is that what you wanted to say?" Connor wanted to keep the conversation going, hold onto whatever chance this was before it slipped away.

"There's more." He hesitated. "I want you to know I'm sorry about what happened between us, Son." His father sniffed, and his voice cracked. "I've regretted it every day since."

Connor had to remind himself to breathe. "You have?"

"Yes." He seemed to think for a moment. "I still don't think buying the airport would've been a good thing for you, but I could've handled it differently. Spent more time talking to you about it, researched it with you. Anyway . . ." He took a slow breath, and a lifetime of pain sounded in his tone. "I'm sorry."

It was his turn, but after so many years, Connor wasn't sure how to voice his feelings. Instead of apologizing, he sat up and pressed the receiver closer to his ear. "I missed you, Dad. Missed you a lot."

"Me, too." Nothing in his father's voice suggested he was upset that the apology hadn't gone both ways. "I hear I have a grandson."

Mention of Max doubled the sorrow welling within him. "Yes. He . . . he looks just like you, Dad. Exactly like you looked when you were a boy."

"Then he must look like you, also."

"He does." Connor stared out the window. "I love him, Dad. I've fallen head over heels for the boy."

His father waited for a bit. "That's the other thing I wanted to talk about."

"Max?" Connor was surprised.

"Yes, Son. When Michele first told me about the boy, I thought you needed to find whatever way possible to keep him. I was ready to pray for Michele to welcome him the way you already had. But then

God talked to me and told me something I needed to remember, something He wanted me to tell you, too."

"Okay . . ." God wanted him to? Connor stood and paced the room, taking slow steps from one side to the other, trying to take it all in. The changes in his father were almost enough to distract him from what the man was saying. "What's that, Dad?"

"God's ways are not our ways, Son. That's the message." His father paused. When he spoke again, his voice was sadder than it had ever been. "You need to send the boy home."

Connor stopped and hung his head. He could still feel Max's arms around his waist, still see him looking concerned as they played catch and talked about Michele. Still feel the way he'd all but taken over his broken heart.

He pinched the bridge of his nose. "I thought that, too, Dad. Until Michele came home today."

"Ah . . . it didn't go well?"

"She's become this . . . this awful person. I don't even recognize her." He looked up and finished his path to the bedroom window. "I think she's going to leave me."

"So you've already made up your mind."

A flicker of anger sparked in Connor's soul, and then died. He'd lost too many years with his father to be angry with him now. "Michele made it up for me."

"Now, Son. What you and Michele have is deeper, stronger, than this type of a test. But there's a problem. You're more willing to let her go because if she leaves, you'll have a reason to keep the boy."

Connor placed his arm against the window and leaned against the cool glass. That was it exactly, wasn't it? He'd given it a try with Michele, and since she'd rejected him, he was ready to move on to Max, right?

"Okay." Defeat rang in his voice. "What am I supposed to do?"

"Believe that God's ways are the best. And that means standing by Michele, standing by her and loving her and helping her through this time. It means sending Max home, Son. As soon as the two weeks are up."

His father was right. He was right and if he followed the man's advice, if he did what God wanted him to do, that meant Max would be gone from their lives in three short days. Three days to love him and bond with him and make enough

451

memories to last a lifetime without him.

It was the only thing he could do, and at that moment he was sure he would do it. Michele would come around eventually, and one day they could find what they'd lost these past weeks. But only if he sent Max away.

"Okay, Dad." He couldn't stay on the phone another minute. "Okay."

"So you'll do it?"

"Yes. He'll go home Friday morning."

"You'll never be sorry."

Connor didn't know about that. But it wasn't the time to say so. "Thanks, Dad. For calling. It's been too long."

"We'll talk again in a few weeks. I want to know how it goes."

"Okay." The irony rattled the walls of Connor's heart. That he would find his father and lose his son all in one week.

"Oh, and Connor?"

"Yes?"

"I wish I could see him. Max, I mean."

"Yeah, Dad." Connor worked his fingertips into his neck, trying to knead out the tightness in his throat. No matter what his father had said about sending Max home, the old man cared. He cared, and in some ways he would carry a permanent ache over losing Max — just as Connor would.

Connor clenched his jaw and then released it. "I wish you could, too."

"Listen." His father's voice cracked. "I may not ever meet Max, but could you do me a favor?" He paused, and Connor could feel the man's sadness through the phone line. "Before you send him home, could you take a picture of him for me?"

"Sure, Dad." Connor bit the inside of his lip. "I'll take one for both of us."

THIRTY

The goldfish feeling in Max's tummy was back.

It was Thursday, and Mr. Evans said after dinner they had to talk. But it wasn't the nice kind of talk they sometimes did about fishing or butterflies or throwing a ball. No, because this time, Mr. Evans only did a small sad smile when he said that.

Tomorrow was two weeks; he heard Mrs. Evans say so, and that meant that maybe the thing Mr. Evans wanted to talk about was him going back home. Max missed Buddy, and so going home was a good thing, except he didn't want to stay there. He wanted to get his bestest dog and get back on a plane to Florida so he could live with the Evans family forever.

Plus for two days Mrs. Evans had been nicer to him. She asked him what his favorite thing to eat was, and he told her blueberry pancakes and whipped cream, or

454

buttered toast. Either one. And yesterday she made him blueberry pancakes for breakfast and today, buttered toast.

And when he couldn't untie the knot in his shoe after the kickball game with 'Lizabeth and Susan, she called him over and put him on her lap while she untangled it all the way. Afterward he told her thank you very much, ma'am, the way his mommy taught him.

And the greatest thing happened. Mrs. Evans smiled at him and said, "Max, you're a very nice boy."

So maybe the Evans family had made a choice to keep him. Because everything was going so good. But when Mr. Evans said after dinner they had to have a talk, his voice didn't sound happy, like he could stay. It sounded sorry but he had to go.

Dinnertime was quiet, except for 'Lizabeth said, "Do you leave tomorrow, Max?" She sounded not happy about the idea.

Then Mrs. Evans gave her a strong look and said, "We'll talk about that later."

That's when Max knew that whatever the talk was about, it wouldn't be good news.

When dinner was over, Mr. Evans took him upstairs to his room and sat next to him on the end of the bed. "Max, I have some news for you."

The goldfish jumped around a little. "Yes?"

"You have to go home tomorrow, Max." His eyes had shiny wet in them, and his voice sounded broken. "Mr. Ogle has found a very nice couple who want to adopt you. They want you to live with them forever."

Angry and scared and wanting to run all mixed together in Max's heart. "But . . . I thought . . ."

"Yes." Mr. Evans closed his mouth very tight and his lips made a straight line. "We wanted you to live here, too. But . . . but God told us it would be better for you to go back to the island."

"Only to get Buddy." Max's throat felt dry, the way it did after a long walk home from the bus stop. "Then I want to come back here." He took Mr. Evans's hand. "I don't want to live with anyone else."

Mr. Evans was quiet for a long time. "I'm sorry, Max. The decision's already been made."

Questions were coming into his mind faster than Max could think. Who was the couple and how did they know about him? How come Mr. Evans let someone else adopt him? And how would he ever find his daddy somewhere out there if he was living with a new couple?

And the biggest question of all. "Mrs. Evans is still mad at me, right?"

"I told you, Max . . . it's because this is what God wants." He dropped his head down some. When he looked up, the water in his eyes was almost spilling over. "But I want you to know that I'll always remember our time together, okay?"

Be strong and brave . . . be strong and brave . . . be strong and brave . . .

"Okay." Max squeezed Mr. Evans's hand. "I'll remember, too."

The talk was over because Mr. Evans said that was all. Then he held out his arms and Max jumped down onto his feet and quick ran up to him for a long hug. After a while, Max pulled back a little. "I have a question."

"Okay." Mr. Evans looked at him. Hurt was in his voice. Hurt and sorry and too bad it didn't work out.

Max could feel his heart beeping hard beneath his shirt. Because this was the question he had all the time he was at the Evans's house, only he didn't know how to ask. And now . . . now he was leaving tomorrow so if he didn't ask, he never would.

"Did you love my mommy, Mr. Evans?"

For a long time, Mr. Evans looked away, out the window probably, but Max couldn't tell. Then he looked back and said, "Your mommy and I were friends for a short time, Max."

"But did you love her?"

This time Max felt him put his hand against the side of his face. "Not as much as I love you."

Max's heart did a somersault inside him, because of two things. First, yes, Mr. Evans had loved his mommy. Not the married kind of love, but at least he loved her. That meant he knew how sad it was that she was gone. And two, Mr. Evans loved him even more!

They hugged again, and then they went back downstairs with the rest of the family. The night was fun with Uno and real actual theater popcorn in the microwave, and a Peter Pan movie. Everything was just perfect, except one thing.

Tomorrow he was going home.

Michele was glad Max was leaving, but she still wasn't ready to sleep in the same bed as Connor.

That night she stayed in Susan's room, and it was after midnight when she heard

458

someone crying. At first she thought it was Elizabeth, because the girl had suffered nightmares the past two nights. She slipped out of bed and padded the few steps to Elizabeth's room, but she was sound asleep. That could mean only one thing, of course.

The crying was coming from Max.

No matter what her feelings about her husband's affair, or the woman who had been Max's mother, her heart broke at the sound of the child's muffled cries. In fact, he had been much easier to be around the past few days. Ever since she'd known for sure that he was going home.

She'd realized something early Wednesday. Connor was right. Max was a very nice boy, well-mannered and kind to the girls, polite and thankful with an easy grin and an adorable face. With no reason to keep her guard up around the boy, Michele found herself actually liking him.

Her cold treatment toward him had been shameful and wrong, and she wished there was a way she could make it up to him. The situation was hardly his fault, not the affair or the interruption his arrival had made in their lives, or the fact that he had his mother's green eyes. He was simply a little boy who had lost his mom, a boy who'd had no say whatsoever in coming to Florida to visit their family.

Earlier that day she had wondered about the boy's grieving process, when he cried for the loss of his mother. Now she knew.

She crept down the hall toward the guest room and pushed the door open. "Max?"

His face was buried in his pillow, but he lifted it a few inches and looked at her. "Yes?"

"Max, honey, why are you crying?" She crossed the room and sat on the edge of his bed. "It's very late."

He rolled over and tucked the covers up to his chin. His eyes were swollen, and in the moonlight she could see tearstains on his cheeks. "I can't sleep."

In that instant, gone were her thoughts about whose son he was or what he represented. All that mattered was that the heart of the boy before her was breaking. Breaking badly. Without giving her actions a second thought, she reached out and ran her fingers along Max's arm. "Are you missing your mom?"

Max nodded and made another couple sobs. "Y–y–yes." He pulled something out from beneath the covers and held it up. "This is my mommy. Sometimes . . . some-

460

times at night I hold her picture against my heart."

Michele's breath caught in her throat.

She kept her eyes from the photograph. She couldn't have made it out in the shadowy light anyway, but just in case . . . This wasn't about Kiahna; it was about Max missing his mommy. Michele's jealousy and her feelings of inadequacy had no place in this conversation.

Max took several quick breaths, his small body still convulsing from the sadness. "She . . . she told me that she'd always be in my heart." He pulled the picture back down under the covers and held it there with one hand. "Do you think that's true, Mrs. Evans? Do you think she's still in my heart?"

"Yes." Michele ached for the boy, ached to pull the child into her arms and hug away the mountain of pain he was under. Instead she caught Max's free hand and held it, the same way she would've held Elizabeth or Susan's hands. "Yes, Max, I'm sure she's in your heart."

Gradually, in lessening sobs and waves of sorrow, Max began to calm down. Michele watched him leave his mother's picture beneath the sheets and blankets. Then he pulled his arm out and dragged it across his face. He kept his other hand tucked safe and small inside hers.

After a minute he peered at her again. "Mrs. Evans?"

"Yes, Max."

"You didn't know my mommy, did you?"

Michele refused to give in to the jealousy that rose up in her heart. *He's a little boy . . . he doesn't have any idea . . .* "No, Max. I didn't know her." She squeezed the boy's hand. "But I'm sure she was very nice."

"She was." He made a few sniffing sounds. "I wanted her to get a husband so we could have a daddy, but she never did. She said I was the only man she needed."

Michele had to keep from letting her mouth hang open. What did he mean she never did? Certainly a woman like Kiahna would've had different men every few months. Casual sex and instability in the home. At least that was the picture she'd had since she learned about her husband's affair.

Twice she ran the boy's words through her head, and the picture still wouldn't come into focus. Max was waiting for an answer, and she kept her voice even. "I'm sure she was telling the truth, that you were all she needed."

"But I still wanted a daddy." Max put his free hand beneath his head so he could see her better. "My mommy loves Jesus very much, did you know that, Mrs. Evans?"

"Really?" Michele's head was spinning. Again, the picture Max was giving her was nothing like the one in her head. Kiahna didn't have men in her life? She loved Jesus? Suddenly something Connor had said came back to her. Kiahna was a nice girl . . . a nice girl . . .

She hadn't believed a word of it. What sort of flight attendant would bring a married pilot home to her apartment? The answer had always seemed obvious — until now. She studied the small boy and bit the inside of her cheek. How important it must be for Max to have times like these, when he could talk about his mother as though she were still alive.

"You believe in Jesus, right?" He gave her a sad smile.

"Yes, Max. I believe very much." But even as she said the words, they sounded tinny, phony. Coated in plastic. She'd been downright mean to a seven-year-old boy who was just weeks from losing his mother . . . she'd spewed bitter words at her husband, never giving him a chance to explain himself or even apologize . . . and when she had a chance to work things out, she'd run to her sister's house.

But she believed in Jesus.

A Scripture came to mind, one that had always haunted her whenever she read the book of James: "You believe that there is one God. Good! Even the demons believe that — and shudder." The point of the Scripture was obvious. Faith without works was a dead faith. Since the news of Connor's infidelity, what had she done to show her love for anyone but herself?

"My mommy gave me a Bible last year." He sat up some and took a white book from his nightstand. "See . . . I read it every day."

The picture continued to grow and fill in. Kiahna had been a believer. Which meant, if nothing else, Michele would be with her in heaven one day. Also, she stayed away from men and taught Max to read the Bible. Suddenly Michele wanted more information about the woman. "Tell me more, Max."

"Really?"

"Yes." She leaned in and with her free hand, she brushed his bangs off his forehead. "Talking about people we love helps keep them alive a little longer."

This time Max's smile was genuine. "I think that, too." Then he took another few breaths, the remains of his sobbing episode, and he told Michele everything he could think of about his mother.

Michele had expected him to say that she was beautiful and thin and well-dressed, that she had a pretty face and that he'd never seen a nicer-looking mommy anywhere. Instead he talked about the fact that she had a special song for him, and about their butterfly days, and how they liked to play at the beach sometimes.

Not once did he mention anything about his mother's looks.

Had Kiahna fretted about her weight, a few pounds one way or another? If she had, did she know now that Max hadn't cared one way or the other?

Suddenly Michele's obsession with her looks, her weight, and the foods she was and wasn't eating, seemed like a silly waste of time. A smoke screen. The truth presented itself, and for the first time she didn't turn away. The real problem back when Connor had his affair was that she'd been absorbed in depression, oblivious to Connor's trouble at work and with his father, unable to encourage him or love him or do anything but pull him down.

Yes, she'd had her reasons. But the way she'd cut herself off from Connor had been wrong. She finally saw the truth for what it was. Her food binges had always been nothing more than a way to hide from her emotional struggles.

The knowledge of Connor's affair had been no different.

Connor never would've left her because of her weight. Love wasn't based on how a person looked. It was how the person talked and played and spent time that mattered. How they lived and loved; that's what people remembered.

Max was saying something, and Michele focused on him once more.

"Know something else, Mrs. Evans?" Max's words were slower than before. He yawned and found her eyes again. "That wasn't all the reason I was crying."

"It wasn't?" Michele still had hold of his hand. "What else was it?"

"Because . . ." This time Max looked straight into her soul. "Because I don't want to say good-bye tomorrow."

Michele reached for Max then, lifting him off the pillow and taking him in her arms. "Oh, Max . . . it'll be okay."

His small body started shaking again. "I wanted . . . I wanted Mr. Evans to be my pretend daddy."

"Your pretend daddy?" Michele's heart was racing now, the knowledge of what the child was going through almost more than she could bear.

"My mommy told me in a letter that I have a daddy somewhere out there. Only . . . only I think it might be too hard to find him because of so many dads in the world. So I asked Jesus if . . . if Mr. Evans could be my pretend daddy."

Michele couldn't contain her tears another minute. They flooded her eyes and she blinked them back so Max wouldn't see them. It took every bit of her resolve to remind herself that sending Max home was the best thing not just for their family but for Max. His school was there, and his friends. And a couple who wanted to love and care for Max forever.

"Max, it'll all work out one day. I promise you that. Jesus has plans for you that are all good."

"But I want to get Buddy and come back h–h–here." He buried his head in her shoulder and wept so hard he could barely breathe. They stayed that way until he grew calm once more. Then he pulled back some. "I wish you would've come camping with us, Mrs. Evans."

They were the most pointed words he could've said to her. Almost as if he knew that, had she come on the trip, she would've fallen in love with him, too.

With her fingertips, she wiped away his tears and said the only thing she could think to say. "I'm sorry I didn't go, Max. I'm so sorry."

"I forgive you." He caught her gaze once more. "And know what?"

"What?" Michele could barely speak, still strangled by the truth of how wrong she'd been that week. Wrong in every possible way.

"Love happens when people forgive." He gave her one more sad, knowing smile. "So that means I love you."

"I love you, too, Max." The moment she said the words, she realized they were true. What was there not to love about this child? He was so much like Connor, and so much his own person at the same time. As she held him and stroked his back, convincing him that life would turn out okay, that Jesus had a plan for his life, she thought about it again. In a just-beginning kind of way, she did love the boy.

If only she'd figured that out sooner.

Because the plan was already in motion, and deep in her soul she knew it was the right one. It had to be. Because by tomorrow at this same time, Max Riley Siefert would be back in Honolulu.

Gone from their lives forever.

THIRTY-ONE

Ramey sat on the sofa and stared at Max and Buddy, standing together a few feet from her. Max had been home three days, and now it was Monday. The Mollers would be there in fifteen minutes for their first meeting with Max and Buddy.

"Well, Ramey, do I look good?"

Buddy lifted his chin and made a soft whining sound.

"Not you, Buddy." Max bent down and patted the dog's head. "I need Ramey to tell me."

"Yes, Max. You look very handsome."

"What about Buddy?" Max had tied a blue scarf around the dog's neck.

"Buddy looks handsome, too."

The dog barked once, and Max dropped to one knee. "No barking, Buddy. The Mollers might not like dogs." He placed his hands on either side of Buddy's face. "Be quiet, okay?"

Ramey hated that they had to do this, hated the idea of parading Max and Buddy before some strange couple, almost as if they were a set of used appliances. She was still praying for a forgiveness miracle for the boy, but it was looking less likely with every day.

No one from the Evans family had called since Max returned home.

She'd talked to Mr. Ogle and agreed to keep Max and Buddy at her apartment until the Mollers's paperwork was completed, if they did, indeed, decide to adopt Max. If not, Max would go to live with the Ogles. But that would mean changing schools, and being fifteen miles from his old neighborhood. Better to make that type of change only once, she and Mr. Ogle had agreed.

And so for now Max was hers.

She was glad, though she would've liked it best if Max had been able to stay with the Evanses. Maybe Kiahna hadn't known the man that well, after all. From her journals, and the letter she'd written in her will, it was clear that she thought Connor Evans was the type of man who would make a good father for Max. But if the man could spend two weeks with the boy and still send him home, then maybe

Kiahna was wrong.

Either way, it felt wonderful having Max back in the apartment with her. She'd missed him, and when he left — whether to the Mollers or to Mr. Ogle and his wife — she would feel his loss far more than she'd realized. The two weeks he'd been gone were the longest she'd been away from him since he was born.

Yes, having him around was more work for her. Sometimes she would get out of breath, and Max would have to get her oxygen tank before she could get up again. But Max was used to that; they made a good team. She would've hated to die without having this last bit of time with him.

"How much longer, Ramey?" Max was finished scolding Buddy. He stood and faced her, shifting his weight from one foot to the other. "I want to get this over with."

Ramey stifled a smile. He'd picked up that line from her, because that's what she'd told Mr. Ogle: "Send them by. I want to get this over with." A needle of guilt pricked her conscience. "Max, that's the wrong attitude, pal. Wrong for me and wrong for you."

"But I told you, Ramey." He dropped to the ground in a heap beside Buddy. The

472

dog immediately lay down and rested his head on Max's knee. "I don't wanna be adopted. If I can't live with the Evanses then I wanna live here with you." He grabbed a fast breath. "And if you get old and die, I wanna live in heaven with Mommy and you." He paused. "Okay, Ramey? Okay?"

"What's wrong is that the Mollers are nice people. They've heard all about you and they think they want you to be their son. That would be a good thing, Max. Try to see it that way."

"Yeah, but —"

A knock sounded at the front door, and the room fell silent. Ramey struggled to her feet. "I'll be right back."

She guessed it was a full thirty seconds before she reached the door. And it was only twenty steps away. She opened it and sized up the people standing before her. "Hello . . . please come in."

"Thank you." The man spoke, and the woman offered a shy smile.

"You must be the Mollers."

"We are." This time the woman took a step forward and looked past Ramey. "Is Max here?"

Ramey studied them for a moment, then turned and led them into the TV room.

They were older than she'd expected, in their early fifties, at least. They both had warm smiles and an anxious look, a mix of nervousness and excitement.

Ramey was enough ahead of them that when she entered the room where Max and Buddy were waiting, she turned around to see the reaction from the Mollers. The woman smiled and gave Max a little wave; the man stood a foot behind her, his eyes kind and glistening. "Hello Max. We're the Mollers."

The woman took a few steps toward Max and held out her hand. "We're so glad to meet you, Max."

Max pulled himself up to his feet. "Hello." His chin stayed tucked close to his chest, but his eyes met the woman's.

Ramey leaned against the nearest wall and took in the scene. *It seems okay, God . . . I guess.* She narrowed her eyes and waited.

Mr. Moller came up alongside Max and pointed to Buddy. "Is this your dog?"

"Yes, sir." Max pulled himself up some. "That's my dog, Buddy. He wants to come too."

"Uh . . ." The man looked up at Ramey and gave a slight shake of his head. "Well Max . . ."

Ramey shrugged at Mr. Moller's distressed look and mouthed the words to him, "Good luck."

Mr. Moller patted Buddy's head. "Max, we can't have dogs." He put his arm on his wife's shoulder. "Mrs. Moller is allergic."

Max's eyes got wide. "But, sir, Buddy's . . . he's my bestest friend."

Mrs. Moller stooped down to Max's level. "Maybe we can get a goldfish, or a turtle. Something in an aquarium." She put her hand along the side of Max's face. "How would that be?"

Ramey winced at what was bound to come next.

"Buddy stays with me." The utter defiance in Max's tone was underlined by his loud, panic-stricken voice. His breathing was hard and fast, causing his small chest to jump as if he'd just run up a flight of stairs. He took hold of the pretty blue scarf on his dog's neck. "Come on, Buddy. They don't want us." Before he pulled Buddy out onto the patio, he turned and shot one more line at the Mollers. "If he stays, I stay."

When the glass door was shut, Mr. Moller looked at Ramey and gave a polite nod. "Thank you for your time."

"I take it you're no longer interested."

Ramey settled back on her heels.

"Oh, no. We're very interested. Children can deal with loss better than adults. He'll miss the dog for a while, but he'll be okay eventually." Mrs. Moller cast a sad look back at Max. "He's probably upset about the whole situation."

"That's exactly it." Ramey liked the woman.

The man held his hand out to Ramey and gave her another smile. "We'll let him take a few days to get used to the idea, and then we'll contact Mr. Ogle."

"Yes." The woman clutched her purse to her midsection. "We're hoping to bring him home soon." She tilted her head. "He's a beautiful child. I'm sorry he's hurting."

Her husband put his hand at the small of Mrs. Moller's back and gave her a slight hug. Over his shoulder he gave Ramey one final look. "We'll be in touch."

For ten minutes after they left, Ramey was still exhaling hard, coaxing her heartbeat back to some kind of normal. Pain radiated from her chest, and for a moment she thought maybe this was it. The heart attack her doctors had been saying could happen at any time.

She shuffled into the kitchen, snatched

476

her nitroglycerin pills from the cupboard next to the sink, poured a quick glass of water, and swallowed two of them. There. That would help. With slow steps, determined not to die with Max and Buddy on the back patio, Ramey crossed the apartment and sat in her favorite chair.

The couple was nice, kind. But how could she let her Max live with anyone who couldn't take Buddy?

Her heartbeat slowed some, and the pain in her chest eased. She huffed hard through her nose and glanced at Kiahna's journal, still on the lamp stand table beside her chair. Kiahna believed in second chances and forgiveness, hadn't she? Wasn't that what she'd prayed for all her life?

Okay, God, so I prayed for it, too. She looked up at the ceiling, because God had to be somewhere beyond the plaster and wood boards. *I asked You specifically for a forgiveness miracle, and this is what You give me?* She pursed her lips. *I have to be honest, God, I'm thinking about forgetting the whole prayer thing altogether. If You're there, I'm not sure You like me enough to listen. Because as nice as they are, let me tell You, God, the Mollers aren't the answer I was expecting.*

She crossed her arms over her round abdomen.

Then she remembered something els Kiahna had written in her journal. Though her life hadn't turned out anything lik she'd planned, she knew that in the darkes times God was always working. Always.

Ramey stared out the patio door at Max lying on the ground alongside Buddy and probably crying his eyes out. She shot another quick look at the ceiling. *Time don't get much darker than this, God* Her gaze shifted to Max again. But what i Kiahna was right? What if somehow God was working out His best miracles ever now, when life looked beyond hopeless?

All right, then, I'll keep on praying God. I'm begging You here, just begging You, God, please . . . give Max a miracle in his life. Just this once. The kid can' catch a break, Lord. I still think the miracle will be wrapped up in forgiveness somehow. So that's what I'm asking You for. Okay? A sheepish feeling filled her heart. *Oh . . . and one more thing. I'm sorry if I sounded rude a minute ago. My dander was up, that's all. I really do think You can do this, or I wouldn't ask.*

She was still too new at talking to God to know how to end the conversation, so she looked at the ceiling one last time and whispered, "Thanks, God. I'll be right here waiting."

Max felt more scared than ever in all his life put together.

Everything in his brain and heart was spinning in circles and landing in a big mixed-up pile. His mommy had told him to always use his manners with strangers, but just now he used his mean voice on the Mollers. So somewhere in heaven she must be disappointed with him. Disappointed was worse than being in trouble, because it meant your mommy was sad inside.

"Don't be sad, Mommy." Max said the words near Buddy's ear, and his dog did a loud huffy breath. "I'm sorry . . . I'm so sorry."

But that wasn't even the only thing mixed up. Also he looked at Mr. Moller's eyes, and he saw a grown-up look that meant he wasn't changing his mind. Max thought about kicking and screaming and throwing himself on the floor. He never did that before, because his mommy would give him that serious look even if he got a whining voice. But once he saw a boy in first grade do that kicking thing, and it worked, sort of. The principal came to first grade and helped take that boy away. So if the boy didn't want to be in class, then it worked, right?

He thought about that. But just when he was maybe going to throw his own fit, Mr. Moller looked at him that way. Smiling, but very serious. Max knew it didn't matter what he did, they were still going to adopt him. But not Buddy . . .

And so here was the confusing thing. What about God? His mommy always told him God had a plan for him. Max wasn't sure if it was a written-out plan somewhere in a desk in heaven, or something God was working on a little more every day. But He had a plan, because that's what his mommy told him, and she never, ever lied.

Plus also, Mr. Evans at the airport hugged him hard and said he loved him and told him the same thing, that God had a plan for him. Even Mrs. Evans told him that. But why would God leave Buddy out of the plan?

He gulped hard and slipped his hand beneath Buddy's new blue scarf. Ramey took him shopping on the weekend for it because sometimes people liked dogs that were pretty. Buddy was always pretty, o' course, but maybe the Mollers wouldn't think so unless he had a nice scarf.

Max also thought maybe they should buy a toenail cutter thing because Buddy's toenails were too long. Even for a dog. Also Mommy used to say it was 'portant to have clean-cut toes. But Ramey said the Mollers probably wouldn't look at Buddy's toes. At least not on the first visit. And plus the cutter was four dollars and ninety-seven cents.

And the most mixed-up thing was that Max didn't care what the Mollers thought of him and Buddy, because he didn't want the Mollers to adopt him. But Ramey said maybe this was his only chance, and that only made him more sad because it wasn't his only chance at all. It was his second chance.

The Evans family was his first chance.

He sank his face against his arm, in the quiet part by his elbow. *God . . . I'm very scared, God. Please help me know what to do next. If I need to cut Buddy's toenails, I will, but please . . . please don't send me to live with the Mollers.*

Another bit of scared came in his heart. He squished himself against Buddy and prayed some more. *Mommy told me that You give people second chances, God. I believe You because Mommy has a second chance right now, with You in heaven.*

He opened his mouth because he really wanted God to hear this part. "But what about me? Please, God . . . could I have a second chance with the Evans family? Or if not, could you show me where to find my daddy somewhere out there?"

Most times when he finished praying, Max would have a slow, warm feeling in his tummy. Peace, his mommy called it. But this time his heart still felt extra thumpy, and he wasn't sure at all about the big pile of things inside him.

He could still hear his mommy's voice, still smell her and feel her skin soft against his. *Be brave, Max . . . whenever you're afraid, be brave . . .*

And that was the worst part of all.

For the first time ever, he couldn't be brave for his mommy. He couldn't even remember how.

THIRTY-TWO

t was Tuesday morning, and Michele was doing everything she could to get their lives back to normal.

She'd let Connor and Max go by themselves to the airport on Friday, and when Connor returned, she met him at the door with a hug. "I'm sorry, Connor." She let her forehead fall against his chest. "I've been terrible."

His eyes were bloodshot, but they filled with a tired kind of hope. "We both have."

"But your affair . . . it was my fault, too. I was . . ." She hung her head for a moment. "I was so caught up in myself I didn't remember to love you."

Connor tightened his hold on her and rested his forehead on her shoulder. "That's okay. You were sick; you couldn't help it. It was me, Michele. All me."

"No." She pulled back and searched his eyes. "I was wrong back then, even if I was sick. And I'm sorry." A moment passed before she could speak. "You needed to know."

For a long while they only looked at each other. Then he nodded, his own eyes damp. "Thank you."

She gave him a single kiss and studied his eyes once more. "And something else. I wasn't ready to hear about Max's mother before. But if . . . if you want to tell me sometime, I'm ready now."

"No." He wore defeat like a mask, as he kissed her forehead. "That's okay. It doesn't matter anymore."

That night they shared a bed but nothing more. The fact that they were together was a start, but Michele wondered if the damage she'd inflicted on Connor's heart was something they'd live with forever. He was still dedicated to her, clearly. Otherwise he would never have sent Max home. But would he ever be in love with her the way he'd been before? In the days since Max left, Michele caught her husband sitting on the front porch the way he had after he first found out about Max. She'd go to him, put her hands on his shoulders, or loop an arm around his neck and try to get a glimpse of what he was feeling.

"Hey . . . pretty night?"

He'd look up, a distant smile tugging at the corners of his lips. "Yes. It's nice out here."

"So" — she'd pull up a chair and search his eyes — "what are you thinking?"

"About life. How strange it is, how one decision can affect so many people for all of time."

Other times his answer was more to the point: "Max. What he's thinking right now."

His words always made her sit back, shocked at what he had become in a matter of days. The old Connor would've given her a standard, "Nothing, dear," and then turned the conversation to her. But not anymore. Now he was an open book, more so than he'd been at any time in their marriage. It was a change that would've been a huge triumph for Michele if it weren't for one thing.

The book in his heart held nothing but pensive sorrow and broken lives.

Half the time Connor seemed consumed with guilt over what he'd done. The way he'd hurt so many people. The rest of the time his sadness came from a place he could neither hide nor deny.

A place that ached for his son.

She no longer hated him for caring about the boy. The connection she'd made with the child his last night in their home was enough to at least feel empathy for her husband.

Even the girls had struggled since Max's departure.

"He was so funny, Mom." Susan found her on Sunday, her tone whiny and frustrated. "No one else'll climb the tree in the front yard with me, except Max. Can't he come back again? Please?"

Elizabeth was more introspective. "I think Dad misses him, don't you?"

"Yes, honey. That's bound to happen. Max was here for two weeks."

"But I think Max wanted to stay longer than two weeks."

"You may be right, but Max has a future in Hawaii. They found a family who wants to adopt him."

"I know." Elizabeth looked out the window at the sky beyond their backyard. "Daddy told me." Then she found Michele's eyes again. "A couple isn't a family, Mom. Not like *we're* a family."

There were times when she wanted to stand on the kitchen counter and yell at all of them. *Get over it, already!* Max wasn't part of their family; he belonged in Honoulu with the couple who wanted to adopt him. It was time to move on.

Other days she wondered what the girls would think if they knew the truth, that Max was actually Daddy's son. That their daddy had been with another woman even after he promised never to do that. Would they like Max as much then?

Every few hours the thought crossed her mind that maybe they should call Mr. Ogle and tell him they'd been wrong. They wanted Max, after all. But that thought would only make a fleeting appearance in her mind. The situation was so much bigger than that, so much more compli-cated. Long after forgiveness had done its work, Max would still be that dreaded re-minder of Connor's worst days.

And what about the kids at school, or their friends at church? "This is Max, Connor's son. Yes . . . we just found out about him. That's right, Connor had an af-fair and never called the girl again. Mmm-mmm, this was the first we knew about the boy."

The idea of trying to explain it made Michele's stomach hurt.

Of course, it would be different if Max had no one, if Mr. Ogle couldn't find anyone to adopt him. But the Hawaiian couple sounded nice enough. So what if they ran a bed-and-breakfast and wanted Max to help out around the grounds. Work was good for kids, and certainly they'd shower him with love, as well.

By Tuesday, Connor was back at work with a layover in Atlanta and a flight home the next afternoon. Then on Thursday he set off for a series of longer legs that would take him away from home until late Sunday afternoon. The assignment was one Connor had asked for, extra hours to make up for the time he'd taken off when Max was with them.

With the girls at school and Connor gone, Michele figured the best thing she could do was clean the house and talk to God about how they were supposed to move on. She worked her way from the kids' bathroom to the guest room where Max had slept while he was there. The sheets had already been changed, but now she dusted the windowsill and the headboard.

She was wiping the rag across the bedside table — the place where Max had kept his white Bible — when she saw it.

A small white envelope lay on the floor beneath the table. Michele knit her brow together. How come she hadn't seen it beore, when she changed the bedding? She reached down, picked it up, and brought it where she could see it better. The three words scrawled across the front made her breath catch in her throat.

For Mrs. Evans.

Michele made a slow drop to the edge of the bed. Who could it be from? Not from . . . not from Max's mother, was it? She slid one trembling finger beneath the flap and made a careful tear along the top. Then she pulled a single page from inside, unfolded it, and began to read.

To Mrs. Evans:

Hello. My name is Ramey, and you don't know me. I've been Max's babysitter for all of his life. Whenever his mother was out of town on a flight, the boy was with me. During that time I haven't been much of a believer. In fact, I haven't believed in God at all, really.

But now as I watch Max, as I think about the months and years he has ahead, I want to believe, ma'am. With all my heart I want to believe.

Marv Ogle tells me that you and your husband are Christians, the same way Kiahna was a Christian.

I've read through some of Kiahna's journal so I might understand Max's situation better, and what I found has given me the beginning of belief. Enough so that I've asked God for a forgiveness miracle for Max.

You see, ma'am, I might not be very educated, but I know it will take a forgiveness miracle for life to work out the way Kiahna and even, I think, God wants it to work out.

The reason I'm writing is because all of this will be hardest on you, Mrs. Evans. You might not have known about Connor and Kiahna's time together. If not, then I'm sure you won't want Max, not at first. He would be a reminder of everything you want to forget.

Michele's hand fell to her lap. She gripped the edge of the bed with her other hand and closed her eyes to ward off the sudden stinging. This . . . this Ramey woman had known her heart exactly. Her soul was heavy, soaked in sadness as she opened her eyes and found her place on the page.

But I found something in Max's Bible that maybe might help. It comes from a part called 1 John, and it says, "As Jesus laid his life down for us, so we must lay our lives down for other people. Anything else is not really love. Not love for God and not love for people."

I don't know if that will help you make a decision, Mrs. Evans. But I can tell you this. Max has been the greatest light in my life for all of his seven years. I'm old and my heart won't go on much longer, but I want Max to be in a family where they know the treasure they are getting. Max is a treasure. I'm praying that you will see so for yourself.

Please call me if you have any questions. Again . . . I'm sorry for whatever pain this has caused you, but Max needs a home. I'd do anything to see that he gets one.

Sincerely,
Ramey Aialea

At the bottom of the letter was the woman's phone number.

Michele reminded herself to exhale. Her hands were shaking so much now that the notepaper made little noises. *Okay, God . . . why? Why do I find this now? What do you want from me?*

Daughter . . . be still and know that I am God. My ways are not yours . . .

The words were straight from Scripture, a part of the Bible Michele hadn't read for years. But now they blew across her terrified soul like a gentle balm. Again and again they came until her hands were no longer trembling.

When she was finally still, the way God wanted her to be, she read the note one more time. The part about Max's Bible and the words from 1 John sliced at her convictions like a sword. A double-edged sword.

Had she laid down her life for anyone? Ever?

For her children, yes, at one point or another. But that was the definition of parenting, giving away self for the sake of your own. Somehow, Michele was certain that wasn't the meaning of the verse. After all, Jesus had laid down His life for people who mocked Him and spat on Him. People who were cruel and biting and unforgiving.

People like her.

Tears formed a layer over her eyes, and

he blinked so she could see the words in he note more clearly. She hadn't cried much these past few weeks, and when she had, the tears had been selfish. Even the night before Max left, her sorrow had been for herself, for the agonizing decision that had been placed squarely on her shoulders.

But this time, the sadness that rose in her heart was nothing but pure God-given remorse.

No, she hadn't laid her life down, not at all. Though Connor had started this ordeal that summer night eight years ago, he was willing to lay his life down whatever way God called him to do it. If that meant taking in Max, then he'd take him. If it meant letting Max go forever, he'd do it.

Even the girls seemed to understand the Scripture better than she did. Yes, they were confused by Max's arrival. But they'd put aside their fears and concerns and uncertainties and almost from the beginning they'd loved him for who he was.

Your ways aren't my ways, God? Does that mean . . . does that mean Max was never supposed to go? She sniffed and set the note back in the envelope. Then she covered her face with her hands and wept for how wrong she'd been, how blind and cold and selfish.

Ramey's words stayed with he
throughout the day. After a few hours sh
washed her face and reapplied her makeup
She didn't want the girls thinking some
thing else was wrong. But a decision wa
taking shape in her soul, a decision tha
felt more right than springtime.

She began making phone calls. B
Thursday morning, after Connor left fo
the airport and his four-day trip, she called
the girls into the living room and sat then
down. She explained that she was taking
another trip, a visit to Hawaii. Her frien
Renee would be there in half an hour t
stay with the girls until whenever Michel
got home.

"Will you see Max, Mommy?" Susar
clapped her hands. "Tell him we mis
him!"

"But don't be gone very long, okay." Eliz
abeth bit the inside of her lip, always the se
rious one. "I don't like when you're gone.'

Then Michele drew a slow breath. *Okay
God . . . give me the words . . .*

"This is the important part, girls. I hav
something to tell you about Max . . ."

Ramey wasn't sure, but she though
maybe this was the miracle she'd beer
praying for.

Michele Evans was set to arrive at her apartment any minute. Her plane came in at two o'clock, and she hoped to arrive before Max walked home from the bus stop.

Ramey waited in her chair, mulling over the events of the past twenty-four hours. The call from Michele Evans came yesterday afternoon. The woman explained that she hadn't read Ramey's letter until the day before; she found it while she was cleaning Max's room.

"I want to talk to you about laying down my life," she said on the phone. "Can I come talk to you tomorrow?"

"Yes." Ramey had almost felt the floor buckle beneath her feet. She had to pinch her knee to convince herself she was even having the conversation. But she had to be honest at the same time. "Mrs. Evans, Max's adoption is already underway. I'm not sure what good it'll do now."

"I'm letting God take care of everything else." The woman's voice had been strong and sure. "He wants me to come, so I'm coming. I want to know more about Kiahna, I want to see pictures of her and Max, so I can know what the boy has lost."

Ramey wasn't sure whether to laugh or cry, but she told Mrs. Evans by all means come. Now, with only a moment or two before the woman arrived, Ramey took the chance to talk to God again.

Okay, so maybe You do hear me up there. And You must love Max a whole lot, because I'm not much of a letter writer. But this woman says my letter made her want to come. She gave a slow shake of her head. *I'm not sure what You're doing, God, but I want a front-row seat to see it happen.*

A gentle knocking sound broke the moment. Ramey whispered a hasty good-bye to God, and then changed her mind and asked Him to stick around. As long as possible, actually. She huffed her way to the door, opened it, and before she could welcome her, they looked at each other for a long moment, and then the Evans woman was in her arms. "Thank you, Ramey. Thank you for opening my eyes."

"Nah . . ." Ramey drew back first. She batted at an errant tear. "It was nothing."

"It was, though. It was everything." The woman stepped inside. "I'm Michele Evans. I wouldn't be here if it wasn't for you."

Buddy rounded the corner and dropped down on his haunches. The heat from the afternoon made his tongue hang out a bit. "That's Buddy."

Mrs. Evans walked up to the dog, scratched him behind the ear, and gave a gentle twist on his blue scarf. "He looks like a nice dog."

"Max loves him to death." Ramey studied the woman for a minute. "Why didn't Mr. Evans come?"

The woman's face fell a bit. "He doesn't know I'm here."

Alarm bells went off in Ramey's soul. "Then you can't exactly make a decision about —"

Mrs. Evans held up her hand. "My husband made his mind up about Max a long time ago, Ramey. And I talked to our girls this morning. Our decision is unanimous."

They talked for a short time before Michele wanted to see pictures of Kiahna and Max. Ramey pointed at the old bookcase. "At the bottom there, the photo albums — they belonged to Kiahna. One is put together from her childhood; the yellow one with the butterfly on the cover has pictures of her and Max."

The woman took the yellow book and held it up. "May I?"

"Sure." Ramey struggled around the sofa and joined Michele. A catch sounded in her voice. "They were something together."

Michele lifted the cover and worked her way through the beginning of the book. "She was very beautiful." She studied a photo of Kiahna holding baby Max. "I knew she would be."

"Yes . . . she could've had any man on the island." Ramey tapped the photograph. "But she wasn't interested. Not once."

The Evans woman caught her eye. "How come, Ramey? I thought . . . I figured she would've had lots of men."

Ramey fought off the defensiveness for Kiahna that pierced her. The woman's misunderstanding wasn't her fault. All she knew of Kiahna was the affair she'd had with Connor. "You don't know the story? What happened with her and your husband?"

Mrs. Evans's face grew a few shades paler. "No. I . . . I never wanted to know until now."

"Kiahna was a rare girl, Mrs. Evans. She was twenty-one when she met your husband, and she'd never been with a man." Ramey squinted at the photographs, as the story came back.

She told the Evans woman everything, details even she hadn't known until reading Kiahna's journal. How the two of them had met at the airport, and Kiahna ad trusted something about him. When the storm came up there wasn't a hotel room anywhere on the island. Kiahna offered her couch only as a way of being kind.

"That's the part I don't understand." The pain in the Evans woman's eyes was deep and tormented. "She had to know what she was getting herself into."

"Fair enough." Ramey nodded her head to the side. "But her journal tells a different story. She was alone; her parents had recently died when she met Connor. He told her he was a Christian, that he shared her devotion to God." Ramey hesitated. "And he told her he lived alone."

"Alone?"

"Yes." Ramey raised an eyebrow. "He said he was married, but his wife lived in Florida and he lived in LA." She lowered her voice and leaned in. "You know something else? He didn't have on a wedding ring, either."

"What?" Mrs. Evans ran her tongue over her bottom lip and leaned back, gripping the sofa arm so tight her knuckles turned white.

Poor woman. Ramey waited before going on. Obviously Mrs. Evans's husband hadn't told her the details. Her face

was as pale as her knuckles, and ange
and hurt no longer took turns with he
expression.

Rather, the woman's face was blank
wide-eyed and desperate.

The look of a person in shock.

THIRTY-THREE

Michele's head was reeling.

All this time she'd blamed Kiahna for what had happened. But now . . . Connor hadn't been wearing his wedding ring? He'd told her he lived alone? She felt a gaping hole in her chest where her heart had been. Was that what he'd been trying to tell her in the days before Max's visit? Even the day she returned from California? He'd said it was all his fault, and now the picture was clear as water.

She looked around Ramey's apartment, desperate for a way to make the room stop spinning. Finally she released her hold on the sofa arm and squeezed her eyes shut for a moment. She still wanted to lay down her life, but she hadn't expected it to be this painful.

When she opened her eyes, she looked at Ramey. "Kiahna had no idea he was married?"

"Not till it was too late." Ramey hesitated. "Kiahna wanted to be a doctor, Mrs. Evans. She didn't want love or marriage or kids until after she finished med school."

"When she found out she was pregnant, why . . . why didn't she tell Connor?"

"He was a married man, Mrs. Evans. He had no plans to see her again; he told her that much before he left the island. Why would she tell him about the baby?"

"So she never did."

"Right." Ramey stared at the photo album. "After Max was born, she had time only for her son and for God."

Understanding flooded Michele's heart. The poor girl! Alone and pregnant, her dreams of med school shattered. Yes, Connor's revelation after the camping trip had been right on. The affair, the entire mess, was all his fault.

And now . . .

Now she could choose to forgive him or make him and Max and all of them pay a lifetime for his sins. She could lay down her life in love, or hold tight to it even if it meant living in misery and bitterness the rest of her days. A soft huff sounded in her throat. She'd already made her decision; it was the reason she'd spent the entire day on a flight to Honolulu.

She thought about her conversation with the girls. They had taken it far better than she'd expected, nodding and listening while she talked to them.

"Remember how Max wanted to find his daddy, the one he knew was somewhere out there?"

"Yes." The girls looked at each other, and then back at her.

"Well, we found out something about that. It turns out that your daddy is Max's daddy, too."

Susan's reaction was instant. "Really! Great, Mom! That means Max has to come back here and be our brother, right?"

A frown shaded Elizabeth's eyes. "So Daddy did love Max's mommy?"

Michele could do nothing but be honest. "For a short time, yes."

That seemed to be all the information they needed. Whatever had gone on with Max's mother and their father, the details didn't matter. Their daddy had always been there for them, would always be there. If it meant Max was their brother now, then all the better.

"Will he come live with us?" Elizabeth's eyes danced with the beginning of a smile. "I think he should, Mom. If he's our brother and Dad's his daddy."

There it was; the simple childlike love that had open arms no matter the situation.

"I want him to. But you both need to pray, okay?"

They agreed to pray, and that was that. Discussion closed. The details she and Connor had fretted about prior to Max's visit were laid out and accepted in as much time as they might've decided what to eat for dinner that night.

The memory of that morning dissolved, and Michele kept flipping pages in the yellow photo album, stopping at certain key shots. Near the back of the book she saw one of Max and Kiahna holding hands at the beach next to Buddy. The photo was taken on a day that must've been not long before her death. Max's hair was windblown, his cheeks tanned from a day in the sun. Kiahna wore a tank top and shorts, and a smile that told the world how she felt about the little boy beside her.

Max had been Kiahna's whole world. She'd made one mistake and paid for it all her life, growing closer to God, teaching Max about the ways of faith, and spending as many hours in the air as it took to take care of her precious son.

Michele shifted her gaze to Max's image

and the look in his eyes. It showed a tender mix of confidence and faith, a trusting that his happy world would keep on that way forever. Beside him, even Buddy looked content with life. Max's love for his dog was clear. He had his hand on the dog's collar, and the dog was leaning into him.

Michele studied the boy, surrounded by all he loved most.

Then in one awful morning everything changed.

Michele could have hidden herself in a hole for the way she'd treated Max while he was with them. If only she'd known this part of the story before . . . Michele swallowed back a wave of emotion. This wasn't the time. She had too much work to do.

"Okay, I need your help, Ramey." Michele closed the photo album and locked eyes with Ramey. "Tell me about the couple, the one that wants to adopt Max."

"They were nice enough." Ramey made a grunting sound and brushed her hand in the air. "But the lady's allergic to dogs."

"No Buddy?" God's ways grew another degree clearer.

Ramey shook her head. "The man said dogs were out of the question." Ramey was breathing hard. She waited until she had control again. "I thought what with Max running out of the room, that they'd change their mind. Maybe agree to keep Buddy outside or something."

"They didn't?"

"No. They thought Max would get over it, adapt or something."

Michele looked at the clock on the wall. According to Ramey, Max would be home in a matter of minutes. "Ramey, I need a favor."

"Whatever I can do." She coughed twice, and her face stayed red.

"I need you to call Mr. Ogle and ask if we can do something drastic."

The older woman seemed to hold her breath. "Drastic?"

"Yes. I need him to stop the adoption."

Max walked home from the bus stop with Jerry from the apartments 'cross the street. Ramey was more tired now, so she couldn't come get him like she used to, but that was okay, even on hot days like this one. As long as he could go back to her and Buddy he would walk a hundred miles.

He slid his feet along the ground and stared at the sidewalk as he went, because he didn't feel much like looking up.

Any day, Ramey had told him. Any day

Mr. Ogle could work out the details and he would be packed up and sent to live with the Mollers. He told Ramey it wasn't fair. But it didn't matter what he thought.

Yesterday night Mr. Ogle even came over and said a 'pology about the Mollers not wanting Buddy.

"They liked you a lot, Max. I've talked to their friends and people in their family. I believe you'll learn to love them."

Max didn't think so. And if they wouldn't take Buddy, Max was sure he wouldn't love them. He'd be too busy missing everyone else. Mommy and Buddy and Ramey. And the Evans family.

Thinking things made the walk go faster. His feet came up to Ramey's door lickety fast this time. He lifted his hand to knock, when he saw a strange sight. The door was open the smallest size, the size of his little finger.

Max shrugged. Maybe Ramey left it open for him so she wouldn't have to get out of her chair. Getting out of her chair was harder for her every day, and sometimes that put a new spot of worry in his heart next to all the other spots of worry.

He pushed open the door very quiet, and he was going to call out her name when he heard some voices. A scared feeling grabbed him by the neck and made his arms start to shake. Was it the Mollers? Had they already come to take him away?

With silent steps he walked into the hall and saw Buddy. "Shhh." Max gave Buddy a serious look. The dog walked up to him, licked his fingers, and lay down on the floor near his feet. That was when Max could finally hear what the people inside were saying.

"Well, I made the call." The person was Ramey, because her breathing was hard and plus it was her voice.

"So . . . what did he say?"

Max froze in place. Even his heartbeep didn't want to work for a breath or two. Because that voice sounded familiar, that's why. He almost thought it was the voice of Mrs. Evans, except that wasn't even possible since Mrs. Evans lived in Florida.

"He called the Mollers while I was still on the phone." Ramey chuckled some. "They weren't very happy at first, but then the truth came out. They didn't really want a boy at first, anyway. They wanted a girl. An older girl."

The woman who sounded like Mrs. Evans made a long breathy sound. "Oh, thank God, Ramey! That's what God was telling me all day yesterday. I knew I had to fly out here and see for myself if Max was supposed to be with them." She stopped and a cracking sound came in her voice. "Or if he was supposed to be with us."

Max felt his heart beeping just fine now. Very fast and very fine. Because now he was sure as could be that the woman in the next room really was Mrs. Evans! She had to be. His feet couldn't stand there another minute. He dropped his backpack and raced speedy fast around the corner and yes. There she was.

"Max!" Mrs. Evans turned and saw him.

"I . . . I heard what you said." His words were short and breathy because he couldn't believe what was happening.

"Is that what you want, Max?" She sank down to the floor and sat on the backside of her shoes. "Do you want to live with us?"

"Yes. I want that with all my heart. Buddy wants it, too."

Mrs. Evans held out her hands and said only, "C'mere, Max."

Tears filled up his eyes, but he didn't care. He ran to her and gave her the tightest, bestest hug in the world. When he pulled back he rubbed at his eyes so he could see better. "You mean it? You want me to be part of your family?"

Long rivers of wet came from Mrs. Evans's eyes, but she smiled anyway. "Yes, Max. We want that forever and ever."

Max thought for a moment, and he remembered something. The rock for Ramey! "Be right back."

He ran into the room where he was staying and dug beneath his pile of clothes. There it was, shiny black with four snowy white stripes.

His fingers slid around it and he ran it back to Ramey. "Here." He opened his hand. "So you don't forget me."

Now wet was in Ramey's eyes, too. She took the rock and hugged him so hard her big arms made his breathing hard. When she let go, she rubbed his head and said, "I could never forget you, Max. Not as long as I live."

"Know what, Ramey?" Max pointed to the rock. "Only God can make rocks like that."

Ramey smiled a special smile, the one she used only for him. "You're right about that, Max."

"So . . ." Max felt his eyebrows raise up. "I'm really gonna live with the Evans family?"

"Yes." Ramey smiled and two tears fell from her eyes. "You got your miracle after all."

Mrs. Evans reached out and took hold of his hand. "Let's get your things, okay?"

And just then, Max could almost see his mommy smiling at him from heaven, because she was right, after all. God really did give second chances, because right then he knew he would never scoot along the ground again.

Forever more, just like his mommy, he would fly.

All the extra emotion wasn't really good for her, but Ramey didn't care.

She wiped at her cheeks as she took in the scene, Max tucked safe in the arms of Mrs. Evans, a perfect picture of the one thing Kiahna believed most in.

Love happens when people forgive.

So what if her heart hurt a little. Love did that to a person every now and then, didn't it? Besides, she was too busy thanking God for sticking around that afternoon, thanking Him for doing the very thing she'd asked of Him. No, the thing she'd demanded, really.

He'd given them a forgiveness miracle.

And even if she lived only another week or two, she would go to heaven a happy woman. Because God had indeed given her a front-row seat to watch it happen.

THIRTY-FOUR

Connor pulled into the driveway at four o'clock Sunday afternoon and made a mental note to himself.

No more long trips.

Even with the strain he still felt around the house, he hated being away from home more than a night or two. Besides, if he was going to work things out with Michele — and he was determined to do so — he needed to spend as much time with her as possible.

He pressed the garage door opener and eased his truck into the space beside Michele's minivan. His body was more weary than usual, tired in a way that couldn't be explained by the long series of flights these past four days. He knew what it was, of course.

It was Max.

He missed the boy so much it was a physical pain, an ache that made him wonder if maybe people could notice a limp in his gait. The scene at the lake when he taught Max how to fish, the one on the big rock when the butterfly landed on Max's pole, the time in the recliner when Max had fallen asleep against his chest . . .

The good-bye at the airport.

All of it played over in his mind a hundred times a day, and no amount of prayer had done anything to dim the pictures. Time would have to handle that task. Or maybe he was doomed to relive the memory of the boy the rest of his days. Punishment for his mistakes, his unbelievably bad mistakes.

He parked the truck, turned off the engine, and climbed out. His bag was in the back, but he could get it later. Right now he needed to see Michele and the girls, needed to know that God had left him with at least the family he'd betrayed. He loved them more than ever before, loved Michele for sticking with him. Her support was more than he deserved.

The garage was cluttered, a job he could tackle in the morning. No doubt the grass needed mowing in the backyard, and tomorrow would be the time to do it. He had two days off before he had to fly again. As he stepped between the cars, another familiar thought came to mind.

How was Max doing? Had he already gone home with the Hawaiian couple, and was he getting to know them? Did he think much of his time in Florida, or the way he'd wanted Connor to be his pretend daddy? Or was he mad at them, smothered in feelings of betrayal and abandonment by everyone who had made an impact on his life?

Connor sighed and it sounded like it came from the heels of his uniform shoes. Thoughts about Max would have to wait. Right now he needed to see his family, needed to feel their arms around him, the reassurance of their love for him even after all he'd put them through.

He heard something coming from the backyard, voices of the girls and maybe even Michele. Normally he would go through the house, but he'd been gone so long this time. Why not go straight into the backyard and surprise them?

The door stuck some, another project to add to the list. But on the second try he pulled it open and stepped down a single stair onto the grass below. The chimney stood like a barrier on his left, blocking out the view of the yard. He was about to move around it and catch the girls off guard when from around the corner something charged him.

Before Connor could react, a yellow Labrador retriever bounced up and licked his hand. Connor stared at the dog, his brow furrowed. What in the world? Had the girls found a stray? That had to be it, but the dog looked familiar, somehow. Maybe he belonged to a neighbor or someone they knew, a house they'd visited sometime.

Then it came to him. He looked exactly like Max's dog, Buddy. Max's best friend. The one in the picture, the one his son had missed so much while he was visiting. Connor leaned against the chimney wall for support and ordered his mind to focus.

Of course this wasn't Max's dog; his mind was merely working overtime.

"C'mere, boy. Let's see if you have a collar." Connor held out his hand and the dog came closer. He had a blue scarf around his neck, and Connor had to run his fingers beneath it to figure out that yes, the dog did have a collar. And a tag, too. He twisted the tag to the top of the dog's back and leaned closer to read what it said.

The tag held just one word.

Buddy.

"Buddy . . ." His heart slipped into an

unfamiliar rhythm and with a burst of adrenaline he rounded the corner —

And there they were.

"Surprise!" The voices rang out in unison, and Connor took in the faces before him.

Michele and Elizabeth and Susan — and *Max* — all running toward him with open arms. And there in the back, eyes locked on him, was his father. He was older, grayer, but seeing him now erased the eight years they'd been apart in as much time as it took to speak a single word. For an instant he remembered the car accident. If the man inside had been his father . . .

God . . . thank You for giving us this second chance. Thank You.

"Dad . . ." Connor mouthed the word, and across the yard the old man nodded his head and gestured toward the others. His turn could come later.

"Oh, Daddy . . . you're home, and look who's here!" Susan and Elizabeth reached him first, and Connor swung them around. As he did he caught Michele's eyes in the back of the group. She was crying and laughing all at the same time.

"Yes." Connor looked at his son and stooped down to his level. It had to be a dream. The scene was too amazing, too wonderful, to be taking place in his own backyard. "Max . . ."

The boy ran to him and jumped into his arms. "I'm back, Mr. Evans! Forever and ever. Mrs. Evans came to Hawaii and got me and Buddy, and Ramey called Mr. Ogle and said no, I didn't want to live with the Mollers, and now here I am. Isn't that a *miracle?*"

Again his eyes found Michele's. She only nodded to him that yes, it was all true. He wasn't dreaming at all, because he could feel Max's hands around his neck. "Yes, Max." He hugged his son tight to his chest. "It's the biggest miracle I could ever imagine."

Elizabeth yelled for the others to join her on the swings, and the children skipped off together. Connor didn't know what to do first, but he saw Michele motion toward his father. With his eyes fixed on the strapping man at the other end of the yard, Connor went to him and the two did something they'd rarely done.

They embraced.

His father placed his hand against the back of Connor's head and held him as if he were a little boy again, held him the way Connor had always wanted to be held. But before his dad could say a word, Connor drew back and searched the man's deep blue eyes.

"I'm sorry, Dad. I . . . I didn't say it the other night, but I'm sorry." His throat was thick, but he was too stunned for tears. "What happened between us . . . it was my fault."

In all his life he'd never seen his father cry. But now, tears fell onto his weathered cheeks, and when he opened his mouth, nothing came out. Instead, while the kids played in the distance, he pulled Connor close one more time and held him as if he might never let go.

When they pulled apart, Connor's brain began firing some of the questions that had been flash frozen in the shock of the moment. "I can't believe you're here . . . how did . . . ?"

His father only nodded at Michele. "She called me, Son. From Hawaii. She told me what was happening, what she wanted to do." This time his father leaned close and kissed him on the forehead. "I told her I wouldn't have missed this for the world." He paused. "Your son's beautiful, Connor."

He looked over his father's shoulder at the boy running in circles around Susan. "Yeah, he is, isn't he?"

"But that woman" — his dad pointed toward Michele — "is beautiful inside and out."

"I know it." Connor glanced at Michele. "I think I need to go tell her so myself."

His father patted him on the shoulder. "Yes, Son, I believe you do."

Connor left his father with the children and pulled his feet through the grass to where Michele stood, not far from the patio door. She still had that sheepish grin, the one that told him yes, everything was exactly how it looked. She had done it all while he was gone on his trip.

"Michele . . . how did you . . . ?" He shook his head. His thoughts formed a logjam in his heart, and he couldn't make himself voice even one of them.

She came to him then, slipped her hands along his sides and wrapped them around his lower back. Her lips met his, but the kiss was a quick one, promising more later on when they were alone. She drew back and placed a single finger to his lips. "Shhh. We can talk about it later."

"But how did you —"

"Later." She smiled at him again, her eyes swimming. "First there's something you have to tell that little boy." She looked beyond him to the children playing near his father. Buddy was frolicking at their feet, thoroughly enjoying his new home. "The girls already know you're his daddy. I told them Thursday morning." Her eyes met his again.

"Were they . . . were they okay? The girls, I mean?"

"Yes." She gave him a look that silenced his fear. "They're fine. Now it's time for you to tell Max."

What? His heart was beating so hard he expected it to burst from his chest and do flips across the yard. Was she serious? Right now? Thirty minutes ago he was trying to figure out how he'd live the rest of his life missing a green-eyed little boy with a face like his own, and now . . . He gave a shake of his head and forced his mind to think straight. What had happened to her in the past few days? A miracle, no doubt, but why?

"Michele . . ." His heart broke for all she'd been through, the price she'd paid for his selfish decisions one night an ocean away from her. "I'm so sorry. Do you believe me?"

"Yes." Her voice was tight with emotion, but her smile was as genuine as he'd ever seen it. "And I forgive you, you know why?"

He had no idea. "No . . . I guess I don't."

"Because love happens when you forgive." She held her finger to her nose and made a sound that was more laugh than cry. "Max told me that."

Once more he looked at her, but she only nodded toward the children. "I have dinner ready inside. I'll bring everyone else in. That way you and Max can be alone for a few minutes." She cupped her hands around her mouth. "Okay, guys, everyone inside to wash hands."

His father must've been in on the plan, because he looped an arm around each of the girls and whispered something to Max. Connor watched the boy grin and look straight at him. Connor nodded and used his finger to call Max to his side.

As soon as they were alone together, Connor begged God for the right words. *Don't let him hate me for not telling him sooner. Please, God . . .*

"Max . . . I have something to tell you." He sat back on his heels, ignoring his dry mouth and the way his throat kept tightening.

"Can you believe it, Mr. Evans?" Max raised his hands high in the air and hooted. "I get to stay forever, and Buddy, too."

"I know." He gave his son an impulsive hug, and then tried again. "What I want to tell you, Max, is that —"

"And guess what!" The boy was vibrating with excitement. "You get to be my pretend daddy now, Mr. Evans. Isn't that just the bestest thing you ever heard?"

"Max." Something in his tone made the boy settle down and catch Connor's gaze.

"Yes, Mr. Evans?" A worried look flashed in his eyes, and Connor had to hold back a smile. He needed to get the news out fast, before the boy misunderstood.

"Remember how your mommy told you that maybe one day you'd find your daddy somewhere out there?"

"Yes." Max's eyes were wide, his breathing still fast. "I remember."

"Well, Max . . . Mrs. Evans and I found out something you should know."

"Okay, but guess what?" Now the boy's eyes were almost full circles. "I don't want that daddy anymore, Mr. Evans. I want you."

"Good." Connor allowed the smile to fill his face. "Because we found out I'm your daddy, Max. The one your mommy told you about."

For a long time, Max only stared at him, searching his face as though maybe this was a joke or perhaps he'd heard wrong. Then he did a giant gulp and his voice fell to a whisper. "You're . . . you're my daddy? My real daddy?"

"Yes, Max."

"So you mean . . ." Max did a little laugh. "You mean God answered all my prayers, every single one?"

Relief spilled across Connor's soul. The boy wasn't upset with him. "Yes . . . and I know why, too."

Max looked bewildered, giddy with joy and stunned all at the same time. "Why?"

"Because somewhere up in heaven, your mommy has been bugging God probably every day to make sure things worked out just like this."

The boy looked like he might soar around the yard and never come down, but instead he flung his arms around Connor's neck and whispered not far from his ear. "Can I call you *Daddy?* Like 'Lizabeth and Susan do?"

"Yes, Son. You can call me that the rest of your life."

Connor was thinking how he'd never been happier, never felt more free, when the girls rushed into the backyard. "Daddy, Daddy . . . look what Grandpa caught!"

With careful movements, Connor's father stepped into the backyard behind the girls. His hand was cupped over something on his wrist, something impossible to make out.

Michele stood a few feet behind him, and Connor winked at her, silently telling her that yes, he'd talked to Max; mission accomplished. She grinned, her face glowing in a way that spoke volumes about their future.

Max ran to the girls. "What is it?" He peered between them at the thing that had stirred up so much attention.

"Well?" Connor chuckled at the sight of his father surrounded by his children. *All* his children. "What'd he catch? A bumpy brown toad?"

"No." Max turned to him and their eyes held. "You won't believe it, Daddy." The boy's face broke into a smile that seemed to go on forever.

"Tell me." Connor stood and made his way closer to the group. The sound of Max calling him *Daddy* still echoed in his heart.

Max took his hand and pointed to the monarch on his father's wrist. "It's a butterfly."

And so it was.

The prettiest butterfly Connor had ever seen.

READER NOTE

Dear Friends,

As always, thank you for traveling with me through the pages of *Oceans Apart*. I pray that the story of Max and Connor and Michele and the steadfastness of Kiahna has touched you as you've read. And I pray that in the process you've felt God working on your own heart.

I certainly felt Him working on mine.

From the beginning I knew *Oceans Apart* would be about forgiveness. I asked myself how it would feel to be Michele, to have a husband I loved and to suddenly, in a moment's time, be asked to forgive him for something as monstrous as unfaithfulness.

Then I let God complicate the story. What if a child was involved?

Suddenly I knew I had to write it out, process the idea by placing it on the pages of this book. Only then would I see that yes, forgiveness is possible. Even when the greatest wrong of all has been committed against you.

Those of you reading this know what I mean. Some of you have rips and holes in your own marriages. Admissions of affairs, unexplained absences, and other areas of pain or betrayal, areas that will never be fixed without forgiveness.

Others of you aren't struggling in your marriage. But perhaps you've been the victim of gossip or unfaithfulness on the part of a friend. I think we can all relate to that, and like Michele, we won't find peace until we forgive. Forgiveness doesn't make a problem go away; it simply gives you the peace Christ intended. Often, when both parties are willing to work on a relationship, healing will come. But sometimes it doesn't.

Even then, forgiveness is the only way to the freedom Jesus wanted for us, the freedom He died for. Without forgiveness, bitter roots grow in our hearts and choke out any good fruit that would otherwise grow there. And we can't have that.

So yes, forgiveness was the obvious life lesson from *Oceans Apart*.

But while I was writing it, God showed me another lesson, one that became almost as important. The lesson of second chances.

Second chances.

The idea that all of us are caterpillars, really. Furry little creatures scooting along the ground wondering why we can't seem to fly. And then God, in all His goodness, encourages us to crawl in a hole, bury our old selves, and die to the life we once knew. If we'll do that, if we'll trust Him with our entire existence, then He'll give us something beautiful in exchange.

He'll give us wings.

The ultimate wings come when we give our lives to Christ and let Him be Lord of our lives, our Savior. Without those wings, a person cannot see heaven — a tragedy none of us need face if only we accept God's gift of grace.

If this idea is confusing to you, if you've never considered Jesus' second chances, then make a phone call. Find a Bible-believing church and find out more about the God who made you, the One who created a plan for your salvation.

But if you've known God and find yourself stuck on the ground again, remember this. Second chances happen throughout our lives. Jesus told us to forgive seventy times seven — in other words, to always forgive. And in return He promised us the same. No matter where you're at in life, no matter what you've done, God waits with open arms, ready to give you that second chance. Even for the seven-hundredth time.

It's a good idea to take Him up on the offer. Because only then will you be able to use the wings He's already given you.

On a personal note, my family is doing very well. Donald is coaching our own boys these days, and loving every minute. He is considering starting a private team, anchored in Bible study and prayer, a team that would involve the families of players and help shape young men not only as basketball players but also as godly, contributing members of society. I remain in awe of his gifts.

Our children are growing like weeds, and this year they seem to have slipped into a warp speed of growth, a kind Don and I have never seen before. Kelsey is beautiful, with long hair and longer legs and a smile and determination that proves she is a one-in-a-million girl. Tyler is still singing and acting, and thrilled that this year Kelsey has joined him on the stage in our local Christian Youth Theater.

. As for the four youngest boys, sports remain their top priority. We manage to slip a bit of reading and arithmetic in as well, but they're happiest when they're playing basketball or soccer, swinging a bat, or rollerblading in our driveway. They have each become professional frog catchers, and I delight to see them run through the back door with a special catch in their hands. I try to take pictures of the best frogs, and if they sometimes hop onto the kitchen floor, well then, that's okay. They'll forget about the frogs soon enough.

This year we also had another addition to our house, two boys — nineteen and twenty-one, respectively. These young men both played sports for Don in years past, but didn't know each other before coming to our house last spring. Each was desperate for structure and Christian guidance. My heart is full beyond belief today as I see the changes they've made, and the godly men they are becoming. And what a blessing to know that God has trusted us — even for a short time — with two more of His own.

As always, I covet your prayers for my writing ministry and especially for my family. You are the other half of this writing life I lead, you who read the books and tell others about them, you who pray for me that I will hear God before each and every book I write.

Thousands of you have written to me in

the past year, and I've read every letter. Sometimes with tears, sometimes with a smile, always with a grateful heart that Christ would give me a story that might touch your life. Amazing. Please contact me and let me know how you're doing. I love hearing from you.

In Christ's amazing grace,
Karen Kingsbury

Email address: *rtnbykk@aol.com*
Website: *www.KarenKingsbury.com*

Visit my guest book to see what other readers are saying about this and other books.

STUDY GUIDE

Think of the beach scene where Michele first learns that her husband has been unfaithful to her. Describe a time when you discovered someone had hurt you. How did you react to the news initially?

What role did God play in how you handled that news?

Read Romans 8:28. God tells us that all things work to the good of those who love Him. Did hurtful events in your life end up bringing about good in your life? Explain.

Kiahna loved to talk to Max about second chances. Describe the time in your life when you first understood God's gift of grace and salvation. Share your personal story with someone, or write it in a journal.

Kiahna felt that she needed a second chance

with God because of what major event in her life? Did she fall easily? What led to her sin?

Think back and remember a time when you fell short of God's best for your life. Describe that time. How did you feel immediately after falling?

What did God bring about to help you realize you could be forgiven?

Describe your second chance after that difficult time.

Read Colossians 3 and 4, and list seven rules for holy living that will help you avoid the type of situation Kiahna and Connor fell into.

Do a search on forgiveness in Scripture. List four verses that act as guidelines on how to handle broken relationships, whenever possible.